A Lasting Promise

A Lasting Promise

A Christian Guide to *Fighting* for *Your Marriage*

Scott Stanley
Daniel Trathen
Savanna McCain
Milt Bryan

JOSSEY-BASS
A Wiley Imprint
www.josseybass.com

Published by Jossey-Bass
A Wiley Imprint
989 Market Street, San Francisco, CA 94103-1741   www.josseybass.com

Jossey-Bass books and products are available through most bookstores. To contact Jossey-Bass directly
call our Customer Care Department within the U.S. at 800-956-7739, outside the U.S. at 317-572-3986,
or fax 317-572-4002.

Jossey-Bass also publishes its books in a variety of electronic formats. Some content that appears in
print may not be available in electronic books.

Unless otherwise noted, all Scripture quoted are from THE HOLY BIBLE: NEW INTERNATIONAL
VERSION®. Copyright © 1973, 1978, 1984 by International Bible Society. Used by permission of
Zondervan Publishing House. All rights reserved. The NEW AMERICAN STANDARD BIBLE®
(Copyright © The Lockman Foundation 1960, 1962, 1963, 1968, 1971, 1972, 1973, 1975, 1977, 1995.
Used by permission.) and the New King James Version (NKJV: Copyright © by Thomas Nelson, Inc.
1982) are used for some passages where the rendering makes the points clearer.

Library of Congress Cataloging-in-Publication Data

A lasting promise : a Christian guide to fighting for your marriage / Scott Stanley . . . [et al.].
  —1st ed.
  p.   cm.
  Includes bibliographical references.
  ISBN 0–7879–3983–8 (paperback)
  1. Marriage—Religious aspects—Christianity.   2. Marriage—Biblical teaching.
I. Stanley, Scott, date.
BV835.L355 1998
248.8'44—dc21   97-45379

Printed in the United States of America
FIRST EDITION
PB Printing   10 9

Contents

Acknowledgments

This book is founded on the contributions of many people who struggle to better understand marriage and to help married couples. First and foremost, we acknowledge our friend and colleague Howard Markman, who had the pioneering vision in the mid-1970s to take the emerging understandings of sound marital research and apply this information in a program that could help couples prevent divorce and preserve lasting, loving marriages. His efforts have borne much fruit over many years in this field. Over the past twenty years, Howard, along with Scott Stanley, Susan Blumberg, and a host of colleagues mentioned here, have worked hard to refine our understanding of marriage and to develop tools and strategies for couples who want to make their marriages all they can be. That work has culminated in the program called PREP, which stands for the Prevention and Relationship Enhancement Program. In fact, this book is based in large part on the earlier book on PREP called *Fighting for Your Marriage* by Howard Markman, Scott Stanley, and Susan Blumberg (1994). The book you are holding presents the integrated, Christian approach to this body of work. We deeply appreciate the contributions of authors Markman and Blumberg that are reflected in this book.

We would also like to acknowledge those marital researchers who have been particularly influential in advancing our understandings of marriage (just to name a few): Clifford Notarius, John

Gottman, Don Baucom, Robert Weiss, Frank Floyd, Danielle Julien, Kurt Hahlweg, Bernard Guerney, Kim Halford, Steven Beach, Amy Holtzworth-Monroe, Sherrod Miller, Caryl Rusbult, Michael Johnson, Patricia Noller, Norm Epstein, and Tom Bradbury.

We also have had the good fortune to connect over the years with many people who have supported us in meaningful ways as our work has developed. Bill Coffin and his colleagues in the U.S. Navy have been immensely supportive and have shared with us insightful suggestions over many years that have made our work better. We also cannot thank our friend Gary Smalley enough for his support and encouragement. It is a rare man who can so freely give help to others in the same field in which he works. Gary is such a man, and we are inspired by his love and his work. We also thank Diane Sollee for her national efforts to put marriage education on the map. She is a great friend and a great supporter.

Over the years, we have been assisted by many colleagues and research associates as we have developed and evaluated the approach that underlies this book. We express our strongly felt appreciation to Lisa LaViolette Hoyer, Amy LaViolette Galloway, Wendy Cowperthwaite, Donna Jackson, Nancy Montgomery, Chris Saiz, Ragnar Storaasli, Mari Clements, Kristin Lindahl, Naomi Rather, Mary Jo Renick, Pat Burton, Brigit VanWidenfelt, Holly Johnson, Hal Lewis, Karen Jamieson-Darr, Paul Howes, Joyce Emde, Pam Jordan, Matt Johnson, Doug Leber, Wayne Duncan, Deb Butte, Natalie Jenkins, Veronica Johnson, Shelle Kraft, Lydia Prado, Laurie Tonelli, Michelle Bobulinski, Michelle St. Peters, Allan Cordova, Antonio Olmos, and Tom Wilkens. We also thank graduate students at Fuller Theological Seminary, who were among the first to be trained in the Christian PREP approach and who provided valuable theological and psychological insights for our work with couples.

We also deeply appreciate the talents and support of the staff at PREP, Inc. Thank you Natalie Jenkins, Sharon Hilty, Veronica Johnson, Phyllis Lemons, Sue Vander Kooy, Gail Herrick, and Janelle Miller.

Some of the key research studies that underlie material in this book have been supported by the University of Denver, the National Institute of Mental Health, and the National Science Foundation. We are grateful for the support of these institutions—support that has enabled us to develop the research basis for the program presented in this book.

Our editor at Jossey-Bass, Alan Rinzler, has been supportive throughout. All told, he's been a major contributor to the quality of this book. He has encouraged us in our goal to make it as effective as possible for couples. We thank Alan and his staff at Jossey-Bass for their support and expertise during this process.

We want to express our deep sense of appreciation for the couples and families who have shared their lives with us in our various research projects. These couples have opened their hearts and their relationships to our interviewers and video cameras. They have shared their struggles and successes, and we hope that the knowledge presented in this book represents some small compensation to these couples, without whom the book could never have been written. We would also like to acknowledge the role that our clients and seminar participants have played in shaping the ideas and case histories presented in the book. We have disguised the identities of the couples in the vignettes presented here through the use of composites and detail changes. Nevertheless, the stories told by many couples over the years are often so strikingly similar that the themes in the case histories we present will speak to a variety of people. We can all learn from each other.

Most important, we thank the Lord for making so many things plainly evident in scripture for our learning and growth. May we all listen closely to the voice of the creator of marriage.

To the three people who remind me of what matters most:
Nancy, Kyle, and Luke
with all my love.
And to Mom and Dad for all your support and love.—SS

To Lynn, who for thirty-eight years has been my best friend, companion, lover, and encourager. Thank you for always believing in me. To our adult children, Scott and Chrissy (and her husband, Dan), for adding love and excitement to our home. To our Lord Jesus, whose grace and vision has been sufficient through it all (I Tim. 1:5, Phil. 1:6).—DT

To those who are the heart of my life—my husband, John, children Bill and Tammy, Rob and Shelley, Rick and Eve, and my special grandchildren Jessica, Zachary, Joshua, and Hailey. And, in memory of my parents who always believed in me and gave me their support.—SM

To Jeannie, for your gracious endurance with me through the tough times in our marriage. The marvelous grace of God and your steadfast love have made it possible for me to finally have something significant to say.—MB

A Lasting Promise

Introduction

Do you want to have a really great marriage? Most people do, but they don't know what steps to take that will make a difference. No book like this will give you all the answers, but we believe you'll find this one full of practical ideas you can put to use in your marriage. *A Lasting Promise* is similar to many other books about Christian marriage in that it is solidly founded on the teachings of scripture. The Bible and historic Christian teaching about marriage provide the plumb line for all we have to say. The Bible has always been, and always will be, the secure foundation for thinking about the most important things about life. But at least two features of this book are not typical of other books on marriage.

First, *A Lasting Promise* is based on a strong body of university-based research about what leads to marriages that fail and what leads to marriages that thrive. Most books about Christian marriage are based on the sound clinical and spiritual insights of their authors, not on empirical research. Because *A Lasting Promise* is founded on a growing body of solid research, it is a book about some of the fascinating interworkings of marriages on the right (or wrong) path. Not surprisingly, most of what research has revealed has already been revealed—at least in principle—in the timeless wisdom of the Bible. That hasn't surprised us.

Second, *A Lasting Promise* is focused on practical action. Unlike many books that are more theoretical or insight-oriented, this one is designed to provide a rich resource of the many things you can do to protect your marriage and make it better. Not only that, the things we will encourage you to do have been shown in research to make a difference for many couples. All good marriages take work. But how can you work effectively? What should you do to make things better? This is where we believe we can help. We intend to give you solid tools you can use to make your marriage stronger, happier, and lifelong. We want to equip you to develop the full promise of your marriage.

WHAT IS PREP?

Much of what we have to offer is based on a nationally recognized program called PREP® (Prevention and Relationship Enhancement Program). Based on twenty years of marital research, the PREP approach focuses on specific attitudes and ways of acting that can make a powerful difference in your marriage over time. This book is also partly based on an earlier, secular book on PREP called *Fighting for Your Marriage* by Howard Markman, Scott Stanley, and Susan Blumberg (1994, Jossey-Bass). A *Lasting Promise* presents the biblically integrated, Christian version of PREP. We'll launch the book with foundational Christian teaching on marriage and build from there around key biblical themes and solid marital research.

This program incorporates principles based on couples research done in the United States and around the world. For example, there is a great deal of evidence that distressed couples show major differences from happier couples in their ability to handle conflict. Such findings have led us to formulate a number of strategies couples can use to help them handle issues more constructively—strategies we will teach you here. But this book is not just about communication and conflict. We will also focus on topics such as commitment, forgiveness, spiritual intimacy, friendship, sensuality, and fun.

Many studies underlying this book were conducted at the University of Denver; some were supported by the National Institute of Mental Health through grants awarded to Howard Markman and

Scott Stanley. A careful analysis of years of research in comparing couples who have significant problems to couples who are happy together and solidly committed resulted in PREP. The results of the analysis and of our work with PREP are presented in this book as suggestions for improving your relationship.

Because of its roots in solid research and its straightforward approach, PREP has received a great deal of attention from couples across the country, professionals in the field of marital counseling, and the national media. You may have been exposed to some of the coverage on programs such as "20/20," "48 Hours," "Good Morning America," "Focus on the Family," "Fox News," "The Today Show," "Moody's Midday Connection," "Oprah," and on networks such as CNN and MSNBC. PREP has been covered in newspapers and magazines such as USA Today, The New York Times, The Washington Post, Woman's Day, Redbook, Psychology Today, and many others. This kind of attention comes primarily from the focus on sound marital research that permeates PREP. This research helps us focus on the kinds of strategies that can be the most powerful for couples. One of our primary goals is to get this information into the hands of couples (possibly like you) who are interested in doing everything possible to prevent marital distress and divorce and to have a great marriage that honors God.

WHAT OUR RESEARCH REVEALS

In one of our key studies, we followed a sample of 135 couples for twelve years; we started following them before they married. These couples came into our laboratory once every year or two and gave us a massive amount of information about satisfaction, adjustment, problem intensity, commitment, demographic information, sexual and sensual enhancement, violence and abuse, family development, and so forth. We also asked couples to communicate about various issues; we recorded their conversations on videotape. These videotaped conversations were subjected to thousands of hours of analysis to assess different communication styles.

This kind of research allows us to look at many factors associated with both marital blessing and marital failure. For example, by *using only data from before these couples married,* we (along with a number of other researchers) have been able to differentiate those who do well over time from those who do not, with 80 to 91 percent accuracy, up to twelve years later (for example, Markman & Hahlweg, 1993; Clements, Stanley, & Markman, 1997). *Let this sink in a moment.* What this means is that, for many couples, the seeds of distress and a future divorce are there early in the marriage and, in many cases, before the couple even says, "I do." Other studies have found similarly high predictions for who will fail in marriage, who will not, and why (see Further Reading and Research References).

Although this kind of finding can be intimidating to some couples, we see such studies as very helpful. Knowing more about how marriages fall apart gives us a clearer idea about where couples can focus their attention in making marriage all it can be. Here, we will direct your attention to dimensions identified in scripture and in research that can greatly affect you and your marriage. *And we'll focus on things that are changeable—things you can do something about in order to experience greater peace and openness in your marriage.*

Not all studies are as encouraging as some of the studies on PREP have been, but many researchers over many years have found that programs focusing on teaching couples more positive and less negative ways to interact consistently show encouraging results (for example, Giblin, Sprenkle, & Sheehan, 1985; Silliman, Stanley, Coffin, Markman, & Jordan, in press). What does this mean for you? There is real reason to believe that learning and practicing the kinds of skills and strategies we present here can have a positive effect on your marriage. The key to this, like anything else, is in acting on what you learn. As James so clearly taught, believing something but not acting on it doesn't accomplish much of anything (for example, James 1:25, 2:15–18, 3:13). You have to put your love in action. We'll show you some powerful ways to do just that.

WHO IS THIS BOOK FOR?

The time-tested techniques of this book are for any couple—from the newly engaged to long-time marrieds—who want to solve problems or prevent them. Some of you may be having significant problems in your marriage. Some of you may have a great relationship now but are interested in *preventing* the kinds of problems encountered by all too many couples in our culture. In fact, PREP was originally devised as a program to help premarital couples prevent serious relationship problems from developing in the first place. But, as we've worked with many couples in our offices and workshops, we've found that the material is just as applicable for those who need to get back on track or who need simply to help their marriage thrive in the years to come.

HOW ARE THINGS GOING FOR YOU?

The following quiz is based on numerous marriage studies. It can help you get a rough sense of how you are doing on some key dimensions. It doesn't cover everything that's important by any means, but it does address key patterns that studies show are related to how a marriage will fare over time. Everyone would occasionally answer yes to some of these questions, but a persistent pattern of yes answers over time can be a warning signal that your relationship needs help. You'll want to begin taking steps to turn things around. Or you may find that you answer no to most of these questions. In that case, you should approach what we have to teach you as a matter of prevention. In other words, take the time to learn the kinds of strategies that can keep your marriage on track and growing over the years to come.

1. Little arguments escalate into ugly fights with accusations, criticisms, name calling, or bringing up past hurts.
2. My partner criticizes or belittles my opinions, feelings, or desires.

3. My partner seems to view my words or actions more negatively than I mean them to be.

4. When we have a problem to solve, it is like we are on opposite
teams.

5. I hold back from telling my partner what I really think and feel.

6. I think seriously about what it would be like to date or marry
someone else.

7. I feel lonely in this relationship.

8. When we argue, one of us withdraws, that is, doesn't want to
talk about it anymore or leaves the scene.

As you read this book, you will understand not only why these
questions are important but what you can do to build and maintain
a great marriage that brings delight to both you and the Lord.

A WORD ABOUT RESEARCH AND THE BIBLE

This book presents a thoroughly Christian model of marriage, using
core teachings about marriage and relationships from throughout
scripture. You may be wondering how we think about the integration of research findings with revealed truth. To highlight the approach to integration taken, we quote from two sources regarding
Christian PREP.

Thomas Aquinas, a Dominican monk, labored in the thir-
teenth century to integrate reason and revelation. Believing
strongly that there was one source of truth (God), he believed
that "nothing discovered in nature could ultimately contra-
dict the Faith" (quoting Chesterton, 1956, p. 93). Essentially,
truth discerned by observation and reason (e.g., science)
should not be incompatible with truth given by God through
revelation. Revelation can be considered to be special (e.g.,
scripture) or general (revelation discerned about the creator

from studying creation, for example, truth discerned through research) [Stanley, 1997].

This approach is based on the belief that God has provided guidelines for marriage in Scripture. Furthermore, he allows us to learn more about the workings of relationships through sound research. The belief guiding the integration of Scripture and research is that "all truth is God's truth," with Scripture being preeminent [Stanley, Trathen, & McCain, 1996].

In other words, sound marital research can discover truth because all truth comes from our Lord. Through scripture, God reveals His heart on marriage and truth about relationships very directly. In the rest of this book, our desire is to present clear truth from scripture. We also will present key research findings that can further illuminate patterns associated with marriages of lasting promise.

To some, coming out with a book on a Christian version of PREP after a secular one has been published could lead to concerns about *proof texting*, a term that, in the most negative sense, refers to using passages of scripture to make points that have little to do with the real meanings of the passages—in other words, making scripture say what you want it to say. We have tried hard to avoid this. However, finding something that seems to be true based on research, then going back to see how it squares with scripture, is a sound strategy of integration. Such a process tests the validity of the newer ideas by holding them up to the light of scripture. As Paul said, "But examine everything carefully; hold fast to that which is good" (I Thessalonians 5:12).

In a world increasingly filled with all sorts of information, this examination is a process that Christians should regularly engage in. This process goes to the heart of what integration is about. If we really believe that there is one source of truth (God) and that we can know truth in two ways—specific revelation (scripture) and general revelation (nature and observation)—there should be a harmony based in the simple fact that God is consistent.

In this book, you'll find chapters with varying levels of depth with regard to biblical content. For example, the first chapter presents a model of marriage in God's design that has nothing to do with research. It's right out of scripture. Likewise, the chapters on forgiveness and spiritual oneness come from a deeper discussion of core eternal truths revealed in scripture. Other chapters, such as those on communication and problem solving, present an integration much more on the level of "proverbial" wisdom. These are common sense concepts, not matters of deep theology. There, the integration amounts more to presenting how recent research findings point in the same directions as age-old biblical wisdom. For example, being "quick to hear, slow to speak, and slow to become angry" is hardly a deep concept, but you'll not likely find a single principle in scripture or marital research that is more important in the day-to-day life of your marriage.

One more point: when and if research ever reveals findings that are inconsistent with revealed truth, we choose to follow scripture. But one of the great blessings to us has been how wonderfully scripture and sound marital research point in the same directions.

HOW TO GET THE MOST OUT OF THIS BOOK

This book starts with the basics, presented in a step-by-step manner, and builds to incorporate a variety of strategies for making marriage all that it can be. We believe that you can learn how to have a good relationship if you are motivated to do so. We provide specific instructions for exercises that can be practiced at home to help you do this. (If your mate is not initially interested in reading this book with you, we have some suggestions for you in the final section.)

We'll introduce a number of very effective tools for handling conflict and disagreements. Like any new skills, these become easier with practice. With each skill or principle, we'll also tell you about the underlying theory and research so you can understand why it works. You will find that these techniques are not really difficult to understand, but *they will take work to master*. We believe it will be worth your effort to make what you learn here a part of your relationship.

We'll focus on the basics as well as the larger picture. We'll try to show you how certain kinds of beliefs and attitudes are related to marital success and failure. We want you to capture a vision for how to nurture what matters most in your marriage—things like expectations, friendship, commitment, and spiritual connection—so that you can take hold of the blessings available to you. These deeper themes are more about how you think and are motivated in your marriage. By combining these deeper themes with a solid focus on the basics, we believe we can encourage you to build and nurture a great marriage. But none of the ideas can help you if the principles are not put into practice. Someone once said that wisdom is putting knowledge into action. That's what we want to help you do. Practicing what we teach is very important. That's how you can put your love in action. And when you are able to do that, you can realize the full blessing and the great *lasting promise* of your marriage.

PART ONE

Handling Conflict/Protecting Your Marriage

In Chapter One, we lay the groundwork for the rest of this book. We offer a view of what marriage is about from God's perspective, as revealed in scripture. Following that chapter are specific suggestions for how you can more fully experience God's blessings in your marriage.

The bulk of this part focuses on how you can handle the difficult issues well. Most couples do not have solid skills or strategies for protecting all of what can be so wonderful in marriage from the conflicts and disagreements that will come up. However, both scripture and research teach us that how we handle the nuts and bolts of life determines the quality of our relationships. So, we start this book with a major focus on how you can protect your marriage from mishandled conflicts. We'll build from there.

1

Oneness

So they are no longer two, but one.

Matthew 19:6

It was a glorious marriage, the kind that fully reflected all the joys and promise a marriage can have. He was delighted with her and she with him. Like so many couples at the start, they felt comfortable and safe with one another. There was deep attraction and a deep knowing of one another. But like too many marriages, what started out with great promise led to great frustration. Over time—a short time for them—barriers grew where closeness had been. Blame and bickering intensified. They grew distant from one another and from the Lord. You know this couple. His name was Adam and her name was Eve.

How do marriages go from such promise to such futility? In part, that's the question we hope this book will answer for you. But much more important, we want to teach you some key principles that can help you build a great marriage and—this is just as important—keep a great marriage alive. God designed marriage to be a place where trust, openness, and vulnerability can thrive. As the world's first couple, Adam and Eve were the first to experience the joys and miseries of marriage. When God designed this first relationship, He made it so it would be nourishing, enriching, and growth producing. Let's take a closer look at what we can learn from Adam and Eve about marriage.

As God was busy creating all of matter, light, and life, He declared everything He made to be good. There was one notable exception. "The LORD God said, 'It is not good for the man to be alone'" (Genesis 2:18). Note that this "not good" in God's eyes came before sin and even prior to the relationship of Adam and Eve. There was no sin, no fall, and there were no consequences of these. Still, it was not good for man to be alone. Why? Simply because God created us for relationships—with Him, in marriage, and with others. But relationships—especially close relationships—are difficult. In fact, it seems that our relationships with those we love most are the very hardest relationships of all to keep on track. Why is this? Let's look at what happened between Adam and Eve in the Garden of Eden for some clues.

As Genesis tells us, Adam and Eve were the last creations of God. They were the pinnacle of His work—a perfect man and a perfect woman, joined together and living in perfect harmony in a perfect setting. We don't know exactly what Eden was like, but imagine having no limits on time or money or any other resource. Imagine you are in the most relaxed setting and experiencing your greatest enjoyment and peace of mind. That dream is probably as close as we can get to Eden, this side of heaven. Here were Adam and Eve in this wonderful setting, anticipating a wonderful life together, knowing God intimately, and without a care in the world. The Bible says, "For this reason a man will leave his father and mother and be united to his wife, and they will become one flesh. The man and his wife were both naked, and they felt no shame" (Genesis 2:24–25).

This passage from Genesis is quoted by Jesus and by Paul as the foundation for our understanding of marriage. By letting Jesus and Paul amplify our understanding of this passage, we can learn a great deal about the nature of marriage as God intended it to be.

ONENESS AND INTIMACY IN MARRIAGE

In Matthew 19, we are told of an occasion when the Pharisees questioned Jesus about divorce. "Is it lawful for a man to divorce his wife for any and every reason?" they asked (Matthew 19:3). At that time, the Pharisees and scribes were debating the conditions under which a man could divorce his wife. In asking Jesus, they weren't seriously interested in the right answer but were more interested in trapping Jesus into giving a "politically incorrect" response that would diminish His popularity with the common people. As on other occasions, this attempt to trap Him failed miserably. Jesus went straight to Genesis to reveal God's heart on the subject. "Haven't you read," He replied, "that at the beginning the Creator 'made them male and female,' and said, 'For this reason a man will leave his father and mother and be united to his wife, and the two will become one flesh'? So they are no longer two, but one. Therefore what God has joined together, let man not separate" (Matthew 19:4–6).

Although this passage is frequently cited to emphasize the seriousness of divorce in God's sight, what Jesus says about being joined together in oneness speaks to the heart of what *A Lasting Promise* is about. In fact, the idea of oneness versus separateness runs through the heart of Christian theology. Although oneness is a major theme in Christianity, it's far from easy to describe. In fact, very different manifestations or forms of oneness are presented for us to ponder—from the Trinity, to the members of the church (as the body of Christ), to the relationship between Christ and the church, and, of course, to marriage as the most fundamental of human relationships.

Oneness means many things to many people, but in His conversation with the Pharisees, Jesus appealed to the ideas of oneness and permanence in answering their trick question regarding the seriousness of divorce. He seems to be telling them that divorce is not God's perfect plan because marriage is fundamentally about two people mysteriously becoming and remaining one for the rest of their lives. Put another way, God's design for marriage is that it be a covenant of spiritual unity in which the souls and hearts of both partners are joined before Him and with Him into a "three-fold cord" providing direction and meaning in the bond of love (Ecclesiastes 4:9–12; Ephesians 5: 31,32). How does that happen? How do two people somehow become one?

The Mystery of Oneness

Historically, Christians have talked about oneness in marriage as a diamond having several facets: spiritual, emotional, intellectual, and physical. We will focus on these dimensions in many ways throughout this book. The foundational teaching about oneness, of course, rests in the physical union of husband and wife, but so much more is implied. What it means for two people to become one is a rich and wonderful mystery. Paul quotes the Genesis passage, then moves right to the concept of mystery as he grapples with what marriage is all about. "'For this reason a man will leave his father and mother and be united to his wife, and the two will become one flesh.' This is a profound mystery—but I am talking about Christ and the church" (Ephesians 5:31,32).

The word in the Greek for *mystery* comes from the idea of astonishment or a shut mouth. When something is a mystery, what can you say? It is hard to describe a mystery like this without first stopping to reflect on its richness. The preeminent point Paul is making pertains to the relationship between Christ and the church, but we believe that Paul is also making a more general point about oneness—that oneness is inherently mysterious. What does oneness in marriage mean? Stop your reading for a moment and ponder this idea. What do you think oneness means in marriage? What might be so wonderful about it that it cannot be easily described?

One thing seems clear. You can't develop true biblical oneness in marriage by having one person's identity disappear or be engulfed by the other, forming one big blob. Some people fear that will happen in marriage; they fear they will somehow lose track of themselves if they grow truly close to another. We've heard it said this way: "The two shall become one . . . but, which one?" But that is not the ideal expressed in scripture. In fact, one of the most powerful images of oneness conveys a wonderful diversity in our unity that is quite the opposite of "blobness." Paul describes the body of Christ as being one but made up of many individual parts, each unique in its own function (I Corinthians 12 and 14). It's a unity (one body), but it has a colorful and wonderful diversity. Although it is mysterious, the concept of diversity in oneness lies at the very core of central understandings in Christianity.

One of the best ways to convey a healthy view of oneness in marriage is with the Me, You, and Us diagram in Figure 1.1.

Note that two distinct persons come together in the marital union: You and Me. But there is also a third, crucial identity of Us that is born out of the connection between Me and You. One person's identity is never to be lost in the other, but God's design is that the two come together in a powerful way to form a new oneness that is unique. Beyond this limited understanding, oneness is mysterious. You can't quite describe it, but you probably know when you and your mate have it and when you don't.

We want to discuss one practical implication of these concepts before moving on. The concept of mystery implies a great freedom in the expression of the unique oneness of your marriage. If you take seriously the idea that this oneness is mysterious, you are freed in the realization that no cookie-cutter model can tell you how you *should* develop oneness in your marriage. You can be creative in the ways you draw together and express your oneness over the years. By doing so, we believe you will be most likely to glorify God in your marriage. Research about successful and happy marriages reveals a great diversity in the ways happy couples relate to each other. But, as you will see in the next chapter, there's almost no creativity in how couples who are doing poorly destroy their oneness. The patterns that unravel a marriage are not very different from one couple to another. Simply put, couples are different in the ways they

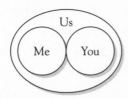

Figure 1.1. Me, You, and Us.

express oneness but fall into well-worn ruts when a marriage is being slowly destroyed.

As much or more than anything else, we will try to keep you out of these ruts by teaching you things that can prevent the attitudes and behaviors that destroy your chances of creatively developing oneness and intimacy in your marriage. In the last chapter of this book, we will focus on ways to help you develop the most mysterious oneness element of all: spiritual oneness.

Permanence in Oneness

When Jesus said, "What God has put together, let man not separate," He clearly conveyed the sense that the oneness of marriage is to be a relationship of permanence (Matthew 19:6). "Until death do us part" is the way this is commonly expressed in marital vows. Scripture leaves us with no doubt that God loves all people, including those who divorce, but that He hates divorce (Malachi 2:16). However, this is not a book about the theology of divorce; it is a book about preventing divorce and enabling you to keep the promise in your marriage. It is a book for couples who want to make their marriages all they can be—marriages that not only will last but will fully reflect the wonderful mystery of oneness with joy, confidence, and growing love.

Naked and Unashamed: Openness in Oneness

Now, we get to the really interesting part. Adam and Eve were in the Garden of Eden, enjoying life and each other. Scripture says this about their marriage at this point: "The man and his wife were both naked, and they felt no shame" (Genesis 2:25).

Naked and no shame. What does that mean to you? What do you suppose that was like? When we ask couples in workshops what this means to them we hear many things: closeness, fearlessness, acceptance, vulnerability, accessibility, freedom, excitement, and innocence.

No one can say what that was like for Eve and Adam, but this passage captures something powerful—something most people strongly desire in their marriages. Although many marriages end up in great pain and frustration, most people seem to genuinely desire the kind of closeness and acceptance implied from God's original model as the first couple experienced it. When looking for a mate, were you looking for someone to argue with? Of course not! Like most couples, you were looking for someone to be your best friend and support—your soul mate. You were not drawn to your partner because of the inevitable conflicts you would have but because you sensed in that person the possibility of a shameless relationship with absolute acceptance—something few have known but all have longed for.

So, here are Adam and Eve, the perfect couple, created for one another, discovering the joy of knowing one another in a perfect world. How long did that last? No one knows. We are told in the third chapter of Genesis of the troubling things that began to happen. But something wonderful was happening prior to the trouble—real oneness.

Although oneness is a mystery, we believe the deepest desire of our souls is to enjoy a deep closeness with God and our loved ones, especially our mates. But for too many couples, the barriers to oneness overtake the sense of connection and hope they began with.

BARRIERS TO ONENESS

Although we are created for relationship, and marriage is the foundation of human relationships, things don't always go the way they should. In marriage as in other relationships, we often succumb to barriers that limit our ability to fully enter into the blessings that God has planned for us. Let's look at several kinds of barriers that get in the way.

Self-Protection and the Fear of Rejection

The things described in Genesis include the perfect couple's temptation, their sin, and their fall from the perfect state. These are important topics to be sure, and they lead theologians to explore weighty matters beyond the scope of this book. Because this is a book on relationships, we will focus on what happened to Adam and Eve in their relationship due to these events.

Adam and Eve were created for each other to live fruitfully in paradise. They had only one admonition from God to observe: they were not to eat from the tree of the knowledge of good and evil (Genesis 2:17). They had a world of exciting possibilities open to them. Only one choice was off limits. That one limit became the point for temptation. People often think of God as limiting us rather than seeing that He wants us to know about the limits we must observe so we can fully partake of the wonderful options that are "in bounds."

Satan tempted the couple to doubt what God had said (Genesis 3:1) and to doubt that God really had their best interests at heart (Genesis 3:4,5). As we all know, Adam and Eve gave in to the temptation and sinned; they ate from the tree that they were not to touch.

Once they had sinned, the couple did a very curious thing: they immediately covered themselves up. "Then the eyes of both of them were opened, and they knew that they were naked; and they sewed fig leaves together and made themselves loin coverings" (Genesis 3:7, NASB).

Consider this. They had seen the tree with their *eyes,* grabbed the forbidden fruit with their *hands,* and eaten it with their *mouths.* So why were they covering what they covered? Tradition and some translations say they made loin coverings. Why did they cover that part of their bodies? Why not make little fig leaf blindfolds (since they had seen the tree with their eyes), or little fig leaf mittens (since they had touched the fruit with their hands), or little fig leaf gags (since they had eaten the fruit with their mouths)? Two answers to this question stand out for us. First, they covered up the part of their bodies that was one of their most wonderful ways of expressing intimacy.

Second, the couple no longer felt the glorious freedom of utter acceptance, so *they covered up where they were most obviously different.* Let that one sink in a bit. Isn't that what we all do all the time?

We cover up our thoughts, feelings, and opinions more when we are with someone who sees things differently. When people are mostly like us, we don't fear rejection. It's the differentness that leads to fear of rejection. In marriage, it's the same way. The same differences that are so much a part of the attraction to begin with become the basis for friction and frustration over time. For too many couples, how these differences are handled leads to ever-increasing barriers to oneness that grow to destroy the whole marriage.

In the next part of the story, God confronts Adam and Eve about their sin. Their reply is noteworthy.

> Then the man and his wife heard the sound of the LORD God as He was walking in the garden in the cool of the day, and they hid from the LORD God among the trees of the garden. But the LORD God called to the man, "Where are you?" He answered, "I heard you in the garden, and I was afraid because I was naked; so I hid" [Genesis 3:8–10].

Do you think God somehow lost track of Adam and Eve, needing to ask where they were hiding? It seems more likely that God wanted them to think about the question, as in "What have you done? Where are you now?" Adam's answer is even more interesting as he displays his motive for hiding—fear. After they had sinned, the fear of rejection drove them to cover up from one another and hide out from God. This was a fear they had not known before their disobedience. Along with sin and shame comes a sense of separateness and the horrifying fear of rejection. That fear lays the groundwork for many barriers in marriage as we seek to protect ourselves from rejection rather than to boldly give ourselves to one another in love.

The Barriers of Sin and Selfishness and the Power of Love

The barriers of sin and selfishness are embedded in the story of Adam and Eve and in our marriage stories as well. The fact is, a marriage brings together two imperfectly motivated people who strongly—and somewhat selfishly— desire intimacy and the other good things of life but who fear being hurt. Often, when we do hurt one another, it is because we have these selfish and self-protective desires motivating us. In fact, James pinpoints such selfish desires as a root cause of destructive conflict.

> What causes fights and quarrels among you? Don't they come from your desires that battle within you? You want something but don't get it. You kill and covet, but you cannot have what you want. You quarrel and fight. You do not have, because you do not ask God. When you ask, you do not receive, because you ask with wrong motives, that you may spend what you get on your pleasures [James 4:1–3].

In following Christ, we are set free to love and serve one another. This love enables us to overcome our basic selfishness. Look how Paul points out that love is the very essence of the law and then contrasts such love with the corrosiveness in relationships where such love is not leading the way.

> You, my brothers, were called to be free. But do not use your freedom to indulge the sinful nature; rather, serve one another in love. The entire law is summed up in a single command: "Love your neighbor as yourself." If you keep on biting and devouring each other, watch out or you will be destroyed by each other [Galatians 5:13–15].

Paul is writing to the church in Galatia, cautioning them to serve one another and to not give in to self-indulgence. Love is contrasted with relationships in which people are consumed by each other. Scripture is filled with such warnings and admonitions because these patterns are so common. Although many of these passages are written about relationships among Christians more generically, the principles apply just as clearly in marriage as elsewhere, if not more so.

To further highlight the point, we note that Jesus elevated the concept of love to the central place in our understanding of what God desires. "This is my commandment, that you love one another as I have loved you" (John 15:12).

Being able to live out this commandment is at the core of Jesus' teaching about how we should relate to one another. Our God-enabled ability to do this affects every human relationship we are in, including marriage, family, church, and those we work with. In many ways, you can think about the things we will be suggesting in this book as tangible ways to put your love in action. *"Lasting promise" love is love that acts. It is love in motion.* This kind of love keeps a marriage open to the fullest blessings in life.

This brings us to an important point. This book is not primarily focused on deep matters of discipleship. In other words, our focus here is not on what you can or need to be doing to know Christ more deeply or follow Him more closely in your own life. Here, we will focus on things that directly relate to your ability to have a healthy, joyous, loving, and lasting marriage. However, if you are genuine and sincere about growing in your ability to serve one another in love, everything else we will share with you will be that much easier to act on. There is no substitute for growing spiritually when it comes to what fuels great relationships, especially your marriage. The desire to change patterns in your marriage ultimately starts at a place deep in your own heart, with a decision to learn how to be different in the way you relate to your mate. Before moving on to the next chapter, which reveals key patterns that can destroy or build up marriages, there's one more barrier to oneness and intimacy that needs to be discussed.

NOT KNOWING WHAT BETTER TO DO

One of the most beautiful things Jesus ever said was, "Do to others as you would have them do to you" (Luke 6:31). Known as The Golden Rule, this statement from Jesus' Sermon on the Mount embodies the call to love in the most simple terms possible. It also puts the emphasis on a simple "do." But wanting to do what's right and knowing how to do it are two different things. We take issue with a common belief among Christians—the belief that if your heart and soul are in harmony with God, you'll somehow automatically know just what to do in your marriage. We don't buy that. Prospering spiritually does not mean that you know how to do the things that nurture a marriage. For example, do you know how to really listen to your mate, even when tensions are high or you disagree? More important, can you stop an argument before damaging things are said? Do you know how to problem solve as a team, how to work through the process of forgiveness together, how to clarify your deepest expectations, how to enhance and deepen commitment? These are things you can learn, and when learned well, they can help you develop and keep the kind of marriage you want most. They are ways to put your love in action.

Perfection is not possible, of course. We will never restore ourselves to Eden. But it is possible to avoid the kinds of pitfalls that snag far too many couples. In the rest of this book, we hope to teach you a number of concepts and techniques that can help you stay together, stay happy, and draw closer to the kind of marriage in which you more fully enter into God's blessings. You don't pick these things up by osmosis. They are things you need to learn and practice in order to receive the benefit and blessing. Give the things we're going to suggest a try. You will be surprised at the power of some fairly simple ideas. Here we go.

EXERCISES

Oneness requires that we do our best to break down the barriers in order to open the paths for intimacy. In further chapters, we will present skills to help you break down the barriers or to keep them out of the way in the first place. To learn these skills you each must make a commitment to read the chapters and practice the exercises. You could do that together, but we understand that is not always possible. In any case, reading (individually or together) and practicing are essential to getting the most out of this book. For your first exercise, address the following.

1. How can you set aside time to read and practice the material? What is realistic for you? It is important that you set goals that are achievable within your schedules, but you should make creating a stronger marriage a priority. Decide what works best for you. For example, you might choose to read the whole book, then go over the exercises together, or you might go chapter by chapter together.

2. Ask God's help in reading and practicing. Pray about your openness to learning about and tearing down your own barriers to intimacy with your partner. You can pray out loud, silently, or whatever works for you. But we believe in the power of prayer and encourage you to avail yourself of God's help in making your marriage all it can be.

3. Write down your goals for working through this material. If you and your partner read each chapter and work on the exercises together, how would you hope this would affect your relationship?

4. Spend some time thinking over this chapter. What do you think about when you think of the concepts of oneness, intimacy, barriers, or of being naked and unashamed? What are some of the barriers you are more concerned about in your relationship?

5. What is your view of what marriage is all about?

"May the Lord make your love increase and overflow for each other" (I Thessalonians 3:12).

2

Four Key Patterns That Destroy Oneness

Reckless words pierce like a sword, but the tongue of the wise brings healing.

Proverbs 12:18

Learning constructive ways to handle your differences is one of the most powerful things you can do to protect the promise that your marriage holds. Much of this book is designed to give you some specific ways to do just that. Researchers from a number of marital study centers have discovered many factors that are associated with couples ending up unhappy or divorced in the future. In this chapter, you'll learn about some of the key negative patterns that put a marriage at risk.

As you learn about these patterns, we believe you'll be better able to avoid them. That is crucial because the kinds of patterns we'll describe here can cement barriers into your marriage, keeping you from the fullness of oneness. In the chapters that follow, we'll teach you some specific tools you can use to prevent negative patterns in your relationship.

THE POWER OF THE NEGATIVE

You might be thinking, "Why focus on the negative? Why not just build up the good things in our relationship?" Good question. Here's the answer. *According to research conducted by our team at the University of Denver, as well as by other researchers around the country, it's the presence of certain negative patterns that can destroy a relationship.* Therefore, if you can eliminate or keep to a minimum some key negative patterns, the positive things in your relationship can blossom and grow. But if you don't control the negatives, they can erase the good effects of just about everything else you have going for you.

Risk Factors for Marital Failure

Researchers have found that the likelihood of divorce is associated with a variety of factors, many of which are already there for couples when they walk down the aisle to say "I do." By looking only at variables from premarriage, a number of researchers have been able to correctly classify those who divorce or end up unhappy many years later. Thankfully, some of the most important elements that raise the risks for a marriage are things that can be changed or prevented with some work.

The key factors that put marriages at risk have to do with how couples think and interact—and, especially, how they handle conflicts in marriage. If you can stop doing the things that put your marriage at risk (or avoid doing them in the first place), we believe you stand a far better chance of experiencing the richest blessings of marriage.

Other factors that influence permanence and happiness are things that are difficult or impossible to change, especially once you are married. These include parents' divorce, young age at time of marriage, premarital cohabitation, differences in religious upbringing, poor financial means, and certain personality characteristics such as neuroticism and impulsivity. If some of these more difficult-to-change factors are present in your marriage, don't be discouraged. When we talk about research findings, we are always talking about differences that tend to be true, but there are always many exceptions. You could be one. Furthermore, these variables combine in very complex ways, making it hard to say how things will turn out for any one couple. What's most important is that if you can focus on the things that can be changed, the unchangeable factors are much less likely to get in the way of a lifetime of blessing in your marriage.

Both scripture and research make it very clear that how you treat one another when you have disagreements or when conflicts arise says a great deal about how your marriage will be in the years to come. The kinds of negative patterns we describe here can wipe out a lot of what's positive. In fact, marital researchers Cliff Notarius and Howard Markman, as well as John Gottman, have estimated that one verbal negative can wipe out the effects of five or even twenty positives. It's much like what Solomon said ages ago. "As dead flies give perfume a bad smell, so a little folly outweighs wisdom and honor" (Ecclesiastes 10:1).

The little negatives can wipe out a tremendous amount of good. After this chapter, we will teach you specific strategies for minimizing negative patterns such as those described here. But first, let's raise your awareness about the damaging patterns to watch out for in your marriage.

Biblical Warnings

We believe that when it comes to how we treat one another (in all relationships, including marriage), scripture says far more about what *not* to do than exactly what to do. Sure, there are passages such as I Corinthians 13 on the wonderful, positive aspects of love, but think of the scores of passages that warn us how not to relate to one another (for example, Proverbs 12:18, 20:3, 29:11; Matthew 5:22, 7:1–5; Galatians 5:13–15; James 4:1ff). The reason so many passages warn us about these kinds of destructive behaviors is that these patterns are so corrosive in all relationships. Their effects are even more damaging in marriage. Before we describe some of the negative patterns in more detail, consider the words of the apostle Peter. "Do not repay evil with evil or insult with insult, but with blessing, because to this you were called so that you may inherit a blessing. For, whoever would love life and see good days must keep his tongue from evil and his lips from deceitful speech (I Peter 3:9,10).

Peter wrote this before there was such a thing as research on marriage. In this passage, he pretty well sums up what we see in study after study. How you treat one another in the moments that make up your marriage has a great deal to do with how many "good days" you are going to see together. We are repeatedly warned throughout scripture about such patterns and behavior, and the modern-day marital research merely sheds further light on the dangers at work here. Let's look at four key patterns that you'll want to avoid.

ESCALATION: WHAT GOES AROUND COMES AROUND

Escalation occurs when partners respond back and forth negatively to each other, continually upping the ante so the conversation gets more and more hostile. In escalation, negative comments spiral into increasing anger and frustration. Research shows that couples who are happy now and likely to stay that way are less prone to escalation; if they start to escalate, they are able to stop the negative process before it erupts into a full-blown fight.

Ted, a thirty-four-year-old construction worker, and Wendy, thirty-two, who runs a catering business out of their home, had been married for eight years when we first saw them. Like many couples, their fights started over small issues.

TED: (*sarcastically*) You'd think you could put the cap back on the toothpaste.

WENDY: (*equally sarcastically*) Oh, and you never forget to put it back?

TED: As a matter of fact, I always put it back.

WENDY: Oh, I forgot just how compulsive you are. You are right, of course!

TED: I don't even know why I stay with you. You are so negative.

WENDY: Maybe you shouldn't stay. No one is barring the door.

TED: I'm not really sure why I do stay anymore.

One of the most damaging things about arguments that are escalating is that partners tend to say things that threaten the very lifeblood of their marriage. As frustration and hostility mount, partners often try to hurt each other by hurling verbal (and sometimes even physical) weapons. As the Bible says in Proverbs 12:18, "Reckless words pierce like a sword." You can see this pattern with Ted and Wendy; the battle quickly heats up to include threats of ending the relationship. Once very negative comments are made, they are hard to take back. These reckless words do a ton of damage to oneness and intimacy and a sense of safety in the relationship.

Although partners can say hurtful things during escalating arguments, such remarks usually don't reflect what they generally feel about each other. You may believe that people reveal their true feelings in the midst of fierce fights, yet we do not believe this is usually the case. Instead, what is said is mostly focused on the immediate goal of piercing the other as a way to protect oneself.

In Ted and Wendy's argument, Wendy mentioned his being compulsive because she really wanted to hit him below the belt. At a more tender moment between them, he had shared his concerns about being so driven, explaining how he had always felt he must try harder to please his father. The escalation of this argument led Wendy to use her intimate knowledge of him to strike a piercing blow. When escalation leads to the use of such knowledge as a weapon, the damage to the future likelihood of tender moments is great. Who is going to share deeper things if the information may be used later when conflict is out of control in the relationship?

You may be thinking, "We don't fight like cats and dogs. How does this apply to us?" Well, damaging escalation isn't always this dramatic. It can be very subtle. Voices don't have to be raised for you to get into the cycle of returning negative for negative. Yet, research shows that even subtle patterns of escalation can lead to divorce in years to come. Consider the following conversation between Max and Donna, a couple of newlyweds in their twenties, who are just starting out in an apartment in Denver.

MAX: Did you get the rent paid on time?

DONNA: That was going to be your job.

MAX: You were supposed to do it.

DONNA: No, you were.

MAX: Did it get done?

DONNA: No. And, I'm not going to, either.

MAX: (*muttering*) Great. Just great.

Being newlyweds, Donna and Max are very happy with their marriage. Imagine, however, the cumulative effect of years of small arguments like this one, gradually eating away at the positive things they now share.

It is important for the future health of your relationship to learn to counteract whatever tendency you have to escalate as a couple. If you don't escalate much, great. Your goal is to learn to keep things that way. If you do escalate a fair amount, your goal is to recognize it and to do whatever you can to stop it.

James addresses this issue bluntly. "If anyone considers himself religious and yet does not keep a tight rein on his tongue, he deceives himself and his religion is worthless" (James 1:26).

You can't say anything you feel anytime you feel it and have your marriage stay healthy. Nor can you really follow Christ well without learning to keep a rein on your tongue.

Short-Circuiting Escalation

All couples escalate from time to time, but some couples steer out of the pattern more quickly and much more positively. Compare Ted and Wendy's earlier argument with that of Maria and Hector. Maria, a forty-five-year-old sales clerk for a jewelry store, and Hector, a forty-nine-year-old attorney who works for the U.S. Justice Department, have been married twenty-three years. Like most couples, many of their arguments are about everyday events.

MARIA: (*annoyed*) You left the butter out again.

HECTOR: (*irritated*) Why are little things so important to you? Just put it back.

MARIA: (*softening her tone*) Things like that are important to me. Is that so bad?

HECTOR: (*calmer*) I guess not. Sorry I was such a pain.

Notice the difference. Like Ted and Wendy, Hector and Maria's argument tended to escalate, but they quickly steered out of it. When escalation sequences are short-circuited, it is usually because one partner backs off and says something to de-escalate the argument, thus breaking the negative cycle. Often, this takes the simple humility of choosing to soften your tone and put down your shield. For her part, Maria softened; she didn't get defensive. For his part, Hector made the decision to back off and to acknowledge Maria's point of view.

Softening your tone and acknowledging your partner's point of view are simple but powerful tools you can employ to diffuse tension and end escalation. As Solomon said, "A gentle answer turns away wrath, but a harsh word stirs up anger" (Proverbs 15:1). Often, a gentle answer is all it takes.

INVALIDATION: PAINFUL PUT-DOWNS

Invalidation is a pattern in which one partner subtly or directly puts down the thoughts, feelings, or character of the other. Let's take a closer look at this pattern. It can take many forms. Here are two other arguments, one between Ted and Wendy and the other between Maria and Hector.

WENDY: (*very angrily*) You missed your doctor's appointment again! You are so irresponsible. I could see you dying and leaving me, just like your father.

TED: (*bruised*) Thanks a lot. You know I am nothing like my father.

WENDY: He was a creep and so are you.

TED: (*dripping with sarcasm*) I'm sorry. I forgot my good fortune to be married to such a paragon of responsibility. You can't even keep your purse organized.

WENDY: At least I am not so obsessive about stupid little things.

TED: You're so arrogant.

MARIA: (*with a tear*) You know, I am really frustrated by the hatchet job Bob did on my evaluation at work.

HECTOR: I don't think he was all that critical. I would be happy to have an evaluation as positive as that from Fred. Besides, why don't you just give it to the Lord?

MARIA: (*with a sigh and turning away*) You don't get it. It upset me.

HECTOR: Yeah, I see that, but I still think you are overreacting.

These examples are as different as night and day. Although both show invalidation, the first example is much more caustic, and hence damaging to the relationship, than the second. With Ted and Wendy, you can feel the *contempt* seeping through. The argument has settled into an attack on character. Jesus taught strongly against such attacks on the character of another. "But I tell you that anyone who is angry with his brother will be subject to judgment. Again, anyone who says to his brother, 'Raca,' is answerable to the Sanhedrin. But anyone who says, 'You fool!' will be in danger of the fire of hell" (Matthew 5:22).

The translation note for the New International Version says that *Raca* is an Aramaic term of contempt, something like calling a person worthless or empty-headed. Of course calling someone a fool is also invalidation. Jesus wants us to know that these attacks on the character of others are way out of bounds.

Although Maria and Hector do not show the contempt displayed by Ted and Wendy, Hector is subtly putting Maria down for the way she is feeling. He may even think he is being constructive or trying to cheer her up by saying, "It's not so bad" and "Trust the Lord." Nevertheless, this kind of communication is invalidating. Maria feels even more hurt now because he has said, in effect, that her feelings of fear and frustration are inappropriate. This kind of invalidation was described by Solomon as "singing songs to a heavy heart," and it doesn't feel too good to be on the receiving end of it (Proverbs 25:20). However, most people do like to hear encouraging words when feeling down, and it's probably wisest to learn together what kind of statements and actions are more encouraging in those circumstances.

The contemptuous invalidation displayed by Ted and Wendy in the first example is more obviously destructive than Hector's more subtle form of invalidation. But any kind of invalidation can set up barriers. Invalidation hurts. It leads naturally to covering up who you are and what you think because it's just too risky to be real. What couple can maintain the ability to be "naked and unashamed" when invalidation is regularly present?

Preventing Invalidation

In either of the previous arguments, the couples would have done better if each partner had simply shown respect for the other by acknowledging that person's viewpoint. Note the difference in how these conversations could have gone.

> WENDY: (*very angry*) I am very angry that you missed the doctor's appointment again. I worry about you being around for me in the future.
>
> TED: (*bruised*) It really upset you, didn't it?
>
> WENDY: You bet. I want to know that you are going to be there for me, and when you miss an appointment that I am anxious about, I worry about us.

TED: I understand why it would make you worried when I don't take care of myself.

MARIA: (*with a tear*) You know, I am really frustrated by the hatchet job Bob did on my evaluation at work.

HECTOR: That must really tick you off.

MARIA: Yeah, it does. And, I also get worried about whether I'll be able to keep this job. What would we do?

HECTOR: I didn't know you were so worried about losing your job. Tell me more.

We have replayed the discussions with similar beginnings but with very different endings. Now, there is acceptance of feelings, respect for each other's character, and an emphasis on validation. By validation, we simply mean that the one raising the concern is respected and heard. You don't have to agree with your partner to validate his or her feelings. Our research shows that *invalidation* is one of the very best predictors of future problems and divorce, but surprisingly, the amount of *validation* doesn't say much about the future health of a relationship the way invalidation does. Again, stopping the negative seems to be more important than increasing the positive. Does that mean validation is not so important? Not really, but it does mean that stopping invalidation is crucial. Respectful validation is probably the most powerful way to eliminate invalidation when you are trying to stay on the higher road. But it takes discipline, especially when you are frustrated or angry. We will teach you some very effective ways to limit invalidation and enhance validation in later chapters.

NEGATIVE INTERPRETATIONS: WHEN PERCEPTION IS WORSE THAN REALITY

Negative interpretations occur when one partner consistently believes that the motives of the other are more negative than is really the case. This can be a very destructive, negative pattern in a relationship. It makes any conflict or disagreement harder to deal with constructively. Margot and David have been married twelve years, and they are generally happy with their relationship. Yet, their discussions at times have been plagued by a specific negative interpretation. Every December they have had trouble deciding whether to travel to her parents' home for the holidays. Margot believes that David dislikes her parents, but in fact, he is quite fond of them in his own way. She has this mistaken belief because of a few incidents early in the marriage that David has long since forgotten. Here's how a typical discussion around their issue of holiday travel plans goes.

> MARGOT: We should start looking into plane tickets to go visit my parents this holiday season.
>
> DAVID: (*thinking about their budget problem*) I was wondering if we can really afford it this year.
>
> MARGOT: (*in anger*) My parents are very important to me, even if you don't like them. I'm going to go.
>
> DAVID: I would like to go, really I would. I just don't see how we can afford a thousand dollars in plane tickets and pay the bill from Joey's orthodontist.
>
> MARGOT: You can't be honest and admit you just don't want to go, can you? Just admit it. You don't like my parents.
>
> DAVID: There is nothing to admit. I enjoy visiting your parents. I'm thinking about money here, not your parents.
>
> MARGOT: That's a convenient excuse. (*storms out of the room*)

Given that we know David really does like to go to her parents' house, can you see how powerful Margot's negative interpretation has become? He cannot penetrate it. What can he say or do to make a difference as long as her belief that he dislikes her parents is so strong? If a negative interpretation is strong enough, nothing will change it. In this case, David wants to address the decision they

must make from the standpoint of the budget, but Margot's interpretation will overpower their ability to communicate effectively.
Fortunately for them, this problem is relatively isolated and not a
consistent pattern in their marriage.

Negative Interpretations Fuel Hopelessness

When relationships become more distressed, the negative interpretations mount and help create an environment of hopelessness
and demoralization. Alfred and Eileen were high school sweet-
hearts. They have been married eighteen years and have three children but have been very unhappy in their marriage for more than
seven years, in part due to the corrosive effect of strong, negative
interpretations. Although positive things happen in their marriage, almost nothing positive that one does is recognized positively
by the other, as seen by this recent conversation about parking
their car.

> ALFRED: You left the car out again.
>
> EILEEN: Oh. I guess I forgot to put it in when I came back
> from Madge's.
>
> ALFRED: (*with a bit of a sneer*) I guess you did. You know how
> much that irritates me.
>
> EILEEN: (*exasperated*) Look, I forgot. Do you think I leave it
> out just to irritate you?
>
> ALFRED: (*coldly*) Actually, that is exactly what I think. I have
> told you so many times that I want the car in the garage at
> night.
>
> EILEEN: Yes, you have. But, I don't leave it out just to tick you
> off. I just forget.
>
> ALFRED: If you cared what I thought about things, you'd
> remember.
>
> EILEEN: You know that I put the car in nine times out of ten.

ALFRED: More like half the time, and those are the times I
leave the garage door up for you.

EILEEN: Have it your way. It doesn't matter what reality is.
You will see it your way no matter what I say.

This may sound like a minor argument, but it is not. It represents a long-standing tendency for Alfred to interpret Eileen's behavior in the most negative light possible. For the sake of argument, assume that Eileen is absolutely correct when she says that she simply forgot to put the car in the garage and that this only happens about one in ten times. Alfred sees it differently, especially in his interpretation that she intentionally leaves the car out to upset him.

Mind Reading

Negative interpretations are a good example of mind reading. *Mind reading* occurs when you assume you know what your partner is thinking or why he or she did something. When you mind read positively, it does not tend to cause any harm. But when your mind reading includes negative judgments about the thoughts and motives of the other, you may be in real trouble, both in your marriage and in your spiritual life. Paul directly warned against attempting to judge the thoughts and motives of others (I Corinthians 4:5). Jesus Christ also issued a stern warning about this tendency to look more for the flaws in others than ourselves.

Why do you look at the speck of sawdust in your brother's eye
and pay no attention to the plank in your own eye? How can
you say to your brother, "Brother, let me take the speck out of
your eye," when you yourself fail to see the plank in your own
eye? You hypocrite, first take the plank out of your eye, and
then you will see clearly to remove the speck from your
brother's eye [Luke 6:41–42].

So, we are strongly warned to be on guard for the tendency to
view or judge others harshly. A marriage would truly be in terrible

shape if either partner routinely and intentionally did things just to frustrate the other. But this is seldom the case. Much more frequently, the actions of our partners that annoy us are either well intended or done with no conscious intention at all. Most of the time, most people think they are doing the best they can. It hurts to be accused of something you never intended to be hurtful. This pattern must be eliminated. When innocent actions of either mate are consistently interpreted negatively and unfairly, the marriage is headed for big trouble—or is already there.

Negative interpretations are hard to detect and counteract. They easily become cemented into the fabric of a relationship because we have a strong tendency toward "confirmation bias," which is the tendency to look for evidence that confirms what we already think is true about others or situations. Many studies show how strong this tendency is in us. So, once formed, negative interpretations do not change easily. Even though we can be completely wrong in our assumptions, we will tend to see what we expect to see.

In the example, Alfred has the expectation that "Eileen does not care one bit about anything that is important to me." Alfred really believes this strongly, which discolors any good things she might do. In distressed marriages, research shows that there is a tendency for partners to discount the positive things they see, attributing them to causes such as chance rather than to positive characteristics of the partner. Because of Alfred's negative interpretations, he attributes the times Eileen does put the car in the garage to his own action of leaving the door open and not to her intention to put it there. She can't win this argument, and they will not be able to come to an acceptable resolution until he can give up his negative mind-set.

Battling Negative Interpretations

You may need to reconsider what you think is true about some of your partner's motives. They may be much more positive than you have believed. Or they may at least be less negative. We are not advocating some kind of unrealistic "positive thinking." You can't just sit around and wish that your partner would change truly negative behaviors. But your negative interpretations are something you have to confront within yourself. Only you can control how you interpret your partner's behavior.

First, you have to ask yourself if your thinking might be overly negative in your interpretation of things your partner does or fails to do. Second—and this is hard—you must push yourself to look for evidence that is contrary to the negative interpretation you usually take. For example, if you believe that your partner is uncaring and generally see most of what he does in that light, you need to look for evidence to the contrary. Does he do some things for you that you like? Could it be that he does nice things because he cares enough to try to keep the relationship strong? It's up to you to consider your interpretation of behavior that others may see as obviously positive. Ask the Lord to remove the plank that might be in your eye.

One more specific point about how you view your mate: as you work through this book and are considering many positive changes in your relationship, make sure you try to give your partner the benefit of the doubt in wanting to make things better. Don't allow inaccurate interpretations to sabotage the work you are trying to accomplish.

Withdrawal and Avoidance: Hide and Seek

Withdrawal and avoidance are different manifestations of a pattern in which one partner shows an unwillingness to get into or stay with important discussions. Withdrawal can be as obvious as getting up and leaving the room or as subtle as "turning off" or "shutting down" during an argument. The withdrawer often tends to get quiet during an argument, look away, or agree quickly to a partner's suggestion just to end the conversation, with no real intention of following through.

Avoidance reflects the same reluctance to get into certain discussions, with more emphasis on the attempt to not let the conversation happen in the first place. A person prone to avoidance would prefer that the topic not come up and, if it does, may manifest the signs of withdrawal just described.

Let's look at this pattern as played out in a discussion between Paula, a twenty-eight-year-old realtor, and Jeff, a thirty-two-year-old loan officer. Married for three years, they have a two-year-old baby girl, Tanya, whom they adore. They were concerned that the tension in their relationship was starting to affect their daughter.

PAULA: When are we going to talk about how you are handling your anger?

JEFF: Can't this wait? I have to get these taxes done.

PAULA: I've brought this up at least five times already. No, it can't wait!

JEFF: (*tensing*) What's to talk about, anyway? It's none of your business.

PAULA: (*frustrated and looking right at Jeff*) Tanya is my business. I'm afraid that you may lose your temper and hurt her, and you won't do a single thing to learn to deal better with your anger.

JEFF: (*turning away, looking out the window*) I love Tanya. There's no problem here. (*leaving the room as he talks*)

PAULA: (*very angry now, following Jeff into the next room*) You have to get some help. You can't just stick your head in the sand.

JEFF: I'm not going to discuss anything with you when you are like this.

PAULA: Like what? It doesn't matter if I am calm or frustrated—you won't talk to me about anything important. Tanya is having problems and you have to face that.

JEFF: (*quiet, tense, fidgeting*)

PAULA: Well?

JEFF: (*going to closet and grabbing sweater*) I'm going out to get some peace and quiet.

PAULA: (*voice raised, angry*) Talk to me now. I'm tired of you leaving when we are talking about something important.

JEFF: (*looking away from Paula, walking toward the door*) I'm not talking, you are; actually, you're yelling. See you later.

Many couples do this kind of dance when it comes to dealing with difficult issues. One partner *pursues* dealing with issues (Paula) and one *avoids* or *withdraws* from dealing with issues (Jeff). Although common, this scenario is very destructive to the relationship. As with the other patterns presented, it does not have to be this dramatic to mean that more problems are to come. Even subtle withdrawal is associated with increased risks of a marriage not making it.

Pursuing and Withdrawing Dynamics: The Gender Dance

The *pursuer* is the one in the relationship who most often brings issues up for discussion or calls attention to the need to make a decision about something. The *withdrawer* is the person who tends to avoid these discussions or pulls away during them. Studies show that men are more likely to be in the withdrawing role, with women tending to pursue. However, in many relationships this pattern is reversed. And in some relationships, the partners switch these roles, depending on the topic. *Simply reverse the points we make here if the gender patterns are reversed between the two of you.*

Why do men tend to withdraw? Some say it's because they are less interested in change and will pull away to avoid dealing with the issues. That may be the case for some men, but we believe something else is happening much of the time: the one who withdraws tends to do so because it does not feel safe to stay in the argument—not emotionally safe. Or the withdrawer may even fear the conflict will turn physical. (If you have concerns about physical conflict and aggression in your relationship, please see "Some Thoughts on Domestic Violence" for important information.)

When this pattern gets going, it tends to be very frustrating for both men and women. When their partner withdraws, women usually feel shut out and begin to feel their husbands don't care about the relationship. For many women, his lack of talking equals a lack of caring. But that's usually a negative interpretation of what the withdrawer is about, which has more to do with trying to stop the conflict than not caring about the relationship. Likewise, men often complain that their pursuing wives get upset too much of the time, griping about this or that and picking fights, as if their wives like to fight. That is also a negative interpretation because what pursuers really want is to stay connected and to resolve issues. Many women say they are really in turmoil until a problem is worked out and harmony is restored. They also want to stay connected. These are not negative motives, just as a man's desire to avoid conflict is not a negative motive.

So, it is important to learn how to stay out of this pursuer-withdrawer pattern. That will take working together. Refrain from taking the most negative interpretation of what your partner does when he or she is either withdrawing or pursuing. A number of studies suggest (including some of ours) that the couples who are the happiest, most relaxed together and who are the best friends are those who do the best job of staying out of this pursuer-withdrawer pattern. So, although these kinds of patterns are fairly normal, they are also not very good for your marriage. You might be best off to accept that we all have some of these problems, but as a couple, work to decrease such patterns . We will give you some tips here for reducing both pursuit and withdrawal and many more strategies as we go on to help you avoid these destructive patterns in your marriage.

Avoiding Withdrawal

If you are seeing this pattern in your relationship, keep in mind that it will likely get worse if you allow it to continue. That is because as pursuers push more, withdrawers pull back more. And as withdrawers pull back, pursuers push harder. Furthermore, when issues are important, trying to avoid dealing with them will only lead to damaging consequences.

Most people have heard the verse that says, "In your anger do not sin: Do not let the sun go down while you are still angry." But do you know the context of this verse? Here it is:

> Therefore each of you must put off falsehood and speak truthfully to his neighbor, for we are all members of one body. "In your anger do not sin": Do not let the sun go down while you are still angry, and do not give the devil a foothold [Ephesians 4:25–27].

In context, this is one of the most direct passages in all of scripture about the importance of not allowing avoidance to grow in relationships. When you do not speak openly and truthfully, anger is likely to grow, and when anger is not being dealt with constructively, it gives the devil a toehold he can use to wreak havoc in your relationship. Don't allow this to happen.

In the case of withdrawal and avoidance, the best step you can take right now is to realize that you are not independent of one another. It takes two to do this tango. For this reason, you will have much greater success if you decide to work together to change or prevent the kinds of negative patterns discussed here. Withdrawers are not likely to reduce avoidance unless pursuers pursue less or more constructively and gently. Pursuers are going to find it hard to cut back on pursuing unless withdrawers deal more directly with the issues at hand. Do a better dance. We can teach you some steps.

HOW POSITIVE FEELINGS ERODE IN MARRIAGE: THE LONG-TERM EFFECT OF NEGATIVE PATTERNS

Contrary to popular belief, positives in marriage do not slowly fade away for no reason in particular. We believe that the chief reason that marriages fail at alarmingly high rates is that conflict is handled poorly, as evidenced by such patterns as those described in this chapter. Over time, these patterns steadily erode all the good things in the relationship until, for many couples, it seems there's nothing left worth fighting for. There are probably many other factors in marriages failing, but none is any more important.

For example, when a couple routinely escalates as issues arise, both may come to the conclusion that it is just as easy not to talk at all. After all, talking leads to fighting—right? Or as issues arise, the partners become more concerned with getting their own way, and invalidation becomes a weapon easily taken in hand. Over time, no issue seems safe. So couples can easily stop talking about anything meaningful, and friendship and intimacy go right out the door.

Many couples have no particular time or strategy in place for talking about problems. So problems tend to come up at the worst times. Even in what starts out as the best of marriages, these ways of handling or avoiding problems can lead to growing distance and a lack of confidence in the relationship. Remember Jeff and Paula from earlier in this chapter? Though a genuinely caring couple, their inability to discuss tough issues—in this case, his anger—has caused a rift that will widen and perhaps destroy the marriage if nothing is done.

At a very basic level, what happens when the differences are not being handled well is that the relationship begins to feel unsafe. When it's not emotionally safe to be around the very person you had wanted to be your best friend, real intimacy and a sense of connection die out. Then the barriers grow into loneliness and isolation—a far cry from being naked and unashamed. There's no lasting promise in a marriage thick with fig leaves.

If you want to keep your relationship strong or renew one that is lagging, you must learn to counteract destructive patterns such as those we have described. Fortunately, this can be done. You can prevent the erosion of happiness in your relationship for the years to come.

In this chapter we have described four patterns in handling conflict that predict future marital discord and divorce. We've made the point that certain patterns of dealing with conflict are particularly destructive in a relationship. How can couples manage their tendencies toward destructive patterns and limit the damage they cause? Later on, we will suggest a set of agreed-upon rules and strategies for handling conflict and difficult issues in your relationship.

Keep in mind that most couples show some of these patterns to some degree. Whether you currently have some of them is not as important as what you are going to do about them. The exercises that follow are a first step toward protecting your relationship from these things that are so damaging.

EXERCISES

Write your answers to the following questions independently from your partner, using a separate piece of paper. The first step in changing patterns is to understand your part in them. When you have finished, we suggest you share your perceptions. However, if this raises conflict, put off further discussion until you have learned more about how to talk safely on tough topics in the next few chapters. Before getting into specific questions about the four negative patterns, consider the following one about your overall impression of how you handle conflict together. When you have a disagreement or argument, what typically happens? Think about the patterns described in this chapter in answering the questions to follow.

Escalation

Escalation occurs when you say or do something negative, and your partner responds negatively, and off you go into a real battle. In this snowball effect, you become increasingly angry and hostile as the argument continues (for example, Proverbs 12:18, 15:1, 20:3, 29:11; Matthew 5:22).

1. How often do you think you escalate as a couple?
2. Do you get hostile with each other during escalation?

3. What or who usually brings an end to the fight? How does it usually end?

4. Does one or the other of you sometimes threaten to end the relationship when you're angry?

5. How do each of you feel when your arguments are escalating? Do you feel tense, anxious, scared, angry, or something else?

Invalidation

Invalidation occurs when you subtly or directly put down the thoughts, feelings, actions, or worth of your partner. This is different from simply disagreeing with your partner or not liking something he or she has done. Invalidation includes belittling or disregarding what is important to your partner, out of either insensitivity or outright contempt. The partner usually feels hurt, discounted, or unimportant (for example, Matthew 5:22; Ephesians 4:29; I Corinthians 13:5).

1. Do you often feel invalidated in your relationship? When and how does this happen?

2. What is the effect on you? How do you feel when this happens?

3. Do you often invalidate your partner? When and how does this happen? How do you feel when doing this?

4. What do you think the effect is on him or her? On the relationship? What are you trying to accomplish when you do this? Do you accomplish that goal?

Negative Interpretations

Negative interpretations occur when you interpret your spouse's behavior much more negatively than she or he intended. It is critical to openly see the possibility that your view of your partner could be unfair in some areas (for example, Matthew 7:1–5; I Corinthians 13:6,7). Your partner can do little to change your negative interpretations. These questions will help you make these changes if you are willing to work at it.

1. Can you think of some areas where you consistently see your partner's behavior as negative? What are the advantages to you in making these negative interpretations?
2. Reflect on this awhile. Do you really think your negative view of your partner's behavior is justified?
3. Are there some areas where you have a negative interpretation but where you're open to considering that you may be missing evidence to the contrary?
4. List two issues on which you're willing to push yourself to look for the possibility that your partner has more positive motivations than you thought. Next, look for any evidence that is contrary to your negative interpretations.

Withdrawal and Avoidance

Men and women often deal quite differently with conflict in relationships. Males are more often prone to withdraw from, and women more prone to pursue, discussing issues in the relationship. But keep in mind, it could be different for you. Perhaps neither of you tends to withdraw or avoid issues, which is often the best pattern. Withdrawal and avoidance just don't work well over time in relationships (Matthew 5:23,24; Ephesians 4:25–27).

1. Is one of you more likely to be in the pursuer role? Is one of you more likely to be in the withdrawer role?
2. How does the withdrawer usually withdraw? How does the pursuer usually pursue? What happens then?
3. When are you most likely to fall into this pattern as a couple? What particular issues or situations bring out this pattern?

4. How are you affected by this pattern?

5. With some couples, one or both partners may both pursue or withdraw at different times. Is this true of your relationship? Why do you think this happens?

We hope these questions have shed further light on how your relationship is affected by these destructive patterns. You should now have a good understanding of them. This will help you to know what patterns to try to counteract, which, in turn, will help you replace such patterns with the positive behaviors and attitudes we will be teaching you.

3

Communicating Safely and Clearly

The Speaker-Listener Technique

Everyone should be quick to listen, slow to speak, and slow to become angry.

James 1:19

Do you really want to communicate well? Most couples do, but many have not learned to communicate well when it counts most—when disagreements arise. There's no danger to your marriage when you see things the way your partner does. The risk comes from differences and conflicts. Handling conflict carefully is critical to the success of your marriage, and communicating well is critical to handling conflict properly. There are two keys: making it clear and making it safe.

MAKING IT CLEAR: THE PROBLEM OF FILTERS

Have you ever noticed that what you are trying to say to your partner is sometimes very different from what he or she hears? You may say something you think is harmless and suddenly your spouse is mad at you. Or you may ask a question such as "What do you want for dinner?" and your partner starts complaining about you not doing your share of the work because she heard something very different from what you meant. Or you may speak through a filter in the first place, muting the intention of what you want to say.

We have all experienced the frustration of being misunderstood. You think you are being clear, but your partner just doesn't seem to get it. Or you are so sure you know what he said yesterday, and today he says something that seems completely different.

Like the rest of us, Tanya and Wellington can relate to this common problem. They married five years ago. Tanya works as a reservation agent for an airline, and Wellington is an accountant for a major firm. Their jobs leave them exhausted at the end of each day. There are no kids yet, so they can usually crash when they get home.

One Thursday night, Wellington was home first and read the paper while waiting for Tanya. He was thinking, "I sure am wiped. I bet she is, too. I'd really like to go out to eat and just relax with Tanya tonight." Good idea, right? This is what happened with his idea (what they are thinking or hearing is in parentheses).

WELLINGTON: (*thinking he'd like to go out to dinner with Tanya, as she comes in the door*) What should we do for dinner tonight?

TANYA: (*hearing, "When will dinner be ready?"*) Why is it always my job to make dinner?

WELLINGTON: (*hearing her response as an attack and thinking "Why is she always so negative?"*) It is not always your job to make dinner. I made dinner once last week!

TANYA: (*negative cycle continues, as Tanya tends to think she does everything around the house*) Bringing home hamburgers and fries is *not* making dinner, Wellington.

WELLINGTON: (*with frustration mounting*) Just forget it. I didn't want to go out with you anyway.

TANYA: (*confused, not remembering him saying anything about going out*) You never said anything about wanting to go out.

WELLINGTON: (*feeling really angry*) Yes I did! I asked you where you wanted to go out to dinner, and you got really nasty.

TANYA: I got nasty? You never said anything about going out.

WELLINGTON: Did too!

TANYA: You're never wrong, are you?

Sound familiar? You can see where things went wrong; Wellington had a positive idea, but conflict blew out the evening. Wellington was not as clear as he could have been in telling Tanya what he was thinking. This left a lot of room for interpretation, and interpret is what Tanya did. She assumed that he was asking her—no, telling her—to get dinner on the table as she walked in the door.

This kind of thing happens in relationships all the time. Many of the biggest arguments you will have together may begin with a simple anger-provoking misunderstanding about what your partner is saying. What gets in the way? Filters.

Filters change what goes through them. A furnace filter takes dust out of the air. A camera filter alters the properties of the light passing through it. A coffee filter lets the flavor through and leaves the gunk behind. In the same way, what goes into our "communication filters" is different from what comes out.

We all have many kinds of filters packed into our heads. They affect what we say, what we hear, how we interpret things, and how we respond. They are based on how we are feeling, what we think, what we have experienced in life, family and culture, and so on. Five types of filters can affect couples as they struggle for clear communication: inattention, emotional states, beliefs and expectations, differences in style, and self-protection.

Inattention

A very basic kind of filter has to do with whether you have each other's full attention. Both external and internal factors can affect attention. External factors are things such as noisy kids, a hearing problem, a bad phone line, and background noise at a party. Internal factors include feeling tired, thinking about something else, feeling bored, mentally forming a rebuttal, and so forth. The key is to make sure you have each other's attention when it counts most.

For important talks, find a quiet place if you can, and don't answer the phone. Make it easier to pay attention to one another, and try not to assume that your partner is ready to listen right now just because you are ready to talk. Ask.

Emotional States

Emotional states or moods become filters, too. Have you noticed that sometimes, when your spouse is in a bad mood, you get jumped on no matter how nicely you say something? A number of studies demonstrate that we tend to give people more benefit of the doubt when we are in a good mood and less benefit of the doubt when in a bad mood. If you are in a bad mood, you are more likely to perceive whatever your partner says or does more negatively, no matter how positive he or she is trying to be.

One good defense against filters is to acknowledge them when you are aware they are operating. Here is an example. It's dinner time. The kids are hungry and complaining. Steve just got home and is reading the mail. Melissa is cooking macaroni in the kitchen.

STEVE: This bill for the phone company got missed again. We better get this paid.

MELISSA: (*snapping with anger*) I'm not the one who forgot it. Can't you see I have my hands full? Do something helpful.

STEVE: I'm sorry. I should have seen you were busy. Rough day?

MELISSA: Yes. I had a very frustrating day. I don't mean to snap at you, but I've had it up to here. If I am touchy, it's not really anything you've done.

STEVE: Maybe we can talk about it some after dinner.

MELISSA: Thanks.

Without using the term filter, Steve and Melissa are acknowledging that one is there. Melissa had a bad day and is on edge because the kids are fussy. They could have let this conversation escalate into an argument, but Steve had the good sense to see that he had raised an issue at the wrong time. He decided not to get defensive and chose to become gentle with Melissa in her frustration. As Solomon said, "A gentle answer turns away wrath, but a harsh word stirs up anger" (Proverbs 15:1). Melissa responded by telling Steve, in essence, that she had a filter going—her bad mood. Knowing this helped him be less defensive in reaction to her mood.

Many kinds of emotional filters can exist inside a person. If you are angry, worried, sad, or upset, it can color your interpretation of and response to what your partner says. Steve's response was helpful because it opened the door for Melissa to clarify her emotional filter and allowed them to de-escalate and be clear with one another.

Beliefs and Expectations

Many very important filters arise from what you think and expect in your relationship. Research and experience tell us that people tend to see what they expect to see in others. This kind of expectation becomes a filter that colors what we see and distorts communication. Studies also show that our expectations can influence the behavior of others. For example, if you believe that your partner is mad at you, she may well sound mad when talking with you, even if she wasn't. We tend to "pull" from others the behavior that is consistent with what we expect. Mental filters, especially negative interpretations, can make things seem a lot worse than they really are.

Alonzo and Heidi were having problems deciding what to do for fun when they had free time. With three kids in elementary school, free time without the kids was valuable to them. They rarely got out to do anything, so both were frustrated. This conversation was typical for them. Note how each of them acted as if they could read the other's mind.

ALONZO: (*really wanting to go bowling but thinking that Heidi was not interested in going out and doing anything fun together*) We have some free time tonight. I wonder if we should try to do something.

HEIDI: (*thinking that she would like to get out but hearing the tentativeness in his voice and thinking he really does not want to go out*) Oh, I don't know. What do you think?

ALONZO: Well, we could go bowling, but it could be league night and we might not get in anyway. Maybe we should just stay in and watch TV.

HEIDI: (*thinking "A-ha! That's what he really wants to do."*) That sounds good to me. Why don't we make some popcorn and watch some tube?

ALONZO: (*disappointed, thinking "I knew it. She really doesn't like to get out and do things that are fun."*) Yeah, OK.

In this conversation, there was no escalation, invalidation, or withdrawal. Nevertheless, they did not communicate well due to the belief and expectation filters involved. Alonzo's belief that Heidi did not want to go out colored the entire conversation—so much so that the way he asked her to go out led her to think that he wanted to stay in. He "knew" that she really did not want to go, which amounts to mind reading—which occurs when you assume you know what your partner is thinking or feeling. It is a specific form of negative interpretation.

In Alonzo's eyes, he could only see that they stayed in once again because that is what she wanted. His mental filter pulled the conversation in this direction and became a self-fulfilling prophecy. Heidi also did a good deal of mind reading. In this conversation, she assumed she knew that Alonzo was tired and really wanted to stay in. The result was a distorted conversation in which neither said what they wanted. If they had been able to communicate clearly, without these filters, they would have realized that both wanted to go out.

Differences in Style

Everyone has a different style of communicating, and different styles can lead to filtering. For instance, one of you may be more expressive and the other more reserved. Styles are determined by many influences including personality, culture, gender, and upbringing. For example, if one of you tends to introversion and one to extroversion, some miscommunication seems likely to come from such a difference. Style differences rooted in family backgrounds can cause great misunderstandings, becoming powerful filters that distort communication.

Sue and Tom came from very different families. His family was very expressive and intense about all manner of emotion. Sue's family was more reserved. As a result, a slight raise of voice could mean great anger in her family, whereas it would hardly be noticed in his. In many conversations, therefore, Sue would over-interpret the intensity of Tom's feelings, and Tom often underestimated the strength of Sue's feelings.

Being more aware of your differing styles can go a long way toward preventing misunderstandings. We recommend that you spend some time talking about your unique styles.

Self-Protection

This last kind of filter comes from the fear of rejection with which we all struggle in some ways. In self-protection, what we really want or feel does not get said out of fear of rejection. Even something as simple as "Wouldn't you like to go see that new movie with me?" can reflect this. Instead of saying it directly ("I'd like to see that new movie. Want to go?"), we often hide our desire because to express it more clearly might reveal more of who we are, thus raising the risk of deeper rejection. This may not matter a lot when it comes to movies, but when it comes to the real issues of marriage—feelings, desires, and expectations—the tendency can lead to a lot of miscommunication. We will say more about this when we get to hidden issues.

Filters and Memory: That's Not What You Heard

Some of the biggest arguments couples have are about what was actually said in the past. How often have you wished that you had a tape recording of a previous conversation? These differences in memory occur in great measure because of the variety of filters that operate in all relationships. Any of the filters discussed here can lead to differences—and arguments—about what was said or done in the past.

Read again the conversation between Wellington and Tanya. Notice that they ended up arguing about what was said at the start of the conversation. He truly thought he had asked her out to dinner, but what he had said was vague. She truly thought he had told her to get dinner on the table, which was also not what he had said. Without a tape recording, no amount of convincing could get either one to back off from their version of the story.

We recommend two things that can protect your relationship from such fruitless arguments about the past. First, accept the fact that your memory is not perfect. This is Humility 101 again. Simply agree that you each may have differing perceptions about the same incident. Countless psychological studies show how fragile human memory is—how susceptible it is to motivation and beliefs. Your memory is not perfect. Accept that you both have filters and that there is plenty of room for things to be said or heard differently than what was intended.

Second, when you disagree about a memory, don't keep arguing about what was actually said in the past. We don't know of a case where that ever helped a couple either solve a problem or draw closer together. Don't get stuck in the past, even if it was five minutes ago. Shift the topic to what you each think and feel in the present.

We hope you understand how important it is to be aware of filters in your communication. We all have filters. Either we react to them with little awareness, which can cause damage to the relationship, or we can learn to spot them when conversations go awry.

MAKING IT SAFE: THE VALUE OF STRUCTURE

"There is no fear in love. But perfect love drives out fear, because fear has to do with punishment" (I John 4:18). To have a great marriage, both of you must be able to fearlessly express your beliefs, concerns, and preferences authentically. The passage from John's writings makes a powerful point. Love is the antidote to fear. If you check out this passage, you'll find that it occurs in the context of teaching about the cross. Such a demonstration of sacrificial love can drive out fear. Likewise, when you maintain an atmosphere of love and respect in your marriage, you increase the odds of interacting without fear of rejection.

In contrast, escalation, invalidation, withdrawal, and negative interpretation (and all kinds of other negative patterns) make it unsafe to express your real heart. You can't be "naked and unashamed" when you feel like you'll be punished for expressing important thoughts and feelings. Filters compound the problem, making it a wonder that couples can ever communicate clearly about anything truly important.

Are marriages necessarily safe? No. Most people start out with the safe haven of a friendly relationship, but many couples don't stay there. By safe we do not mean risk-free. There is a direct relationship between risk and intimacy in relationships. If you are going to share what you are concerned with, hurt by, or hoping for, you are going to take risks. You cannot be accepted deeply without offering something deep for your partner to accept. Conversely, you can take the risk, share deeply, and be rejected. This hurts a lot because you have chosen to risk a deeper part of yourself in the relationship. But if it goes well, you find a wonderful, soul-satisfying acceptance of who you are—warts and all.

When you disagree or think you do, rejection seems more likely and more can go wrong. For your relationship to grow through conflict (instead of being damaged by it) you'll need to be aware of destructive patterns. But that's not all we have to suggest.

One way to make it safer to draw together and deal with issues well is to use agreed-upon rules to help you in important conversations. We call this adding structure to your interaction. With adequate structure, you can talk about difficult or important matters with less chance of damage to your relationship. When less is at stake or you are not in conflict, you don't need much structure. Just communicate in whatever way you are most comfortable. But during the tough times, a bit of structure can get you through without damage and may even lead to greater closeness.

THE SPEAKER-LISTENER TECHNIQUE

When it comes to great communication, you can't beat the simple advice of James. "Take note of this: Everyone should be quick to listen, slow to speak, and slow to become angry, for man's anger does not bring about the righteous life that God desires" (James 1:19–20).

That is easier said than done, right? In fact, this may be hardest do to in marriage because of the great potential to feel hurt by those we love. The Speaker-Listener Technique offers you an alternative way of communicating when issues are hot or sensitive, or likely to get that way. Any conversation in which you want to increase clarity and safety can benefit from this technique. Most couples (although not all) can decide whether to go out for Chinese food without this technique, but many can use more help when dealing with sensitive issues like money, sex, and in-laws. It's the structure of the technique that makes it work. Here are the rules.

Rules for Both of You

1. *The speaker has the floor.* Use a real object to designate the floor. When giving seminars, we hand out small cards or pieces of linoleum or carpet for couples to use. You can use anything, though—the TV remote, a piece of paper, a

paperback book, anything at all. If you do not have the floor, you are the Listener. As Speaker and Listener you follow the rules for each role. Note that the Speaker keeps the floor while the Listener paraphrases, keeping it clear who is in which role all the time.

2. *Share the floor.* You share the floor over the course of a conversation. One has it to start and may say a number of things. At some point, you switch roles and continue back and forth as the floor changes hands.

3. *No problem solving.* When using this technique you are going to focus on having good discussions. You must consciously avoid coming to solutions prematurely.

Rules for the Speaker

1. *Speak for yourself.* Don't mind read. Talk about your thoughts, feelings, and concerns, not your perceptions or interpretations of the Listener's point of view or motives. Try to use "I" statements, and talk about your own point of view.

2. *Talk in small chunks.* You will have plenty of opportunity to say all you need to say, so you don't have to say it all at once. It is very important to keep what you say in manageable pieces to help the Listener actively listen. If you are in the habit of giving long monologues, remember that having the floor protects you from interruption, so you can afford to pause for the paraphrase to be sure your partner understands you. A good rule of thumb is to keep your statements to just a sentence or two, especially when first learning the technique.

3. *Stop and let the Listener paraphrase.* After saying a bit, perhaps a sentence or two, stop and allow the Listener to paraphrase what you just said. If the paraphrase was not quite accurate, you should politely restate what was not heard in the way it was intended to be heard. Your goal is to help the Listener hear and understand your point of view.

Rules for the Listener

1. *Paraphrase what you hear.* To paraphrase the Speaker, briefly repeat back what you heard the Speaker say, using your own words if you like, to make sure you understand what was said. The key is that you show your partner that you are listening as you restate what you heard, without any interpretations. If the paraphrase is not quite right (which happens often), the Speaker should gently clarify the point being made. If you truly don't understand some phrase or example, you may ask the Speaker to clarify or repeat, but you may not ask questions on any other aspect of the issue unless you have the floor.

2. *Don't rebut. Focus on the Speaker's message.* While in the Listener role, you may not offer your opinion or thoughts. This is the hardest part of being a good Listener. If you are upset by what your partner says, you need to edit out any response you may want to make, so you can continue to pay attention to what your partner is saying. Wait until you get the floor to state your response. As Listener, your job is to speak only in the service of understanding your partner. Any words or gestures to show your own opinions are not allowed, including making faces. Your task is to understand. Good listening does not equal agreement. You can express any disagreement when you have the floor.

Here are some ideas about what good paraphrases sound like. Suppose your spouse says to you, "I really had a tough day. Mom got on my case about how I handled the arrangements for Dad's party. Ugh!" Any of the following might be an excellent paraphrase:

"Sounds like you had a really tough day."

"So, your mom was critical of how you handled the party, and really got on you about it."

"Bad day, huh?"

Any one of these responses conveys that you have listened and displays what you have understood. A good paraphrase can be short or long, detailed or general. At times, if you are uncertain how to get a paraphrase started, it can help to begin with "What I hear you saying is. . . . " Then fill in what you just heard your partner say. Another way to begin a paraphrase is with the words, "Sounds like. . . . "

When using the Speaker-Listener Technique, the Speaker is always the one who determines if the Listener's paraphrase was on target. Only the Speaker knows what the intended message was. If the paraphrase was not quite on target, it is very important that the Speaker gently clarify or restate the point and not respond angrily or critically. One more key point: When in the Listener role, be sincere in your effort to show you are listening carefully and respectfully. Even when you disagree with the point being made by your partner, your goal is to show respect for and validation of his or her perspective. That means waiting your turn and not making faces or looking bored. Showing real respect and honor to one another is the goal. You can disagree completely with your mate on a matter and still show respect. In fact, we are told in scripture to show respect no matter what (I Peter 2:17). Just wait until you have the floor to make your points.

Two more points—first, when using the Speaker-Listener Technique, it is important to stay on the topic you mean to discuss. Many issues in marriage can become involved in one conversation, but you'll do better on important matters if you try to stay on the issues at hand. Also, don't try to problem solve prematurely. Focus on having a good discussion where you can get the issues on the table.

Using the Speaker-Listener Technique

Here is an example of how this technique can change a conversation that is going nowhere into a real opportunity for connection. Peter and Tessie are in their mid-thirties, with four kids ages two to ten. For years they have had a problem dealing with issues. Peter consistently avoids discussing problem areas. If cornered by Tessie he withdraws by growing quieter.

In this case, Peter and Tessie have been locked in the pursuer-withdrawer cycle about the issue of preschool for Jeremy. However, they have been practicing the Speaker-Listener Technique and are ready to try something different. Let's see what happens.

> TESSIE: I'm really getting tired of leaving Jeremy's preschool up in the air. We have got to deal with this, now.
>
> PETER: (*not looking up from the TV*) Oh?
>
> TESSIE: (*walking over and standing in front of the TV*) Peter, we can't just leave this decision hanging in the air. I'm getting really angry about you putting it off.
>
> PETER: (*recognizing this would be a wise time to act constructively and not withdraw*) Time out. I can tell we need to talk, but I have been avoiding it because it seems that talking just leads to fighting. Let's try that Speaker-Listener Technique we have been practicing.

The technique they will use now is not a normal way to communicate. But it is a relatively safe way to communicate clearly on difficult issues. Each will get to talk; each will be heard; both will show commitment to discussing the problem constructively. If one of you tends to withdraw, and that person moves constructively toward the pursuer in this positive manner, the effect on the relationship is often very positive. It contradicts the pursuer's belief that the withdrawer does not care about the relationship.

The conversation proceeds, with Peter turning off the TV and picking up a piece of carpet they use for the floor.

> PETER (Speaker): I've also been pretty concerned about where we send Jeremy to preschool, and I'm not sure this is the year to do it.
>
> TESSIE (Listener): You have been concerned, too, and you're not sure he's ready.

PETER (Speaker): Yeah, that's it. He acts pretty young for his age, and I am not sure how he would do, unless the situation were just right.

Note how Peter acknowledges that Tessie's summary is on the mark, before moving on to another point.

TESSIE (Listener): You're worried that he wouldn't hold his own with older-acting kids, right? (*Tessie is not quite sure she has understood Peter's point, so she makes her paraphrase tentative.*)

PETER (Speaker): Well, partly that's it, but I'm also not sure if he's ready to be away from you that much. Of course, I don't want him to be too dependent, either.

Note how Peter gently clarifies. He's moving toward Tessie in the conversation rather than away from her. In general, whenever the Listener feels that clarification is needed, he can use the next statement to restate or expand upon what he was trying to get across.

TESSIE (Listener): So, you are feeling torn about him needing me a lot and him needing to be more independent.

PETER (Speaker): That's right. Here, you take the floor. (*Floor switch*)

TESSIE (now the Speaker): Well, I appreciate what you are saying. Actually, I hadn't realized you had thought this much about it. I was worried that you didn't care about it. (*As the Speaker, Tessie now validates Peter in the comments he has made.*)

PETER (Listener): Sounds like you're glad to hear that I am concerned.

TESSIE (Speaker): Yes. I agree that this is not an easy decision. If we did put him in preschool this year, it would have to be just the right place.

PETER (Listener): You're saying that it would have to be just the right preschool for it to be worth doing this year.

TESSIE (Speaker): Exactly. I think that it might be worth trying if we could find a great environment for him. (*Tessie feels good with Peter listening so carefully and lets him know it.*)

PETER (Listener): So you would try it if we found just the right setting.

TESSIE (Speaker): I might try it. I'm not sure I'm ready to say I would try it.

PETER (Listener): You're not ready to say you would definitely want to do it, even with a perfect preschool.

TESSIE (Speaker): Right. Here, you take the floor again. (*Floor switch*)

As you can tell, they have been practicing quite a bit. They are both doing an excellent job following the rules and showing concern and respect for each other's viewpoints. Couples can have discussions like this on difficult topics, even when they disagree. The key is in making it safe and in showing respect for your partner's thoughts, feelings, and opinions.

The Advantages of Using the Speaker-Listener Technique

The Speaker-Listener Technique has many advantages over unstructured conversation when discussing difficult issues. Most important is the way it counteracts the destructive styles of communication described in Chapters One and Two. This is crucial. It's not that this technique is the be-all-and-end-all of good communication. It's just one very simple way to be "quick to hear, slow to speak, and slow to become angry" and thereby limit the damage that patterns such as the danger signs can cause. In fact, we do meet couples who try this and do not like it. We don't get defensive about it or push it, we simply say to them, "That's fine, as long as you have some other way to have respectful, good conversations on difficult issues. If you can do that, you don't need this technique, though you may find many other things we have to teach you useful, so keep on listening."

You may be thinking, "This sure is artificial." Agreed. In fact, that's the key reason it is so effective. The truth is, what comes naturally to couples when difficult issues come up is often destructive and quite the opposite from being "quick to hear, slow to speak, and slow to become angry." Again, James shows his tendency toward purifying bluntness. "If anyone considers himself religious and yet does not keep a tight rein on his tongue, he deceives himself and his religion is worthless" (James 1:26).

This technique is designed to help couples keep a tight rein on their tongues. That's why it works. When you choose to use it, you are making the choice to limit the defensive responses that come naturally and to submit yourself to a more caring, disciplined approach to understanding your mate. You are unleashing your ears and reining in your tongue. Keep in mind that although these rules are simple, simple does not always mean easy. Structure can make it easier, but sometimes it just takes hard work to communicate well.

There are benefits of agreeing to use this technique for important discussions in a number of areas. Using the technique limits a great number of problems in communication:

1. *Escalation.* The structure of the technique makes it much harder to get into escalation. In fact, it will be nearly impossible to escalate if you both follow the rules and work at showing respect.

2. *Invalidation.* The simple process of paraphrasing prevents invalidation because the Speaker gets immediate feedback that he was heard. You can enhance the validation by saying "I see what you mean" or "That makes sense to me" at the end of a paraphrase or when you get the floor. This does not mean that you agree, just that you can see it from your partner's perspective.

3. *Pursuers and withdrawers.* For people who tend to withdraw from talk when conflict is possible, the structure makes it safer to remain in the conversation. With a clear sense that both of you are committed to keeping things from getting out of hand, there is less to be anxious about. For people who are usually in the pursuer role, structure in conversations ensures that you will be heard and that issues will be addressed. This gets you both closer to a win-win situation and out of hopeless win-lose cycles. And remember, the happiest couples tend to not show these pursuer-withdrawer dynamics as much, if at all. You can beat these patterns that are both common and not very good for your marriage. But, you have to work together.

4. *Filters.* The Speaker-Listener Technique makes it much easier to identify filters as soon as they come up. They will be evident in the paraphrases. The Speaker will have a nonthreatening opportunity to say "That's not quite what I said. I said 'such and so.' Could you paraphrase again, please?" All manner of filters can be reduced using this technique, especially negative interpretations.

When you choose to use these skills as well as the ground rules we will present later, you are choosing to protect your relationship from destructive conflict by using more structure. But practice is the key. With regular practice, several positive things can happen. First, the technique will become easier and less artificial over time, so it is readily available when you need it. Second, if you practice this for a while, you'll find yourselves communicating better with each other, even when not using the rules. As yeast affects an entire loaf of bread, your new skills will find their way into all your conversations. You'll be limiting the damaging patterns and fostering great communication. We see many couples who work with this a while, practice it, then hardly ever need it because the practice completely changed the way they talk about important matters. They shift much more naturally into a better, more respectful flow when important matters arise. As we have worked with thousands of couples, this is one of the most beautiful transitions to watch.

If you want to strengthen your marital promise and reduce your chances of divorce, learn to move toward each other and to deal constructively with those issues that have the potential to drive you apart. We will cover many other important principles in this book, but none is more critical.

EXERCISES

"Whatever is true, whatever is noble, whatever is right, whatever is pure, whatever is lovely, whatever is admirable—if anything is excellent or praiseworthy—think about such things. Whatever you have learned or received or heard from me, or seen in me—put it into practice" (Philippians 4:8,9).

What Paul clearly taught here was that it is important not to simply know the right things to do but to put what had been learned from him into regular practice. That's our point here. We have strategies that can help you in your marriage, but to get any real benefit, you must put these strategies into practice in your relationship.

One of the most powerful ways we know to get couples to change how they communicate on sensitive or conflicted topics is by getting them to practice the Speaker-Listener Technique. Although this technique is not a miracle worker, it does work very well. To make something become a part of your normal behavior, it must be practiced . . . and practiced. At first, it may feel uncomfortable, but as with anything new, it becomes easier over time. When learning a new skill, the goal is to learn it well enough that it becomes a habit, something you can instinctively do. Begin with the basics. When playing the piano, you do not start with difficult pieces but with simple ones, learning one note at a time. Allow yourself to approach using the Speaker-Listener Technique in this way—tackling easy topics first, then progressing to the more complex, difficult ones.

Remember, practicing this technique can help you in two ways. First, you'll have the technique to use when things get rough (James 1:19). Second, practicing this regularly can change the way you talk together in general, even when not using all the rules formally. So, practicing will help you to put this all into practice.

1. Practice this technique several times a week for fifteen minutes or so each time (each of you taking a turn as Speaker and Listener). If you do not set aside the time to practice, you'll never find this powerful technique very helpful.

2. During the first week, try the technique with only nonconflictual topics. Talk about anything of interest to either of you: your favorite vacation, news, sports, your dreams for the future, concerns you have at work, and so on. Try to stay away from topics on which you know you have issues. Your goal right now is not to resolve a problem but to practice new skills.

3. After about three successful practice sessions about nonconflictual topics, choose minor conflict areas to discuss. Sometimes couples are poor at knowing what will or won't trigger a fight. If the discussion gets heated on a topic you choose, drop it. (It won't go away, but you can deal with it when you've practiced more together.)

   Practice several discussions in which you exchange some thoughts and feelings on these issues. For now don't try to solve problems, just have good discussions. Your goal is to understand each other's point of view as clearly and completely as possible. In the process, you may solve some problems because all that was needed was to understand what the other person was thinking. That's OK, but don't set out or intentionally try for solutions. You're focusing on good discussions right now. You'll learn and practice problem solving in the next chapter.

4. When you are doing well on the last assignment, move up to tougher and tougher issues. As you do, remember to work at sticking to the rules. The technique will work if you work at it.

4

Problem Solving

He who answers before listening—that is his folly and his
shame.

Proverbs 18:13

We all want to solve problems that affect our relationships.
This is natural. But we have not addressed problem solving until
this point because most couples try to solve problems before they
have really heard each other's views about them. This often leads
to discouragement, as haste really does make waste (for example,
Proverbs 19:2). Understanding—before solving—is crucial for
maintaining respect and connection in your relationship. This
chapter presents a straightforward approach to problem solving
based on understanding and respect.

THREE KEY ASSUMPTIONS

We need to look at three key assumptions about problems and marriages over time. Couples who understand these assumptions are
likely, in our view, to do better over time than those who have
never thought about these points.

Assumption One: All Couples Have Problems

Jesus summed this up quite clearly when He said, "In this world you
will have trouble" (John 16:33). He didn't leave anyone out when
He said this. Now think about marriage. Have you ever wondered
why some couples seem to deal with the challenges of marital life so

effectively? This is not because they are problem-free. Although some couples have more problems come their way than others, all couples have problems to cope with. Count on it.

However, the kinds of problems couples deal with do change over time. Engaged couples report that their typical problem areas are jealousy and in-laws. These issues reflect a developmental task couples experience early in a relationship: that of establishing boundaries with those outside their relationship. By the first year of marriage, couples begin to report other problems as being more important, such as communication and sex. These are issues central to how the two partners deal with each other. In these very simple data, you can see how couples shift from working on defining "who is us and who is not us?" to "how are we treating one another?" No matter what stage of the relationship they are in, most couples also struggle with money. In fact, money is the most common argument-starter for couples. Our key point is this: It's not what your problems are, it's how you handle them that will matter most in your marriage.

Assumption Two: It Is Best to Handle Problems as a Team

For some couples, mutual respect and skill combine to produce a powerful sense of teamwork as they work on solutions that will enhance life together. You have a choice when dealing with a problem. Either you will nurture a sense that you are working as a team against the problem, or you will operate as if you are working against each other. Our research clearly shows that it is a bad sign when two people feel as though they are on opposite sides when dealing with issues. People don't get married to have an enemy at home.

Jeremy and Lisa are a couple who have the sense of teamwork flowing in their marriage. They were talking about how to handle the feeding of their newborn baby (Brent) while Lisa, a nurse, was at work. Jeremy had recently lost his job as a store manager.

LISA: I am worried about breast feeding.

JEREMY: What do you mean? Can't you do that when you're at home, with me giving him a bottle during your shift?

LISA: No. That's not going to work because I'll fill up with milk. I make milk whether he drinks it or not, you know.

JEREMY: I had no idea that would be a problem. You mean you can't go through your shift without him nursing?

LISA: Not without being very uncomfortable.

JEREMY: Oh! What can we do to make this work out?

LISA: Well, either Brent nurses on my break or I need to pump.

JEREMY: What's better for you? I could help either way.

LISA: Would you be willing to bring him over to work at lunch time? If he'd nurse well then, that would tide me through the day, and you could give him bottles the rest of the time.

JEREMY: Sure, I'd be glad to bring him over. No problem, with me out of work for now.

LISA: That would help a lot. I'd also get to see him during the day. Let's give it a try this week.

Notice how Jeremy and Lisa are working together. They are listening to each other, and there is a sense of respect and cooperation. This is the way they have learned to approach all kinds of problems—as challenges to be faced together. We can't overstate the importance of mutual respect in having this kind of "teamwork" marriage. This is so important that both men and women are specifically called upon in scripture to nurture respect for the other.

However, each one of you also must love his wife as he loves himself, and the wife must respect her husband [Ephesians 5:33].

Husbands, in the same way be considerate as you live with your wives, and treat them with respect [I Peter 3:7].

Contrast the respectful and harmonious tone of Jeremy and Lisa's discussion with that of Shandra and Eric. Shandra, the owner of her own dry cleaning business, and Eric, a real estate agent, are the parents of two middle schoolers. They have repeated arguments about housework, which generally go like this:

SHANDRA: (*calmly*) We need to do something about keeping the house neater. It's such a mess most of the time . . . it's depressing to be here.

ERIC: (*a bit annoyed*) Look, that's your job. My work requires me to be out a lot more than you. I just don't have the time, and you know it! Keeping the place picked up is more your job than mine.

SHANDRA: (*hurt and angered*) Says who? There's a lot more to do than you seem to think. And did you forget that I work, too? Besides, you don't even clean up after yourself!

ERIC: I'd do more around here if you could generate more money in your business. You know, when you're home, you spend lots of time watching the tube. You could use your time better.

SHANDRA: (*anger growing*) I need some breaks . . . but that's not the point. I work just as hard as you outside the home, and you should . . . you need to do more of your share.

ERIC: I'm not going to give up my free time because you aren't using yours well. We had a deal. It's fair and that's all I have to say.

SHANDRA: What deal? When did I agree to do all the work around the house?

ERIC: You said I wouldn't have to do any more work around here when you began devoting more and more time to your business. That was the deal.

SHANDRA: (*looking him in the eye and now very angry*) That was when you used to do a lot more than you do now.

ERIC: (*turning away, indicating the conversation is over for him*) I don't agree, and I'm not talking about it any more. A deal's a deal.

This discussion ends with Shandra discouraged and Eric annoyed that she even brought up the problem. There is a definite lack of teamwork. Eric refuses to accept his part in this problem. He sees her as trying to take something away from him, not as a partner working to make life as good as it can be for both of them. Likewise, Shandra sees Eric as the problem, not as a teammate who is working with her to solve the problem.

All too often, people approach problems as if their partner were the enemy to be conquered. There will be a winner and a loser, but who wants to lose? The good news here is that you don't have to be locked into the cycle of one trying to win at the expense of the other. You can learn how to work as a team to live in respect and harmony with each other. We'll show you how.

Assumption Three: Rushed Solutions Are Poor Solutions

Solomon was one of the wisest persons who ever lived because he asked God specifically for wisdom. (We are all invited to do that. See James 1:5. In fact, stop for just a moment if you will, and ask God for wisdom in your marriage.) Solomon was right on target about problem solving in relationships. "He who answers before listening—that is his folly and his shame" (Proverbs 18:13). "It is not good to have zeal without knowledge, nor to be hasty and miss the way" (Proverbs 19:2).

Many well-intentioned attempts at problem solving fail because couples do not take the time needed to understand the problem together. They get hasty and miss the way. If it is a decision about which movie to see, not much is lost in a hasty solution except maybe the time spent sitting through a boring film. But if you are deciding something more important, such as how to parent or how to divide up the household responsibilities, it's critical that you take time to discover a solution based on mutual understanding. That takes listening.

Two major factors propel couples to rush to premature solutions: time pressure and conflict avoidance. Most of us are not all that patient. We want the solution now. Unfortunately, quick fixes seldom last. This often reflects the hurried pace of our lives. Sometimes, couples rush to a solution that is destined to fail because of their desire to avoid further conflict. That's what happened in this next example.

Frances and Bjorn have been married twenty-four years. They have two children, one in college and one a senior in high school. Bjorn sells insurance and Frances volunteers for a Christian organization. Money hadn't been a problem until college bills began accumulating. Bjorn's issue is financial—specifically that Frances devotes so much time to a job that doesn't pay. The following is a typical attempt to solve the problem.

> BJORN: (*testily*) I noticed that the credit card bill was over $600 again. It worries me that we can't keep up. I'm doing all I can, but . . .
>
> FRANCES: (*giving no indication that she is paying attention to Bjorn; saying nothing*)
>
> BJORN: (*frustrated*) Frances, did you hear me?
>
> FRANCES: Yes. I didn't think we spent that much this time.
>
> BJORN: If we had some income coming in from your work, it would help.
>
> FRANCES: Why don't we just get rid of that credit card? Then you wouldn't have to worry about it any more.
>
> BJORN: We could do that, and also we could plan to put aside an extra $150 a month in my retirement plan. What about you getting a part-time job?

FRANCES: I don't want to think about that now. For now, let's just try to get rid of the credit card and save more.

BJORN: OK, let's see what happens.

End of discussion. The one good thing about this discussion is that they had it. However, what are the chances that they came to a satisfactory resolution of their money problem? Two months later, nothing was changed, no more was saved, the credit card was still being used, interest was accumulating, and they were no closer to working together on the budget. This example illustrates what couples do all the time: make a quick agreement so that conflict is avoided. Solutions arrived at in this manner rarely last because all the important information is not on the table. And that is a "folly and a shame," as Solomon noted thousands of years ago. With Bjorn and Frances, crucial concerns were not addressed by their hasty solution.

Furthermore, there were no specifics about how their agreement would be implemented. Bjorn and Frances rush to solutions because they hate conflict. For them, this is a relatively big fight. Both are uncomfortable with disagreements. Finding a solution can be a relief when spouses are talking about issues that cause distress. However, when settling on a solution prematurely, the likely payback is more conflict later.

HOW TO HANDLE PROBLEMS WELL

The approach we teach to solving problems is structured. In other words, we recommend a specific set of steps that successful problem solvers follow. (Some of the thoughts we present here are adapted from ideas presented in earlier works such as *We Can Work It Out: Making Sense of Marital Conflict* [1993] by Notarius and Markman; *A Couple's Guide to Communication* [1976] by Gottman, Notarius, Gonso, and Markman; and earlier PREP and Christian PREP materials.) Although the steps that follow are straightforward, don't be misled by their simplicity. You must be willing to work together, to be creative and flexible, and to experiment with change. Under these conditions, you'll be able to discover solutions to most of the problems you have to grapple with together.

The steps to handling problems well include

1. Problem discussion
2. Prayer
3. Problem solution
   A. Agenda setting
   B. Brainstorming
   C. Agreement and compromise
   D. Follow-up

We'll follow the outline and describe the steps for handling problems next. We will give detailed examples to help you get a feel for the process.

Problem Discussion

Problem discussion is the critical first step to laying the foundation for the next steps of prayer and problem solution. Although you may not agree about how to solve a problem, a good discussion can lead to a clear sense that you're working together and respecting each other. Whether the problem is large or small, you should not move on to problem solution until you both understand and feel understood by each other. This means that you have each expressed your significant feelings and concerns on the topic and that you each believe the other has seen your point of view clearly, whether they agree or not. Problem discussion and problem solution are two distinctly different steps. As we said earlier, premature problem solving leads to poor solutions and poor follow-through. Give important matters the time they are due.

We recommend that you use the Speaker-Listener Technique for this problem discussion step. It is best that you place a premium on validation in this phase. Problem solution can proceed much more smoothly in an atmosphere of mutual support. We have re-peatedly seen that when good discussions precede problem solving, problem solving as a team can go quickly and smoothly, even on some of the most difficult issues.

Sometimes when discussing problems it can be helpful to have a specific way to share gripes constructively. One way to do this is to use what Gottman, Notarius, Markman, and Gonso call an XYZ statement (*A Couple's Guide to Communication* [1976]). With the XYZ statement, you put your gripe or complaint into this format: When you do X in situation Y, I feel Z. X is the behavior you are ad-dressing; Y is the situation (or context) in which it occurred; Z is the feeling you have about this behavior. This format gives your mate specific information rather than a vague complaint. It also en-courages you to take responsibility for your feelings. For example, suppose you had a concern about your partner making a mess at the end of the day. Which of the following statements do you think gives you a better shot at being heard?

"You are such a slob."

(Or)

"When you drop your pack and jacket on the floor (X) as you come in the door at the end of the day (Y), I feel frustrated (Z)."

It's pretty simple. Although no one likes to hear criticism, this simple technique can up your chances of sharing it in a construc-tive way.

Before we move on to the next step in the model, remember that the key to what we are saying here is to not move from discus-sion to solution unless you both agree that the issue has been fully discussed. In many instances you'll find that, after an excellent dis-cussion, there's really no problem solving to be done. Just having a good discussion is enough. That's because, on many issues, what we all really need most is simply to be heard and respected. But when you do need to find a specific solution, the steps we outline here work powerfully.

Prayer

It is wise to invite the Lord to be a participant in finding solutions to important problems. Couples who approach the problem prayerfully as a team of three (God and the couple) instead of just two, experience more spiritual intimacy and obtain the Lord's help with the problem. Most of us know the following passage very well: "Trust in the LORD with all your heart and lean not on your own understanding; in all your ways acknowledge him, and he will make your paths straight (Proverbs 3:5,6).

It's easy to get so familiar with such a great passage that we don't think about the meaning of it. This is a truly great and powerful principle, and it is just as true in marriage as anywhere else. So, we are recommending that you acknowledge God as you seek solutions on key problems. The promise is that He will make your paths straight.

There are many ways to apply this principle. Even if you are sensitive about praying out loud, don't let that stop you. Pray silently, or pray just a sentence out loud. Or pray out loud together. Whatever style works for you, the key is "acknowledging" the Lord. There's no format attached to the this promise in Proverbs. Take hold of it in a way that works for the two of you.

Problem Solution

The following steps work well for couples, provided that the work of problem discussion has been done. Prayer can leave you all the more ready to find a solution together. As you enter the problem-solving steps here, we do *not* recommend you use the floor. Drop all the structure of the Speaker-Listener Technique, and just follow the flow of the following steps.

Agenda Setting. The first step in the problem-solution phase is to set the agenda. The key here is to make it very clear what you are trying to solve at this time. Your discussion may have taken you through many facets of an issue. Now you need to hone in on one facet to focus on. The more specific the problem you are tackling, the better your chances of coming to a workable solution. Many problems in marriage seem insurmountable, but they can be cut down in size if you follow these procedures.

For example, you may have had a good problem discussion about money, covering a range of issues such as credit cards, checkbooks, budgets, and savings. As you can see, the problem area of "money" can contain many "sub" problem areas to consider. Focus on the more manageable pieces, one at a time. It is also wise to pick an easier piece of a problem to work on first. You might initially decide who should balance the checkbook each month, then deal with budget plans later. Some of the best possible agendas for problem solving answer a time-limited question such as "How are we going to handle getting the kitchen cleaned up differently this week?" Then, you have focused on finding a solution to try and then evaluate.

At times, your problem discussion will have focused from start to finish on a specific problem. In this case, you won't have to define the agenda for problem solving. For example, you may be working on the problem of where to go for the holidays—your parents' home or your spouse's. There may be no specific smaller piece of such a problem, so you will set the agenda to work on it as a whole.

Brainstorming. There are several rules regarding brainstorming:

> Any idea can be suggested. One of you should write them all down.

> Don't evaluate the ideas during brainstorming, verbally or nonverbally. This includes making faces.

> Be creative. Suggest whatever comes to mind, no matter how ridiculous it might seem.

Have fun with it if you can. This is a time for a sense of
humor: all other feelings should be dealt with in the
problem discussion.

The best thing about this process is that it encourages creativity. Write down all the ideas you can. If you can edit out your tendency to comment critically on the ideas, you will encourage each other to come up with some great suggestions. Wonderful solutions can come from considering some of the wildest ideas that come during brainstorming.

Agreement and Compromise. In this step, the goal is to come up with a specific solution or combination of solutions that you both agree to try. We emphasize the word agree because the solution is not likely to help unless you both agree to try it. We emphasize specific because the more specific you are about the solution, the more likely you will be to actually implement it.

Some people have trouble with the idea of compromise. We have even been criticized for using the term. Obviously, compromise implies giving up something you want for the sake of the relationship. To some, compromise sounds more like lose-lose than win-win. But we believe that compromise is sometimes necessary. Paul tells us to "look not only to your own interests, but also to the interests of others" (Philippians 2:4). Good compromises can allow you each to do this for the other.

Great marriages are about oneness, teamwork, and respect. You may see things differently on issues, but that is OK. Many times, the best solution will be a blend of each of your strengths. You are not going to have a great marriage if either of you gets his or her way all the time. You can count on that.

Follow-Up. Many couples make agreements to try out a particular solution for a specific period of time, especially when the problem has been an ongoing one. At the end of the "trial solution" it is important to follow up about how the agreement is working out.

Following up has two key advantages. First, solutions often need to be tweaked a bit to work in the long term. Second, following up builds accountability. Often, we don't get serious about making changes unless we know there is some point of accountability in the future. Sometimes, there needs to be a lot of follow-up in the problem solution phase. At other times, it's not really necessary. You reach an agreement and it works out, and nothing more needs to be done.

Some couples choose to be less formal about follow-up, but we think that is a risk. Most people are so busy that they don't include this step, so the solution just doesn't happen. It is an old but true saying, "If you fail to plan, you plan to fail." Good plans include good follow-up.

A DETAILED EXAMPLE: BJORN AND FRANCES

It did not take Frances and Bjorn very long to realize that their problem solving regarding their credit card, her volunteer work, and their retirement savings was not working. They decided to try the steps we are suggesting.

First, they set aside the time to work through the steps. Let's follow them through the process.

Problem Discussion with the Speaker-Listener Technique

FRANCES (Speaker): I can see that we really do have to try something different. We aren't getting anywhere on our retirement savings.

BJORN (Listener): You can see we aren't getting anywhere, and you are also concerned?

FRANCES (Speaker): (*letting Bjorn know he had accurately heard her*) Yes. We need to come up with a plan for saving more and using credit cards less.

BJORN (Listener): You agree we need to save more and can see that the credit cards may be part of the problem.

FRANCES (Speaker): I can also see why you are concerned about my volunteer work, but it is really important to me.

BJORN (Listener): Sounds like you can appreciate my concern, but you also want me to hear that it's really important to you.

FRANCES (Speaker): Yeah. That's exactly what I am feeling. Here, you take the floor, I want to know what you're thinking.

BJORN (Speaker): I have been anxious about this for some time and worry that without saving more, we won't be able to maintain our lifestyle in retirement.

FRANCES (Listener): You're really worried, aren't you?

BJORN (Speaker): Yes, I am. You know how things were for Mom and Dad. I don't want to end up living in a two-room apartment.

FRANCES (Listener): You're worried we could end up living that way, too.

BJORN (Speaker): I'd feel a lot better with about three times as much saved.

FRANCES (Listener): Too late now. (*catching herself interjecting her own opinion*) Oh, I should paraphrase. You wish we were much further along in our savings than we are.

BJORN (Speaker): (*feeling he is really getting her attention*) I do. I feel pressure about it. I really want to work together. (*letting her know he wants to work as a team*)

FRANCES (Listener): You want us to work together to reduce the pressure and plan for our future.

BJORN (Speaker): (*suggesting some alternatives*) Yes. We'd need to spend less, save more, and use the credit cards more wisely. And it would make a big difference if you brought in some income.

FRANCES (Listener): You feel we need to save more, spend less on credit cards, and that it's important for me to make some money.

BJORN (Speaker): Yes. I think income is a bigger problem than outgo.

FRANCES (Listener): Even if we could spend less, you think we need more income if we want to live at the same level in retirement. Can I have the floor?

BJORN (Speaker): Exactly! Here's the floor. (*Floor switch*)

FRANCES (Speaker): (*responding to Bjorn's clarification*) Sometimes I think that you think I am the only one who overspends.

BJORN (Listener): You think that I think you are at fault for spending too much. Can I have the floor again? (*Floor switch*)

BJORN (Speaker): Actually, I don't think that, but I see how I could come across that way (*validating Frances's experience*). I think I overspend, too. I just spend it in bigger chunks.

FRANCES (Listener): Nice to hear that (*validating his comment, feeling good at hearing him take responsibility*). You can see that we both spend too much, just differently. You may buy some big things we don't need, and I buy more small things.

BJORN (Speaker): Exactly. We are both to blame and we can do better.

FRANCES (Listener): We both need to work together. (*Floor switch*)

FRANCES (Speaker): I agree that we need to deal with our savings. My biggest fear is losing the work I love. It's been the most meaningful thing I've done since the kids got older.

BJORN (Listener): It's hard to imagine not having that—it's important to you.

FRANCES (Speaker): Yes. I can see why more income would make a big difference. But, at the same time, I would hate to lose what I have.

BJORN (Listener): You enjoy it, and you are doing something really meaningful.

FRANCES (Speaker): Exactly. Maybe there is some way to deal with this so that I could do some of what I am doing and help us save what we need for retirement at the same time.

BJORN (Listener): You are wondering if there could be a solution that would meet your needs and our needs at the same time.

FRANCES (Speaker): Yes. I'm willing to think about solutions with you.

They discontinue the Speaker-Listener Technique.

BJORN: OK.

FRANCES: So, are we both feeling understood enough to move on to the problem-solution step?

BJORN: I am. How about you?

FRANCES: (*nodding her head*) Yes.

Here, they are agreeing that they have had a good discussion and that they are ready to try some problem solving. They are consciously turning this corner together to move into problem solving.

Prayer

BJORN: Before we try to solve this, I'd like for us to ask God to help us with the solution.

FRANCES: I'd like that also.

Bjorn and Frances pray a moment silently, asking for God's help and wisdom in reaching a solution to their income and spending problems.

Problem Solution

Bjorn and Frances now go through the four steps of problem solution.

Agenda Setting.   Here, the important thing is for them to choose a specific piece of the whole issue to solve. This increases their chances of finding a solution that will really work this time.

> FRANCES: (*putting down the remote control they use to designate the floor*) We should agree on the agenda. We could talk about the retirement accounts, but that may not be the place to start. I also think we need to discuss spending money and credit cards.
>
> BJORN: You're right. We are going to need several tries at this entire issue. It seems we could break it down into bringing in more and spending less. I'd like to focus on "bringing in more" first, if you don't mind.
>
> FRANCES: I can handle that. Let's problem solve on that; then we can talk later this week about spending.
>
> BJORN: So, we're going to brainstorm about how to boost the income.

Brainstorming.   The key here is to generate ideas freely.

> FRANCES: Let's brainstorm. Why don't you write the ideas down?
>
> BJORN: OK . . . You could get a part-time job.
>
> FRANCES: I could ask the board of directors to make my work into a paid position. I'm practically a full-time staff member anyway.
>
> BJORN: We could meet with a financial planner to get a better idea of income we need. I could also get a second job.

FRANCES: I could look into part-time paying jobs similar to what I already do.

BJORN: Jack and Marla do something like that. We could talk to them.

FRANCES: I feel this list is pretty good. Let's talk about what to try doing.

Agreement and Compromise. Now, they sift through the ideas generated in their brainstorming. The key is to find an agreement that both can get behind.

BJORN: I like your idea of talking to the board. What could it hurt?

FRANCES: I like that too. I also think your idea of seeing a financial planner is good. But I don't think it is realistic for you to work more.

BJORN: Yeah, I think you are right. What about talking to Marla and Jack?

FRANCES: I'd like to hold off on that until I am sure I'm interested.

BJORN: Okay. What about exploring paid part-time jobs where you could be doing something that has meaning for you?

FRANCES: I'd like to think about that. It'd be a good option if they don't have room in the budget where I am. I wouldn't want to do more than half-time, though. I would hate to give up all of what I'm doing now.

BJORN: And I wouldn't want you to. If you had a part-time income, I'll bet we could cut back enough to make it all work.

FRANCES: So, how about I talk to the board, you ask Frank about that financial planner they use, and I'll also start looking around at what kinds of part-time jobs there might be.

BJORN: Great. Let's schedule some time next week to talk about how we are doing in moving along for the solution we need.

FRANCES: Agreed.

They set a specific time and place to meet.

Follow-Up. At the end of the week, Frances and Bjorn met to discuss what they were finding out and what to do next. To her surprise, the board member she talked with seemed eager to try to work out something. In the meantime, she'd gone ahead with looking into various part-time jobs that would meet her needs. Bjorn had scheduled a meeting with a financial planner for the following week.

In this case, the solution became a process made up of a series of smaller steps and agreements. Things were moving on an issue that had been a problem between them for a long time, mostly because it felt good to work together and they were no longer avoiding a tough issue.

Later, they went through the steps again and came to a specific agreement about spending less. They decided how much less to spend and agreed to record all the credit card purchases in a checkbook register so they would know how they were doing compared to their target. In contrast to their problem solving about income, which was a process lasting several weeks, this specific solution on spending was implemented right away, without much tweaking needed.

We'd like to tell you that this model always works this well, but at times it does not. What do you do then?

WHEN IT'S NOT THAT EASY

In our experience with couples, a few common dilemmas often come up when dealing with problems. For example, friction is likely and things can get heated. If things get so heated that you are resorting to negative behavior, it is time for a Time Out. More on that in the next chapter. If you can get back on track by staying with the structure (for example, the Speaker-Listener Technique), great. If not, you need a break until you can keep it constructive.

You can get bogged down and frustrated during any segment of the problem-solution phase. Getting stuck can mean you have not talked through some key issues, or one or both of you is not feeling validated in the process. If so, it's usually best to cycle back to problem discussion. Simply pick up the floor again and resume your discussion. It is better to slow things down than to continue to press for a solution that may not work.

Also, keep in mind that the best solution you can reach may not always be the end solution. At times, you should set the agenda just to agree on the next steps needed to get to the best solution. For example, you might brainstorm about the kind of information you need to make your decision.

WHEN THERE IS NO SOLUTION

Some problems have no mutually satisfying solutions. However, we feel strongly that there are far fewer unresolvable problems than some couples might think. Nevertheless, suppose you've worked together for some time using the structure, and no solution is forthcoming. You can either let this lack of a solution damage the rest of your marriage or you can plan for how to live with the difference. The biblical idea here is the notion of forbearance. Sometimes, couples allow the rest of a good marriage to be damaged by insisting there must be a resolution on a specific unresolved conflict. Instead, you can choose to simply live together graciously in the absence of a solution. Paul summarized this idea beautifully. "If it is possible, as far as it depends on you, live at peace with everyone" (Romans 12:18).

It's not always possible to be at peace with others, but you are called to seek peace as far as it depends on you. In marriage, one of the most powerful ways you can facilitate this is if you go back through the problem-solving steps with this agenda: How are we going to protect the rest of our marriage from the fallout from this unresolved problem? This agenda rejoins the two of you in a common goal—protecting your marriage. You would be literally agreeing to disagree. Solutions that can move you forward come from both teamwork and tolerance. You can't always have your spouse be just the way you want him or her to be, but you can work as a team to deal with your differences.

Here, we have given you a specific model that works well to help preserve and enhance your teamwork. We would not expect you to use such a structured approach for minor problems. We do believe that you can benefit by using this model when dealing with more complex matters, especially those that could lead to unproductive conflict and the danger signs discussed in Chapter Two. This is one more way to add structure when you need it most and to preserve the best in your relationship. Although you can solve problems a variety of ways, the model will work well to help you preserve and enhance your teamwork in solving the problems that come your way.

In the next chapter we conclude this part of the book, which has focused on handling conflict. We will build further on the techniques presented so far to help you prosper in your relationship together. The ground rules we will present next will help you take control of the conflict in your relationship rather than allowing it to take control of you.

EXERCISES

We have two things for you to practice here. First is the XYZ concept. Second, we have a form you can use to gauge your problem areas. Third, and most important, we want you to practice the problem-solving model presented here.

XYZ Statements: Constructive Griping

Let's look at one more example of this technique to make sure you get the idea. Say you were angry about a comment your spouse made at a party last Saturday night. Here's a contrast:

> "You are so inconsiderate."
>
> (Or)
>
> "When you said that what I did for work wasn't really that hard (X) to John and Susan at the party last Saturday (Y), I felt very embarrassed (Z)."

Unless you are careful, it is all too easy to fall into a nonspecific attack on character. Such statements are guaranteed to cause defensiveness and escalation. The XYZ statement is far more constructive. A specific behavior is identified in a specific context. The "I feel Z" part requires you to take responsibility for your own feelings. Your partner does not make you feel anything in particular, so it is important to simply say "I feel . . ." not "it (or you) make(s) me feel . . . " You are in charge of how you feel. People sometimes use "I feel" to mean "I think" and follow with interpretations about the specific behavior. This may be stated as, "I feel like . . . " or "I feel that . . . " These kinds of statements follow with another thought, not a feeling. It works best if you stick simply to "I feel . . . " Use the following to practice XYZs:

1. Spend some time thinking about things that your partner has done or regularly does that bother you in some way. On your own paper, list your concerns as you normally might state them. Then practice putting each of your concerns into the XYZ format (When you do X in situation Y, I feel Z).

2. Next, do the same thing, except list things your partner does that please you. You will find that the XYZ format also works

great for giving positive, specific feedback. For example, you might say something like "When you came home the other night with my favorite ice cream, I felt loved." Share such encouraging statements with your spouse.

3. For those of you who have some difficulty identifying words that reflect feelings, here is a list to help: happy, sad, mad, angry, delighted, frustrated, anxious, tense, nervous, joyful, peaceful, content, irritated, annoyed, euphoric, gleeful, disturbed, on edge, warm, depressed, safe, bothered.

Problem Area Assessment

The following problem inventory is a measure of common problem areas in relationships. The inventory was originally developed by Knox in 1971, and we have used it for years in our research as a simple but relevant measure of the problem areas in couples' relationships. As we'll explain, filling these forms out will help you practice the problem-solving skills we have presented. You should each fill out your own form independently.

Consider the following list of issues that all relationships must face. Please rate how much of a problem each area currently is in your relationship by writing in a number from 0 (not at all a problem) to 100 (a severe problem). For example, if "children" were somewhat of a problem, you might enter 25 next to "children." If children were not a problem in your relationship, you might enter a 0 next to "children." If children were a severe problem, you might enter 100. If you wish to add other areas not included in our list, please do so in the blank spaces provided. Be sure to rate all areas.

_____ Money	_____ In-Laws
_____ Recreation	_____ Alcohol and drugs
_____ Jealousy	_____ Sex
_____ Communication	_____ Children (or potential children)

_____ Friends   _____ Religion

_____ Careers   _____ Other _____

_____ _____   _____ _____

Practice Problem Solving

For practicing this model, it is critical that you follow these instructions carefully. When dealing with real problems in your relationship, the chances of conflict are significant, and we want you to practice in a way that enhances your chances of solidifying these skills.

1. Set aside time to practice when you won't be interrupted. Thirty minutes or so should be sufficient to begin using the sequence on one of the problems you want to solve.

2. Look over your problem inventories together. Construct a list of areas in which each of you rated the problem as being less serious. These are the problem areas we want you to use to practice the model at the start. We want you to practice with more manageable problems and look for specific solutions. That will boost your skills and help you gain confidence in the model.

3. We recommend that you set aside time to practice the Problem Discussion/Prayer/Problem Solution sequence several times a week for a couple of weeks. If you put in this time, you'll gain skill and confidence in handling problem areas together.

4. Keep this chapter open when practicing, and refer back to the steps that are recommended.

5

Ground Rules for Protecting Your Marriage from Conflict

If it is possible, as far as it depends on you, live at peace with everyone.

Romans 12:18

As we have seen in previous chapters, selfishness, upbringing, gender differences, and personal choices made during arguments can damage your oneness if you don't learn to manage the inevitable conflicts and differences that *will* arise in marriage. Without using some skill to overcome negative patterns, the resulting anger can seriously damage your relationship. Now that you understand some powerful techniques for communicating and solving problems, we turn to our six ground rules for protecting your relationship from mishandled conflict.

ANTICIPATE PROBLEMS AND STAY IN CONTROL

A couple of biblical perspectives should be kept in mind as you consider these ground rules. First of all, you should anticipate problems and conflict. Some Christians believe that Christian couples should never have trouble getting along. We see this as an unrealistic expectation that can create discouragement. Christians are fallen people who struggle with sin and selfishness. No one will be perfect this side of eternity, including you and your spouse. Even when we have the best of intentions, our humanness gets in the way. There would not be so many admonitions in scripture about how to get along with others if this weren't such a common problem. Conflict is simply an inevitable part of our relationships with other fallen people, including our mates.

Take Responsibility for Yourself

We also live in a fallen world. There are times of greater stress in our lives. We get tired and irritable. We are not always at our best in the middle of life's trials, and we will blow it at times. Part of reaching Christian maturity is accepting the reality of our imperfection while striving to become holy. Truth is, we will never perfectly understand another person this side of heaven, even when we are doing all the right things. The important thing is to take responsibility for your own behavior, even when your partner doesn't seem to want to get along. You can choose to be polite and to use good skills, even when your spouse won't. If you can run what you are about to say to your mate through this test, you are in great shape: "Do not let any unwholesome talk come out of your mouths, but only what is helpful for building others up according to their needs, that it may benefit those who listen" (Ephesians 4:29).

You might say, "You have got to be kidding me." Nope. We don't think Paul was kidding when he wrote this. This goes back to a key point from the first chapter: most relationships can withstand a limited amount of negative interaction. The Lord Jesus, the apostles, Solomon, and David (just to name a few) all gave significant warnings about the destructiveness of certain ways of treating others. You will certainly not be perfect, and you will slip from time to time and say things poorly or say things that are possibly rude or inconsiderate. But if you really accept how important it is to limit the "reckless words that pierce like a sword," you will be creating a climate that fosters openness and closeness in your marriage. That can help you fully develop the promise your marriage holds for the two of you.

Sometimes, handling issues well comes down to an act of obedience to the Lord, as you choose whether or not to edit out your own negative responses and to take control of the things you say and the way you say them. You are already doing a lot to build each other up by choosing to read this book and trying the things we recommend. In fact, it is very important to encourage one another in your efforts to strengthen your marriage (I Thessalonians 5:11). You could say little things like "It really helped me the way you brought that up" or "Thank you for taking the time to listen to what I was upset about." Recognizing your partner's efforts to communicate well can go a long way to keeping your efforts on track.

Take Control of Your Issues

One more crucial point: the guidelines that follow can help you control the difficult issues in your relationship rather than having them control you. We end Part One of the book with this topic for two reasons. First, the ground rules sum up many key points we have made so far. Second, these rules will give you the opportunity to agree on how you will handle conflict together to protect your marriage. In sports, ground rules specify what is allowed and not allowed, what is in bounds and out. Although we don't wish to evoke the image of competition in using the term *ground rules*, these are powerful tools for helping you work as a team to protect and strengthen your marriage.

SIX KEY GROUND RULES

A couple could have many kinds of ground rules. The ones we recommend here are not the only ones that may benefit you. However, they contain six keys for keeping a marriage on track that are very doable and very beneficial.

Ground Rule No. 1:

> **When conflict begins to escalate, we will call a Time Out and either try talking again, using the Speaker-Listener Technique, or agree to talk later at a specified time about the issue, using the Speaker-Listener Technique.**

If we could get the attention of every Christian couple and have them all agree to only one key change in behavior, this ground rule would be it. It's that important! This one simple rule can protect and enhance relationships. Why? Because "A fool gives full vent to his anger" (Proverbs 29:11). Scripture clearly teaches us that escalating and venting at one another is foolish. Furthermore, research on marital health, mental health, and physiological health simply does not support the idea that venting is healthy. In fact, it's deadly for relationships and for your own health.

This ground rule gives you an agreed-upon way to stop arguments that are not productive—nothing more, nothing less. But this is a powerful thing to do. Why should you continue in an argument that you both know will be damaging for your marriage? You can also use Time Outs for talks that are off track but that have not escalated. An example of this is to say "I'm not sure we're really hearing each other right now. Maybe we should take a break."

To use this ground rule effectively, we suggest you refer to it with a specific term such as *Time Out*. That helps you both interpret correctly what is going on—to see that when your partner says "Time Out," he or she is not just trying to avoid an issue. When you use Time Out, you are taking a stand against destructive behaviors and deciding to do something constructive instead. You're making an effort to keep yourself under the Lord's control.

It is important to approach this as something you are doing *together* for the good of your relationship. Sure, one of you may call Time Outs more often than the other, but if you both agree to the rule, you are really doing the Time Outs together. This is critical. You can't stop escalation effectively without working together when the situation warrants it. Anybody can walk out, but that just fuels more escalation and later hostility. But when either of you calls Time Out, you are working together to stop the destructive process on the spot.

You should work as a team to call Time Out the moment you realize that you, your partner, or both of you are getting out of control. Time Out is called on the communication, not on the other person. The bad conflict is the enemy, not your partner. Don't simply say "Time Out" and leave the room. Such unilateral actions are usually counterproductive. Instead, say something like "This is getting hot; let's stop the action and talk later, OK?" By including your partner in the process, you are using this skill as a team to de-escalate frustration and anger.

Time Out is not avoidance. Another key to this ground rule is that you are agreeing to continue, not avoid, the discussion—pro-ductively. That can be either right now or in the near future, after a cooling-off period. If you are a pursuer, this part of the ground rule addresses your concern that Time Outs could be used by an avoider to prevent discussions about important issues. This ground rule is designed to stop unproductive arguments, not all dialogue on an issue. You do need to discuss difficult issues, but do it in productive ways. In agreeing to use the Speaker-Listener Technique when you come back to talking about an issue, you are agreeing to deal with the problem more effectively.

The Time Out itself can give withdrawers confidence that con-flict won't get out of hand. Some withdrawers become much better able to tolerate conflict, knowing they can stop it at any time. And using the Speaker-Listener Technique also makes it safer for with-drawers to deal with issues that come up by providing that all-important structure. This ground rule will work without using the Speaker-Listener Technique, but we are convinced that using the Speaker-Listener Technique can be one very effective way to structure talks about difficult things.

When you decide to talk later, try to set the time right then, perhaps in an hour, or maybe at a specific time the next day. If things had already become really heated when the Time Out was called, you may find that you can't even talk then about when you'll come back to the discussion. That's OK. You can set a time after things have calmed down between the two of you. The time while you're waiting is a great opportunity to think about the parts of this problem that concern you. Better still, it is a great time to pray for the Lord's wisdom and grace to work on this problem as a team working against a common enemy. This is much better than ob-sessing about how you can "win" the argument. Give it a try.

Luke and Samantha have been married for twenty years and have two teenage sons. Before learning these techniques, they had frequent, intense arguments that ended with shouting and threats about the future of the relationship. Both came from homes where open, intense conflict was relatively common, so changing their pattern was not easy for them. As you will see, they still escalate rather easily, but now they know how to stop it when the argument gets going.

SAMANTHA: (*annoyed and showing it*) You forgot to get the trash out in time for the garbage pick-up. The cans are already full.

LUKE: (*also annoyed, looking up from the paper*) It's no big deal. I'll just stuff it all down more.

SAMANTHA: Yeah, right. The trash will be overflowing in the garage by next week.

LUKE: (*irritated*) What do you want me to do now? I forgot, so just leave it alone.

SAMANTHA: (*very angry now, voice raised*) You aren't getting a lot of the things done around here that you are supposed to.

LUKE: Let's call a Time Out. This isn't getting us anywhere.

SAMANTHA: OK. When can we sit down and talk more about it? How about after church tomorrow?

LUKE: OK. As soon as we finish lunch and get the dishes in the dishwasher.

This ground rule is simple but its impact can be powerful. Samantha and Luke used Time Out very effectively to stop an argument that was going to be destructive. Later, they did sit down and talk, using the Speaker-Listener Technique, about Samantha's concern that Luke was not meeting his responsibilities at home. Then, using the problem-solving techniques we presented in the last chapter, they were able to come up with some new ways to get the chores done as a team.

In this next example, another couple used this ground rule to save an important evening from potential disaster. Byron and

Alexandra have been married for six years and have no children. They want kids but Alexandra has had trouble getting pregnant. This has added plenty of strain to their marriage. They had decided to take a weekend trip to a cottage in the mountains; they wanted to get away and spend a relaxing—perhaps romantic—couple of days together. Each of them had both been looking forward to this time together for months. This conversation transpired on their first evening, as they got into bed together:

ALEXANDRA: (*feeling romantic and snuggling up to Byron*) It's so nice to get away. No distractions. This feels good.

BYRON: (*likewise inclined, and beginning to caress her*) Yeah, should have done this months ago. Maybe a relaxed setting can help you get pregnant.

ALEXANDRA: (*bristling at the thought*) Help *me* get pregnant? That sounds like you think it's my fault we're not getting pregnant. Why did you have to bring that up?

BYRON: (*anxious and annoyed at himself for spoiling the moment*) I don't think it is your fault. We have been through that. I just meant . . .

ALEXANDRA: (*angrily*) You just meant to say that there is something wrong with me.

BYRON: Hold on. Let's take a Time Out. I am sorry that I mentioned pregnancy. Do you want to talk this through now, or set a time for later?

ALEXANDRA: (*softening*) If we don't talk about it a little bit, I think the rest of the evening will be a drag.

BYRON: OK, you have the floor. (*He picks up the remote control from the night stand and hands it to her.*)

ALEXANDRA (Speaker): I got all tense when you brought up pregnancy, and I felt like you were blaming me for our infertility.

BYRON (Listener): So mentioning that subject raised unpleasant feelings, and more so because you felt blamed.

ALEXANDRA (Speaker): Yes. That whole thing has been just awful for us, and I was hoping to get away from it for the weekend.

BYRON (Listener): It's been really hard on you, and you wanted to just forget about it this weekend.

ALEXANDRA (Speaker): And I wanted us to focus on rediscovering how to be a little bit romantic, like it used to be.

BYRON (Listener): Just you and me making love without a care.

ALEXANDRA (Speaker): (*feeling really listened to and cared for*) Yes. Your turn. (*Floor switch*)

BYRON (Speaker): Boy do I feel like a turkey! I didn't mean to mess up the moment, though I see how what I said affected you.

ALEXANDRA (Listener): You feel bad that you said anything. You did not mean to mess things up between us tonight.

BYRON (Speaker): You got it. And I really don't think it is your fault we are not pregnant. Whatever is not working right in our bodies, I don't think of it as you or me messing up. When I said what I said about you getting pregnant, I think of "us" getting pregnant, but really, it's you that will actually be pregnant. That's all I meant.

ALEXANDRA (Listener): (*with a smile*) You didn't mean to be such a turkey!

BYRON (Speaker): (*chuckling back*) That's kind of blunt, but yeah, that's what I'm saying. (*He hands her the floor.*) I think we should just avoid that whole topic for the weekend.

ALEXANDRA (Listener): You think we should make infertility an off-limits topic this weekend.

BYRON: Yes! (*Floor switch*)

ALEXANDRA (Speaker): I agree. I would like to pray about it together though. OK. Where were we? (*tossing the remote on the floor*)

BYRON: (*big smile*) You were calling me a turkey.

ALEXANDRA: (*playfully*) Oh yeah. Come over here, turkey.

BYRON: (*moving closer to kiss her*) I'm all yours.

Notice how effectively they used the Time Out to stop what could have turned into an awful fight and a weekend full of barriers and distance. Alexandra was too hurt to just shelve the issue. She needed to talk right then, and Byron agreed. Using the Speaker-Listener Technique to do so helped them diffuse the tension and come back together, and it saved their special weekend.

Ground Rule No. 2:

When we are having trouble communicating, we will engage the Speaker-Listener Technique.

This ground rule gives you a specific way to put James 1:19 into practice. "Everyone should be quick to listen, slow to speak and slow to become angry" (James 1:19). The objective here is to use a way to communicate safely and clearly when you really need to do it well. With this ground rule, you are agreeing to use more structure when you need it, in order to

Ensure there are no misinterpretations.

Help each of you be "quick to listen and slow to speak."

Keep the conversation slowed down, so that each of you is heard.

Make it safe enough for you to talk about your deeper concerns.

It is good to use this ground rule when you are planning to talk about a topic that has been "hot" for you in the past. For example, suppose that you wanted to talk about how money is being spent. You know from your history that these talks usually get difficult. You could raise the issue this way. "Dear, I am pretty concerned about money right now. Let's sit down and talk using the floor." Such a statement tells your mate that you are raising an important issue and that you want to talk it out using added structure. This is the most common use of this ground rule. Like the wise man in Proverbs who foresees the evil and prepares himself, you can learn to engage the skills before things go downhill on a tough subject. This is being proactive rather than reactive.

At other times when things may have already escalated, a Time Out might be helpful. But with this ground rule in place, you can choose to move right into the issue using the Speaker-Listener Technique. In the next example, Allison and James used this ground rule to get back on track. On this occasion, their new skills made a big difference. On this particular evening, they went out to dinner and got into an argument about their friends before even ordering.

ALLISON: (*matter of factly*) This reminds me. Dick and Barb asked us over for dinner next Saturday. I told them that I thought we could do it.

JAMES: (*very angrily*) What! How could you tell them we'd go without even asking? You know that I really dislike being around her.

ALLISON: (*angry, but speaking in a low, serious tone*) Lower your voice. People are turning to look at us.

JAMES: (*just as loud as before and just as angry*) So what? Let them stare. I am sick and tired of you making decisions without talking to me first.

ALLISON: Don't talk to me like this.

JAMES: How 'bout I don't talk to you at all?

At that point, James got up and left the restaurant and went out to the car. He paced a bit, fuming and muttering about how difficult

Allison could be at times. Then he got in the car, intending to drive away and leave her at the restaurant. "Wouldn't that serve her right?" he thought. As he cooled off for a moment, he thought better of that idea. He got up, walked back into the restaurant, took his seat across from Allison, picked up a menu and handed it to her, and said, "OK, you have the floor."

This might have been a good moment for a total Time Out, but instead, he decided he wanted to talk this one out right now, but more productively. Allison went with it, and they had an excellent discussion of the issue. Their transition to greater structure took them from what could have been a real meltdown to a victory in an area where there had been defeat in the past. Experiences like this serve to boost your confidence in your ability to work together and keep your relationship strong. And studies show that having such a confidence is part of a great marriage.

Ground Rule No. 3:

When discussing an important issue, we will completely separate Problem Discussion from Problem Solution.

"He who answers before listening—that is his folly and his shame" (Proverbs 18:13). It seems that we all tend to violate this biblical principle. Too often, we rush to find to a solution, only to find that the solution fails because it was premature. This results in a sense of hopelessness about the problem and sometimes about the marriage itself.

Go back to Chapter Three and review the conversation between Tessie and Peter about Jeremy and preschool. Notice how they had a great discussion but did not seek a specific solution. They each expressed and heard one another's concerns. They were ready to try problem solving on this issue. Let's pick it up from where they left off.

TESSIE: I think we are ready for problem solving. What do you think?

PETER: I agree. I'm feeling like we had a good talk and got a
    lot out on the table. How about we pray about it a moment?

TESSIE: Wonderful idea. Let's do that.

They paused for a moment, while each uttered a very simple and direct prayer asking God to help them find the best solution. Thus, they made the transition from Problem Discussion to Problem Solution with an acknowledgment of God in the process. Now they were ready to move forward.

Peter and Tessie have learned the value of "hearing a matter before answering it." Discussion and solution are different processes with different goals. Problem Discussion is about understanding each other. Problem Solution is about taking action together. Each works better when you give place to both in your marriage.

Ground Rule No. 4:

We can bring up an issue at any time, but the listener can say "This is not a good time." If the listener does not want to talk at that time, he or she takes responsibility for setting up a time to talk in the near future (usually within twenty-four to forty-eight hours).

This ground rule ensures that you will not have an important or difficult talk about an issue unless you both agree that the time is right. There is no point in having a discussion about anything important unless you're both ready to talk about it.

Sadly, most couples talk about their most important issues at the worst times: dinnertime, bedtime, when getting ready for church on Sunday, when it's time to get the kids off for school, as soon as you walk in door after work. . . . You get the picture. These are times when your spouse may be a captive audience, but you certainly don't have his or her full attention. In fact, these are often the most stressful times in life. So they are not good times to talk things out.

This ground rule assumes two things: that (1) you each are responsible for knowing when you are capable of discussing something and giving your full attention to your partner and (2) you can each respect the other when he or she says "I can't deal with that right now." There simply is no point in trying to have a discussion unless you are both ready to hear one another.

Perhaps you are thinking, "Isn't this just a prescription for avoidance?" That is where the second part of the ground rule comes in. The one who is not up to the discussion takes responsibility for making it happen in the near future. This is critical. Your partner will have a much easier time putting off the conversation if she has confidence that you really will follow through, usually within twenty-four to forty-eight hours. This may not always be practical, but it works as a good rule of thumb.

And what about late at night? This is a tricky time for many couples because many of us are so busy that bedtime can seem like the only time to talk. Many times, though, it's a bad time to try to have important discussions. You may be thinking, "Doesn't the Bible say to 'not let the sun go down on your anger'?" (Ephesians 4:26). Yes, but note that it says to not let the sun go down on your anger, not that you have to resolve the issue before you sleep. Some issues just are not going to be resolved late at night. When you are working together so well that you can agree to put off an issue until tomorrow and have confidence that it will be dealt with, that goes a long way toward reducing anger and frustration—and you can go to sleep.

Here's one example. Martina and Alex are a couple with two children, a five-year-old girl and a two-year-old boy. As is typical of many couples with young children, they have little time for sleeping, much less for talking things out. Most days their only moments alone are at bedtime, after both kids are finally bathed and in bed.

ALEX: I can't believe how Mary wants to hear the same Bible story ten times in a row. I thought she'd never get to sleep.

MARTINA: It's the same with naps. You'd think she would be bored to death with those stories.

ALEX: I would. Speaking of boring things, we need to talk about those life insurance decisions. I know that agent will call back any day.

MARTINA: I know it's important, but I just can't focus right now. I think I could focus about ten minutes on the TV, and that's about it.

ALEX: Pretty wiped, eh? Me, too. Well, when would be a good time to talk about this?

MARTINA: No guarantee I will be alive, but I think I might have the energy around lunch time tomorrow. Could you come home? Maybe we'll get blessed and catch Matt on his nap.

ALEX: Sounds good. Let's watch TV and crash.

It is now Martina's responsibility to bring it up again tomorrow and to make sure this talk happens. This should be pretty easy to do, because their agreement is very specific. They may be too tired and busy for there ever to be a perfect time to talk this out, but some times are better than others. At any rate, they are not going to bed angry, and they are not trying to push a talk at a bad time.

As one variation of this ground rule, you may want to come to an agreement that certain times are never good for bringing up important things. For example, we have worked with many couples who have agreed that neither will bring up anything significant within thirty minutes of bedtime. Other couples also include the time getting ready for church, transition times when preparing for or arriving home from work, date times, mealtimes, and so forth. However, the next ground rule is absolutely necessary if you are going to protect these special times from conflict.

Ground Rule No. 5:

We will have weekly couple meetings.

This ground rule is a tangible way to "keep short accounts" and to avoid the roots of bitterness that grow when problems are never resolved. Sadly, most couples do not set aside a regular time for dealing with key issues and problems, although most marriage experts advise us to do so. Our view on this sage advice is that the advantages of having a weekly meeting time far outweigh any negatives.

First, this is a tangible way to place high priority on your oneness by carving out time for its protection. We know you are busy. We all are busy. But if you decide that this is important, you can find the time to make it work out.

Second, following this ground rule ensures that even if there is no other good time to deal with issues and problems in your marriage, you at least have this weekly meeting as your "default setting." You'll be surprised at how much you can get done in thirty minutes or so of concentrated attention on an issue, especially when you are using the skills and techniques we recommend in this section of the book.

Third, having a weekly meeting time takes much of the day-to-day pressure off your relationship. This is especially true if you have become tangled up in the pursuer-withdrawer pattern. If something happens that brings up a gripe for you, it's so much easier to delay bringing it up until another time, *when you know there will be another time*. Pursuers can relax, knowing they will have their chance to raise their issue. Withdrawers are encouraged to bring up concerns they have, because they have a meeting for doing this in a controlled way.

You may be thinking that this is a pretty good idea. But to put this good idea into action, you must be consistent in taking the time to make the meetings happen. You may have the urge to skip the meetings when you are getting along better. We have heard this repeatedly from couples. Don't succumb to this temptation. Keep your promise to meet.

If you get to a meeting and have little to deal with, fine. (Believe it or not, that day will come.) Have a short meeting, but have a meeting. Use these meetings to air concerns, have discussions about important issues, plan for events coming up, or just take stock of how your relationship is going. When a specific problem is in focus, work through the problem-discussion and problem-solution steps presented in the last chapter. When nothing is more pressing, practice some of the skills presented in the program. Keep the appointment and use the time to keep your relationship strong.

Ground Rule No. 6:

We will make time for the great things of marriage—fun, friendship, sensuality, and spiritual connection. We will agree to protect these times from conflict and the need to deal with issues.

Just as it's important to set aside times to deal with issues in your relationship, it's critical that you set aside times for enjoying the God-given blessings of marriage. You can't be focusing on issues all the time and have a really great marriage. You need some nurturing and safe times for relaxing—having fun, talking as friends, making love—when conflict and problems are always off limits.

For now, we'll emphasize two points embodied in this ground rule. First, set aside specific times in your schedule for these great things. Second, if you're already spending time together in these ways, don't use that time to bring up issues that you have to work on. And if an issue does come up, table it for a later time, such as your couple meeting.

The example we presented earlier in this chapter with Alexandra and Byron makes this point well. They were out to have a relaxing and romantic weekend, and it wasn't a good time to focus on one of their key issues. Using Time Out and the Speaker-Listener Technique helped them to get refocused on the real reason they had gotten away. But it's better still if you agree to keep such issues off limits during such positive times in the first place.

If you agree to use these ground rules, you are agreeing to control the difficult issues in your marriage rather than allowing them to control you. Instead of having arguments whenever things come up, which are usually the worst times, you are agreeing to deal with the issues when you both are able to do it well, when you are both under control.

One of the most destructive things that can happen to a marriage is to have the growing sense that you are walking in a mine field. You know the feeling. You begin to wonder where the next explosion will come from, and you don't feel in control of where you're going. You no longer feel free to just "be" with your partner. You don't know when you are about to set off an explosion, but you know right away when you just did. It just doesn't have to be this way, or ever get to be this way in the first place. These ground rules will go a long way to getting you back on safe ground. They work. You can do it.

EXERCISES

Together, discuss each of these ground rules. You may want to modify one or more of them in some way to make them work better for you. We also suggest that you review the passages of scripture discussed in this chapter. The key is to take a hard look at these rules and give them a chance to work in your relationship. You don't need to work these things out exactly as we suggest, but we believe that couples taking hold of the promise in their marriages are able to protect their marriages in these kinds of ways. Many couples can do this naturally, without much help from a book or others, but many cannot. We want to help all couples to be able to protect their marriages better, so that's why we ask you to give these ground rules great consideration. Here are our suggested ground rules for handling issues.

1. When conflict begins to escalate, we will call a Time Out and either try talking again, using the Speaker-Listener Technique or agree to talk later at a specified time about the issue, using the Speaker-Listener Technique.

2. When we are having trouble communicating, we will engage the Speaker-Listener Technique.

3. When discussing an important issue, we will completely separate Problem *Discussion* from Problem *Solution*.

4. We can bring up an issue at any time, but the listener can say "This is not a good time." If the listener does not want to talk at that time, he or she takes responsibility for setting up a time to talk in the near future. (You need to decide how "the near future" is defined.)

5. We will have weekly couple meetings. (Schedule the time now for your regular weekly couple meetings. There is no time like the present.)

6. We will make time for the great things: fun, friendship, sensuality, and spirituality. We will agree to protect these times from conflict and the need to deal with issues.

PART TWO

Going Deeper

In this part, we begin to move to deeper themes that affect the life of a marriage. We'll look at deeper motivations and issues that drive conflicts as well as expectations that affect nearly everything else in your marriage. The material on commitment and forgiveness speaks to some of the most powerful themes in both scripture and research regarding good relationships, especially marriage. Here, we want to help you better understand your deeper motivations and to develop the kind of mind-set that honors God and builds great marriages.

6

Issues and Events

Accept one another, then, just as Christ accepted you, in order
to bring praise to God.

Romans 15:7

So far, we've focused on how you can manage conflict and disagreements in your marriage. Now we want to offer some help in
dealing with everyday happenings and long-term arguments. All
couples experience frustrating events, and all couples have difficult
issues. In this chapter, we'll help you understand how issues and
events are connected and how important it is to deal with them
separately. Then we'll discuss the deeper, often hidden issues that
affect relationships.

ISSUES VERSUS EVENTS

The four major issues that most married couples say cause problems
are money, sex, communication, and children. Other things couples
commonly fight about are in-laws, recreation, alcohol and drugs, religion, careers, and housework. We call all these things issues. Actually, issues are not the things that couples argue about most
frequently. What they do argue most often about are the small, day-
to-day happenings of life. We call these events. We want to help
you handle events and issues separately and then separate the issues
that are more apparent—like money, communication, sex—from
the deeper, often hidden, issues that affect your relationship. An example will help you see what we mean.

Ellen and Gregg are a couple with big money issues. One day, Ellen came home from work and put the checkbook down on the kitchen counter as she went to the bedroom to change. Gregg got livid when he looked at the checkbook and saw an entry for $150 made out to a department store. When Ellen walked back into the kitchen, tired after a long day at work, she was looking for a hug or a "How was your day?" Instead, the conversation went like this:

GREGG: What did you spend this $150 on?

ELLEN: (*very defensive*) None of your business.

GREGG: Of course it's my business. We just decided on a budget, and here you go blowing it.

All of a sudden they were into a huge argument about the issue of money. But it happened in the context of an event—Gregg discovering that Ellen had spent $150. (It was actually for a new sweater for Gregg to celebrate his new job offer. But that never came up.)

Arguments about events like this are common. Issues and events work like the geysers in Yellowstone National Park. Underneath the park are caverns of hot water under pressure. The unresolved issues in your relationship are like these cauldrons of pressure. The issues that give you more trouble contain the greatest amount of heat. The pressure keeps building up when you aren't talking about them in constructive ways. Then events trigger the messy eruption.

Many couples deal with important issues only in the context of triggering events. For Ellen and Gregg, so much negative energy is stored up around the issue of money that it's easily triggered. They never sit down and talk about money in a constructive way, as a separate issue, but instead argue like this when checks bounce, bills come, and so forth. They never get anywhere on the big issue because they spend their energy just dealing with the crises of the events. What about you? Do you set aside time to deal with issues ahead of time? Or do you wait until events trigger them?

Another couple, Tom and Samantha, had avoided talking about the intrusion of relatives in their relationship. One evening, they went to a baseball game—the first time they'd been out for three or four weeks. On the way, Tom got a call on their cell phone from his mother. When the phone call ended, Samantha confronted him.

SAMANTHA: Why do you always let her interfere with our relationship? This is our evening out.

TOM: (*really hot under the collar*) There you go again, blasting me when we're going out to have fun for a change.

SAMANTHA: (*sounding indignant*) Well, I didn't know we were planning to bring your mother along!

TOM: (*dripping with sarcasm*) Ha-Ha. Real funny, Sam.

Their evening was destroyed. They never even made it to the ballpark. They spent the night arguing about his mother calling and whether or not she was too involved in their lives.

Events tend to come up at the most inopportune times—you're ready to leave for work, you're coming home from work, you're trying to get everyone ready for going to church, you're going to bed, you're out to relax, the kids are fighting, friends are coming over, and so forth. Events come up at times like these, but these are usually the worst times to deal with the issues.

How to Deal with Triggering Events

We're suggesting that you edit out this tendency to argue about the issue right then, when an event triggers it. Don't try to deal with important issues only in the context of triggering events. The key to this is saying to yourself, "I don't have to deal with this right now. This isn't the time. We can talk later." There are times when simply dropping the matter for the moment is the wise strategy—as Solomon in all his wisdom tells us, "There is a time for everything, and a season for every activity under heaven . . . a time to be silent and a time to speak" (Ecclesiastes 3:1,7).

This is not deep theology here; it's simple wisdom. In the argument just described, Samantha could have said, "That phone call from your mother really set off an issue for me. We need to have a talk about it later." In this way, the event is acknowledged, but the issue is left for a time when you can deal with it more effectively. Likewise, Tom could have said, "Listen, let's take a Time Out. I can see you are feeling hurt, but let's wait for a better time to talk about the issue. How about tomorrow after dinner?" If they had been practicing the skills we've presented so far, they could have saved their evening by containing the event so that it didn't trigger the explosive, unresolved issues about his mother and their time together. That's what we mean by separating issues from events. It's a very wise thing to do.

When an event does happen, you could also try to have a brief but effective talk about the issue for just a few minutes, agreeing to have a more thorough discussion later. You might say, "Let's talk about what just happened a few moments and then try to move on and have a nice evening together." You can use the Speaker-Listener Technique so you are sure both are heard. Then let it go until later. If you do talk right then about the issue, be "quick to hear, slow to speak, and slow to become angry" (James 1:19).

One reason people focus on events and let them turn into issue discussions is that "later" never happens (avoidance). So the person who is most bothered by the issue doesn't feel he can wait. When this happens a lot, it feels like you're living in a marital minefield, with the issues being the explosives and the events being the triggers. You never know when you're going to step on another mine. One effect of living in a minefield is that you feel tense around one another most of the time rather than open and relaxed. What you want most is to simply enjoy each other as best friends. But instead you end up feeling up-tight around each other a lot of the time. The effect on your marriage can be devastating.

Practicing the things we've been teaching makes it more likely you'll handle events better as you take the time to deal with important issues. Separate them from the events. The goal is to control where, when, and how you will deal with the issues in your relationship.

HIDDEN ISSUES

It's often easy to recognize the issues being triggered by events because they are pretty closely connected to one another. With Ellen and Gregg, his looking at the checkbook started the event, and the issue was money. That's not hard to figure out. But sometimes couples get into fights about trivial events that don't seem to be attached to any particular issue—like the toilet seat being left up.

Arguments about these kinds of things are signs that you aren't getting at the real issues. It's not about money, it's not about careers, it's not about housework, it's not really about his leaving the toilet seat up. The real issues are deeper and more elusive. We call these hidden issues. Hidden issues often drive our most frustrating and destructive arguments. For example, Samantha and Tom ended up arguing about his mother and his willingness to take calls from her at any time. But the real issue is probably that Samantha feels she is not as important to him as his relatives.

When we say these issues are often hidden, we mean they are usually not the things being talked about openly, even though they are the really important issues. But they get lost in the flow of the argument. For instance, you may be very aware of feeling uncared for, but when certain events come up, that's not what you talk about, just as Samantha may have been aware that she felt Tom didn't think she was as important as his mother. But that's not what they talked about. They couldn't see the forest (the hidden issue) for the trees (the events).

To summarize, events are everyday happenings such as dirty dishes or a bounced checks. Issues are those larger topics, like money, sex, and in-laws, that all couples must deal with. Hidden issues are the deeper, fundamental issues that usually lie underneath the arguments about issues and events. We see at least six hidden issues in our work with couples: power, caring, recognition, commitment, integrity, and acceptance. There are surely others, but these six capture a lot of what goes on in relationships. As you will see, because these issues are the things closest to our hearts, they often have a deeper spiritual significance.

Hidden Issues of Control and Power

With control issues, the question is power and status. For instance, who decides who does the chores? Are your needs and desires just as important as your partner's, or is there an inequality? Is your input important or are major decisions made without you? Who's in charge? If you deal with these kinds of issues a lot, you may be dealing with the hidden issue of control.

This hidden issue tends to come into play when decisions come up—even small ones. For example, what happens if one of you really wants to order pizza and the other really feels like having Chinese food? This is an event without a lot of long-term significance. Nevertheless, if either of you is unyielding in what you want, you can have a lot of conflict about something as simple as what's for dinner. You can feel like the other is trying to control you or like you need to be in control. A power struggle can come out of just about anything.

Whatever the topic or disagreement, control issues are least likely to damage your relationship when there's a good sense of being a team and when each partner's needs and desires are considered in decisions. Such teamwork reflects love and humility. Control and power arguments reflect selfishness. James really nailed it when he wrote:

> What causes fights and quarrels among you? Don't they come from your desires that battle within you? You want something but don't get it. You kill and covet, but you cannot have what you want. You quarrel and fight. You do not have, because you do not ask God. When you ask, you do not receive, because you ask with wrong motives, that you may spend what you get on your pleasures [James 4:1–3].

As James says, a lot of power battles arise from selfish motives, as we struggle to get our way, to have what we want, and to obtain our own pleasure. But even when one partner's motives are pure, the other may still react negatively due to their own past experiences. Some people are hypersensitive about being controlled by others because they have experienced a very controlling authority figure somewhere in the past, usually a parent. So they tend to mistrust their mates, operating with the negative interpretation that their mates are trying to control them. Couples who do well struggle less with such mistrust.

It's no accident that money is rated the number one problem area in our studies at the University of Denver. So many decisions in our lives revolve around money. If you have significant power or control issues in your marriage, it's likely you struggle a lot with money as well as any number of other things. Money in and of itself isn't the deeper issue, but it's an issue that provides many events for triggering the deeper issues of control and power.

Also, any time you must make a decision together, especially if it's an important one, the control issue can be triggered. Working together as a team is the best antidote to control battles.

Hidden Issues of Needing and Caring

A second major arena where we see hidden issues emerge involves caring. Here, the main theme is the extent to which you feel loved and cared for by your partner. The caring issue is what's involved when you feel that important emotional needs aren't being met.

Jill and Nelson repeatedly fought over who should refill the orange juice container. But juice wasn't the real issue. As it turned out, Nelson had always seen his mother refilling the juice container as a demonstration of her love for him. Because Jill wouldn't do it, he felt it meant she didn't love him—a hidden issue about caring. So he was always pushing her to refill the orange juice. He was very aware of feeling uncared for, but in their arguments about orange juice he didn't talk about it. Instead, he focused on what he saw as Jill's stubbornness.

For her part, Jill was thinking, "Who's he to tell me to mix the orange juice? Where does he get off saying I have to do it?" Jill had a hidden control issue, thinking he was trying to force her to live a certain way. That really wasn't his motive, but she was very sensitive about control because she'd previously been married to a domineering man. Our mutual hidden issues often underlie our arguments. For Nelson and Jill, a good discussion about it finally touched on the hidden issues. As a result, they ended up feeling much closer, and who filled the juice container no longer seemed all that important.

NELSON (Speaker): So for me, it's really not about wanting to control you. I've been so primed by my upbringing to connect refilling the juice with love that I've put this pressure on you to do it to be sure that you love me.

JILL (Listener): (*summarizing in her own words*) So for you, the key issue is wanting to know I care, not wanting to control me?

NELSON (Speaker): (*going on to validate her*) Exactly, and I can see how you'd be feeling controlled without knowing that.

(*Floor switch*)

JILL (Speaker): You're right. I've really felt you wanted to control me, and that's a hot button, given what I went through with Joe.

NELSON (Listener): So it really did seem to you that I just wanted to control you, and that's an especially sensitive area given what you went through with Joe.

JILL (Speaker): You got it. I want to be your partner, not your hired hand.

NELSON (Listener): (*capturing what she's saying in his own words*) Sounds like you just want us to work as a team.

JILL (Speaker): Yeah! That's really important to me.

As you can see from the end of their conversation, talking about the deeper concerns paved the way for greater connection instead of alienation over empty juice containers. This is another example of its being very hard to solve the problem about the event (refilling the orange juice) unless a couple is communicating well enough to get the hidden issues out in the open. But it's hard to talk about such issues if you can't talk safely. The key is to be able to talk about deeper issues in a safe way rather than letting them operate as powerful pressure points in arguments.

Hidden Issues of Recognition

The third type of hidden issue involves recognition. Are your activities and accomplishments appreciated by your partner? Although caring issues involve concerns about being cared for or loved, recognition issues are more about feeling valued by your partner for who you are and what you do.

Consider Burt and Chelsea, a couple who enjoy running their business together—most of the time. Burt is president and treasurer of their corporation, and Chelsea is vice president and secretary. One day they were having a business lunch together when someone asked him a question about the company. His quick response was, "I'm the only officer in this company." His wife, the vice president, was sitting next to him. Chelsea was furious and embarrassed.

We don't know why Burt failed at times to recognize her role in the company. Perhaps he had a control issue that was seeping out when he made such a comment. Perhaps he does think "I can do it all" and really does disregard her contributions to the company. But whatever his real reason for saying it, such events will make Chelsea's involvement less and less rewarding. She may even pull away from him and her work in the business over time. If they want to prevent further damage to their relationship, they had better talk openly about this key issue.

Such examples are common. For example, many men tell us they don't think their wives appreciate how hard they work to earn income for the family. Likewise, we hear many women say that they don't feel their husbands appreciate all the work they do around the house, whether or not the women work outside the home. In either case, spouses may try hard for a while to get recognized for what they do for the family but eventually burn out if no appreciation is expressed.

It appears that some of the apostles struggled with the recognition issue. Even after years of walking with Christ, Jesus' most trusted companions got into an argument about who deserved the highest place in His kingdom (Matthew 20:17–28). Jesus rebuked them, linking this desire for recognition with the desire to have power over others, and He admonished them to focus instead on serving one another (Matthew 20:26,27). Such advice couldn't be more apt in marriage. Ironically, one of the best ways to serve your mate is to recognize his or her contributions to your marriage. That's a gift you can give to your mate that will return to you in kind. How long has it been since you told your partner how much you appreciate the things she or he does?

Hidden Issues of Commitment

The focus of this fourth hidden issue is on the long-term security of the relationship. The question that is felt but not usually asked is "Are you going to stay with me?" One couple we worked with, Alice and Chuck, had huge arguments about separate checking accounts. He would complain bitterly about her having a separate account whenever the bank statement arrived and he saw her balance.

For Chuck, the hidden issue was commitment. As a child, his mother had taken him and left his father. He knew prior to leaving that his mother had begun to put money in her own bank account, which he was told not to tell Daddy about. His mother left his father after she'd saved up several thousand dollars in her account. Now, when the statement for Alice's account would arrive, he'd associate it with thoughts that Alice could be planning to leave him, based on his childhood experience. That was not at all her plan. But because he had never talked openly about his fear, she wasn't given the opportunity to alleviate his anxiety by affirming her commitment. The issue kept fueling explosive conflict in events connected to it.

When your commitment to one another feels secure, it brings a deep kind of safety to your relationship. This is safety that comes from feeling secure about each other's promise to always be there for you, to lift you up in tough times, to cherish you for a lifetime, no matter what. As we said in the first chapter, the oneness that God planned for marriage is a oneness of permanence, not because God loves restrictions but because he cares about our need to have a relationship that we can count on.

Many people who have gone through divorce (their own or their parents') or other forms of abandonment as children, struggle with fears about commitment. Do you worry about your partner's long-term commitment to you and the marriage? Have you talked about this openly, or does this issue find indirect expression in the context of events in your relationship? In Chapters Eight and Nine, we'll be focusing in much more depth on how commitment issues affect relationships.

Hidden Issues of Integrity

The fifth type of hidden issue deals with integrity. Have you ever noticed how upset you get when your partner questions your feelings or motives? These events can spark great fury.

With Byron and Gladys, arguments frequently included making hurtful statements about each other's intentions. Most often, they were sure that what the other meant was negative. Both are therapists, so you'd think they'd know better. They had a serious problem with negative interpretations about each other. Here's a typical example.

GLADYS: You forgot to pick up the dry cleaning.

BYRON: (*feeling a bit indignant*) You didn't ask me to pick it up, you asked me if I was going by there. I told you I wasn't.

GLADYS: (*really angry at what she sees as his lack of caring about what she needs*) You did say you'd pick it up, but you just don't give a rip about me.

BYRON: (*feeling thoroughly insulted*) I do care, and I resent you telling me I don't.

Her caring issue is pretty out in the open here, though they are not exactly having a constructive, healing talk about it. But his issue has more to do with integrity. It's not as much in the open, but it's there. He feels insulted at her calling him an uncaring, inconsiderate husband who never thinks about her needs. He really does care. So he feels judged. Each winds up feeling invalidated.

As we pointed out earlier, it's not wise to argue about what each other really thinks, feels, or intends. In fact, Paul tells us not to judge the thoughts and motives of others, only their actions (I Corinthians 4:3–5). Don't tell your partner what's going on inside unless it's your inside! To do otherwise is guaranteed to trigger the issue of integrity. And almost everyone will defend their integrity when it's questioned.

Acceptance: The Bottom Line

One primary issue seems to underlie all the others listed here: the desire for acceptance. Sometimes, this is felt more as a fear of rejection but the fundamental issue is the same. At the deepest level, people are motivated to find acceptance and to avoid rejection in their relationships. This reflects the deep need we all have to be both respected and connected. Consider again the foundational teaching we looked at in the first chapter. Adam and Eve did not know fear, only openness and no shame, until they sinned.

Then the eyes of both of them were opened, and they realized they were naked; so they sewed fig leaves together and made coverings for themselves. Then the man and his wife heard the sound of the LORD God as he was walking in the garden in the cool of the day, and they hid from the LORD God among the trees of the garden. But the LORD God called to the man, "Where are you?" He answered, "I heard you in the garden, and I was afraid because I was naked; so I hid" [Genesis 3:7–10].

This fundamental fear of rejection drives so many other hidden issues. And the fear is real. Marriage involves imperfect people who can hurt one another deeply and even reject one another at times. You can see this fear of rejection come up in many ways. For example, some people are afraid that if they make their real desires known, their partner will reject them. Perhaps one partner asks for what he wants indirectly rather than directly. For example, he might say, "Wouldn't you like to make love tonight?" rather than, "I would like to make love with you tonight." Many people are indirect about what they ask of their partners. Their desires are not stated clearly because of a fear of rejection.

The issue of acceptance is so critical that we are specifically called on in scripture to accept one another: "Accept one another, then, just as Christ accepted you, in order to bring praise to God" (Romans 15:7).

Passages like these are not specific to marriage, but we can think of no other relationship in which acting on what we are called to do matters so much. No matter what our differences or problems, we are called to accept our mates with a richness that frees them to feel safer in the relationship. And even more important, as we accept one another in this way, the result is that God's acceptance of us is modeled to the world in perhaps the fullest expression of grace that can be known. And when His marvelous grace is seen in human relationships, He gets the praise.

Recognizing the Signs of Hidden Issues

You can't handle hidden issues like acceptance unless you can identify them. There are four key ways to tell when hidden issues may be affecting your interaction.

Wheel Spinning. One sign of hidden issues is when you find your-selves talking about some problem over and over again but getting nowhere fast. It's as though you're spinning your wheels. These re-peated struggles can be very discouraging. If an argument starts with you thinking "Here we go again," you should suspect hidden issues. You aren't getting anywhere on the problem because you probably aren't talking about what really matters—the hidden issues. So you go around and around in a hopeless circle.

Trivial Triggers. A second way to identify hidden issues is when minor things blow up out of all proportion. The argument between Jill and Nelson is a great example. The refilling of the orange juice container seems like a trivial event, but it triggers horrendous argu-ments driven by the issues of power and caring.

Avoidance. A third sign of hidden issues is when one or both of you is avoiding certain topics or levels of intimacy. It could be that walls have gone up between you. This often means that important, unexpressed issues are affecting the relationship. Perhaps it seems too risky to talk directly about feeling unloved or insecure. Trouble is, those concerns have a way of coming up anyway.

Couples avoid many topics, reflecting hidden issues in relation-ships. For example, we have talked with couples from different cul-tural or religious backgrounds who strongly avoid talking about these differences. We think this usually reflects concerns about ac-ceptance. They wonder, "Will you accept me fully if we really ex-plore our differences here?" Avoiding such topics not only allows hidden issues to remain hidden, it puts the relationship at greater risk because these important differences can have a great impact on marriage.

Other common but taboo topics in marriage include issues of sex, weight, and money. There are many such sensitive topics that people avoid dealing with in their relationships out of fear of rejec-tion. What issues do you avoid talking about?

Score Keeping. A fourth sign of hidden issues in your relationship is when one or both or you start keeping score. We'll talk more about the dangers of score keeping in Chapter Nine. For now, the key is that score keeping reflects something that needs attention in your relationship. It could mean you are not feeling recognized for what you put into the marriage. It could mean that you are less committed, as we'll explain later. It could mean you are feeling controlled, so you're keeping track of the times you think your partner has taken advantage of you. Whatever the issue, it can be a sign that important things are not being talked about, just documented.

Handling Hidden Issues

Recognizing the signs that hidden issues are operating is an important first step. But what can you do once you realize one is affecting your relationship? The most important thing you can do is simply to talk about these hidden issues constructively, perhaps at a time set aside just for this purpose. This will be easier if you are cultivating an atmosphere of teamwork using the kinds of techniques we've presented thus far. We strongly recommend using the Speaker-Listener Technique when you are trying to explore such sensitive areas.

One other important strategy is deal with the issue in terms of problem discussion, not problem solution. Be aware of the tendency to jump to shallow solutions. In our opinion, the deeper the issue, the less likely that problem solving will be the answer. What you need first and foremost is to hear each other and understand the feelings and concerns. Such validating discussions have the greatest impact on hidden issues because they work directly against the fear of rejection. If you haven't been talking about the real issue, how could your problem solution address what's really at stake? No more powerful form of acceptance exists than really listening in an understanding way to the thoughts and feelings of your mate. Safe, open, "no-fig-leaf" talks have real power to overcome this fear and to heal the wounds of the past.

An Example: Simon and Rachel

We round out this chapter with an example of how the really important, deeper issues will come out if you are communicating clearly and safely. Simon and Rachel are newlyweds who came to one of our workshops. Both were working long hours to make ends meet. When they did have time together, they'd frequently run into difficulties with TV, especially because he'd watch a great deal of sports. She was very upset about this. Many events arose around the TV, but much more important hidden issues were involved. As you will clearly see, Rachel was really concerned about caring, and Simon was concerned about acceptance.

They could have argued forever on the level of the events, for example, who would control the TV. They made much greater progress when talking about the issues in the safety of the Speaker-Listener Technique. This was one of the first times they used the technique. You'll see their skills were a little rough around the edges at this point, with some mind reading and less than ideal paraphrasing. Yet, they ended up talking about the real issues.

We hadn't told them to focus on hidden issues, but they came out anyway. We find that this happens regularly when couples are doing a good job with the Speaker-Listener Technique.

> RACHEL (Speaker): It seems like you spend more time with the television than conversing with me. There are times when you can stay up late to watch television, but if it comes down to spending time with me, you're tired. You can go to bed and fall right to sleep.
>
> SIMON (Listener): So you are saying it's more comfortable for me to watch television than it is to be with you?
>
> RACHEL (Speaker): (*with a clear sigh of relief at being heard*) Yeah.

Rachel is not feeling accepted or cared for by Simon. This comes out clearly here, yet in the past when they'd argued about the

TV, they never got to what was really going on. When he paraphrases that it seems to her that he's more comfortable watching TV than spending time with her, he really hits home. In one sense, his paraphrase goes way beyond her words, but it seems to reflect exactly what the matter seems like to her. She can tell from the quality of his paraphrase that he's really listening to her. This does more to address her hidden issue of wanting to know he cares than all the problem solving in the world could do.

It's not clear whether he agrees that he's more comfortable watching TV, but it is clear that he heard her. If he is uncomfortable with her, it may be the result of how they've been mishandling the hidden issues around the TV events. They go on.

SIMON (Listener): Can I have the floor? (*Floor switch*)

SIMON (Speaker): Before we were married, you never had any gripes about me watching sports.

RACHEL (Listener): So what you are saying is that in the beginning I didn't mind the fact that you watched sports so much. We did spend a lot of time together, and that seemed to satisfy me.

SIMON (Speaker): Right, and also before we were married, even though we spent time together, you never really had the opportunity to see that I did watch football as much as possible.

RACHEL (Listener): So what you are saying is that I didn't get to see you watching football as much as I do now.

SIMON (Speaker): Right. But you did know about me playing sports, that I was actively involved in sports, not just football.

RACHEL (Listener): So what you're saying is that because you played sports in your previous time of knowing me that I should have known that you would really be sports-oriented as far as watching it all the time.

SIMON (Speaker): Yes and no. I'm not saying that you should have known, but you saw that was a part of me, whether you want to accept it or not.

RACHEL (Listener): OK, so what you are saying is that I saw this part of you being involved in sports, so this is something that I should have known was going to come about throughout the relationship. Is that what you're saying?

SIMON (Speaker): More or less.

When Rachel complained about Simon watching so much football, he felt she was attacking a core part of his identity. So for him, the fundamental hidden issue revolves around acceptance of who he is and recognition of this part of him. He gets this out in the open in his statement, "You saw that was a part of me, whether you want to accept it or not."

After enough discussion on these deeper levels they went on to engage in some effective problem solving about time together and time watching TV. But without dealing more directly with the hidden issues first, we don't believe they could have done this.

GOING DEEPER WITH CHRIST

Hidden issues are complicated, mostly because they involve fear about the deeper issues of our souls. Most of our deeper desires and fears are legitimate; some are not—they are more based in self-protection. Either way, we believe that people are less prone to be triggered by hidden issues if they have no unresolved hidden issues with the Lord. For example, when you know at a deep level that you are perfectly cared for and accepted in Christ, there is a lot less likelihood that you'll be triggered about acceptance and commitment in your relationships with others, especially your mate. After all, there is such a deep security that comes from knowing who you are in Christ that there's much less to be threatened by with other people. Whole books have been written on this subject, so we'll not try to do that here. However, as we end this chapter, we present a meditation on the person and character of Jesus Christ as we think about the deeper issues we have considered here.

Some Reasons We Need Have No Hidden Issues with Our Lord

Jesus has no hidden issues, so He is completely open with us. He cannot be triggered by hidden issues because He has a totally secure identity. Because we are forgiven in Christ, the Father can pour out His love on us. Experiencing this love can drive out the fear that causes us to be defensive about hidden issues (I John 4:18). If we deeply believe His love for us, we may well have fewer hidden issues with Him and with others as well.

The passages that follow are merely a few examples of the things we know about the Lord that should challenge our own defenses and deepest fears about our relationship with Him. As we continue to grow in the experience of His wonderful and absolutely perfect acceptance and love for us, we can become less defensive and be released to express the same radical love that He showed to others. This is probably the single most powerful thing you can do to protect the promise of your marriage.

Power

Contrast Jesus' model of power with the world's. What do we have to fear from someone who has given His very life for us?

> Jesus called them together and said, "You know that the rulers of the Gentiles lord it over them, and their high officials exercise authority over them. Not so with you. Instead, whoever wants to become great among you must be your servant, and whoever wants to be first must be your slave—just as the Son of Man did not come to be served, but to serve, and to give his life as a ransom for many" [Matthew 20:25–28].

Caring

Jesus' care for us is indisputable, but do we really believe it?

> As the Father has loved me, so have I loved you. Now remain in my love [John 15:9].

> Greater love has no one than this, that he lay down his life for his friends [John 15:13].

Recognition

What more recognition could we expect than to realize that the Lord of the universe has valued us to the point of making us coworkers with Him in His labors?

> As you sent me into the world, I have sent them into the world [John 17:18].

Commitment

Want someone you can depend on forever and completely?

> Keep your lives free from the love of money and be content with what you have, because God has said, "Never will I leave you; never will I forsake you" [Hebrews 13:5].

Integrity

To whatever degree you do or even do not have integrity, it's not something you need to defend (or would even be able to defend) with the one who sees right into the depths of your soul, yet still accepts you completely. While we can't read the minds of those around us, the Lord knows our hearts and souls like no other.

> O Lord, you have searched me and you know me. You know when I sit and when I rise; you perceive my thoughts from

afar. You discern my going out and my lying down; you are familiar with all my ways. Before a word is on my tongue you know it completely, O Lord [Psalm 139:1–4].

Acceptance

Meditate on the profound acceptance of being called Jesus' friend.

I no longer call you servants, because a servant does not know his master's business. Instead, I have called you friends, for everything that I learned from my Father I have made known to you [John 15:15].

———

Our goal in this chapter has been to give you a way to explore and understand some of the most frustrating things about intimate relationships. You can prevent a lot of damage by learning to handle events and issues with the time and skill they require. Using the model presented here along with all the skills and techniques presented in the first section of the book will help you do just that.

For all too many couples, the hidden issues never come out. They fester and produce fear, sadness, and resentment that can erode and eventually destroy the marriage. It just doesn't have to be that way. When you learn to discuss deeper issues openly and with emphasis on validating each other, the things that had been generating the greatest conflicts can become the things that deepen your oneness and draw you closer together.

EXERCISES

In order to help you look at your own relationship, we recommend that you first pray for your relationship and for your mate or prospective mate. Hidden issues are hidden because they are difficult to think and talk about. Instead of allowing anxiety or fear to build barriers, ask God to help you build and maintain a deeper connection. God is eager to hear your requests about everything (Philippians 4:6), including your marriage, and this is a powerful antidote to anxiety.

Confronting our fears can make us fear them less and give us insight into what drives our behaviors. Confronting your hidden issues and then sharing with your partner can only increase your level of intimacy, as long as this is done in love. Work through the following questions individually, then plan time to talk together about your impressions.

1. Take some time to reflect on the reasons we covered a few pages back as to why there need be no hidden issues with the Lord. Meditating more deeply on who Christ is and what He has done for you is the most powerful basis we can imagine for breaking down barriers in relationships. Paul prayed that the Philippian Christians' "love would abound more and more in knowledge and depth of insight" (Philippians 1:9). Although some kinds of knowledge can puff you up with pride (I Corinthians 8:1), a deeper knowledge of Jesus Christ can help you be more fully able to love. And a clear, constant love can make your relationship less susceptible to issues triggered by the events of life.

2. Think about these signs of hidden issues. Do you notice that one or more of these come up in your relationship? What do you notice happening most often: wheel spinning? trivial triggers? avoidance? score keeping?

3. Next, we'd like you to consider which hidden issues might be triggered most often in your relationship. Note if there are certain events that have triggered or keep triggering the issues. Make a list of the common triggering events for issues of power and control, caring, recognition, commitment, integrity, and acceptance.

4. Set aside time to talk together about your observations and thoughts. Most couples have certain hidden issues that come

up repeatedly. Identifying these can help you draw together as you each learn to handle those issues with care. Also, as you discuss these matters, you have an excellent opportunity to get in some more practice with the Speaker-Listener Technique.

7

Unmet Expectations and What to Do About Them

Hope deferred makes the heart sick, but a longing fulfilled is a tree of life.

Proverbs 13:12

In the last chapter, we explained how hidden issues can fuel conflict and create distance between partners. Now we're ready to build on those concepts by focusing on expectations: what they are, where they come from, and whether or not they are reasonable or doable. This chapter includes a very important exercise that will help you explore and share your expectations for your relationship. In fact, this entire chapter is designed to prepare you for the exercise. It's that important.

THE POWER OF EXPECTATIONS

We bring into our relationships an array of hopes and dreams from a variety of sources. Expectations are profoundly powerful, as they reflect what we long for and how we wish things would be. When they are fulfilled, they are a "tree of life." But when what we expect does not happen, the hope deferred makes our hearts sick. To a large degree, we are disappointed or satisfied in life based on how well what is happening matches what we expect. Therefore, expectations play a crucial role in determining our level of satisfaction in marriage. To experience the full promise in your marriage, you'll need to get a strong grip on your expectations and how they affect your relationship.

In the first part of the book, we discussed how expectations can become powerful filters that create negative interpretations of what is happening. In this chapter, we want you to think about expectations as the ways you think things are supposed to be in your relationship. For example, you have specific expectations for such minor things as who will refill the orange juice container or who will balance the checkbook—the stuff of events. You also have expectations about common issues such as money, housework, in-laws, and sex. In addition, you have expectations about hidden issues—what it means to be loved, how power will be shared (or not shared), and what commitment means in your relationship. Because expectations touch on such important matters in life, many also have direct spiritual overtones. Expectations affect everything.

Bumping into Walls

Discovering expectations in marriage can be like moving into a beautiful new house. This house looks wonderful from the outside, but you soon discover that it has a feature you may not have counted on: many of the key interior walls are invisible. Although you cannot see all the walls clearly at the start, you bump into them and find that you have to move slowly to keep from smashing your head against them. Over time, you learn to mark these invisible walls as your awareness grows of their presence. But for some time, it can look like marriage in mime, as you feel for the invisible walls you know are there.

This is what unclear and unmet expectations can be like. You can either become aware of them and seek to clarify, meet, or modify them, or you will experience a lot of conflict and pain from continuing to bump into these invisible walls. The process can either lead to growth or frustration. Unmet expectations provide great potential for conflict because they so clearly highlight that you and your mate are, in fact, different people with differing needs and desires and views about marriage. On the positive side, it can help you move from "me-ness" to "we-ness" when you work together to clar-ify the expectations in your marriage. This chapter will help you make this move.

Expectations and Conflict

Consider Sue and Mike. They have been married about a year and things have gone pretty well. Sue, however, is upset about the way Mike goes out once or twice a week with his longtime guy friends, often to sporting events and sometimes to movies. This drives Sue nuts. During their premarital counseling this issue was discussed as an example of the scriptural teaching about "leaving and cleaving" and about a man's duty to love his wife and put her first. But in some ways Mike has remained stuck to some of the single lifestyle. Sue, on the other hand, has expectations of more time together now that they are married. Sometimes, the event of him going out triggers huge arguments between them, like this one:

> SUE: (*feeling agitated*) I don't see why you have to go out again tonight. You've been out a lot lately.
>
> MIKE: (*obviously irritated and rolling his eyes*) How many times do we have to argue about this? I go out once a week and that's it. I don't see any problem with that.
>
> SUE: Well I do. All of your guy friends are single, and I know they keep their eyes open for girls.
>
> MIKE: So?
>
> SUE: So they are looking for girls and you're married.
>
> MIKE: (*angered, feeling attacked and accused of being loose*) We don't go out hunting for girls. I don't like it that you don't trust me.
>
> SUE: I just don't think a married man needs to be out so often with his single friends. Women notice a group of men, and you can't tell me your friends aren't interested.

MIKE: (*turning away and walking out*) You sound jealous. I have to leave now; I'll be back by ten.

Sue and Mike are arguing about an expectation. She didn't expect that he'd still go out with his friends so often after they got married. She associates their going out with being single, not being married. Mike expected to cut back time with friends but not to stop seeing them altogether. These nights out mean a lot to him. He sees nothing wrong, except that Sue isn't handling it very well.

This is an example of the tension and frustration a couple can run into when what they envision doesn't happen. What's much more important is that their expectations don't match, and this fuels conflict. You can easily imagine that hidden issues of caring and control are also at work. She could be wondering if he really cares to be with her, considering that he still wants to go out regularly with his friends. He could be feeling that she's trying to control him—a feeling he does not respond to warmly. They each think the other's expectations are unfair and unrealistic.

Expectations and Hidden Issues

When hidden issues get triggered by events, it's usually because some expectation was not met. Underlying power issues are expectations about how decisions and control will be shared—or not shared. Underlying caring issues are expectations about how one is to be loved. Underlying recognition issues are expectations about how your partner should respond to who you are and what you do. Underlying commitment issues are expectations about how long the relationship should continue and, most important, about safety from abandonment. Underlying integrity issues are expectations about being trusted and respected. Under it all, are the core expectations about being accepted that we all have. And, as was true for Adam and Eve, it's not always safe in marriage. We fear rejection.

WHERE EXPECTATIONS COME FROM

Expectations build up over a lifetime of experiences. Most expectations are based in the past but still operate in the present. The three primary sources for our expectations are family of origin, previous relationships, and the culture we live in.

Family of Origin

You picked up many expectations unconsciously as you grew up. Your family experiences laid down many patterns—good and bad—that became the models for how you think things should or will be. Expectations were transmitted directly by what your parents said and indirectly by what you observed. No one comes to marriage as a blank slate.

Let's look at several examples. If you observed your parents avoiding all manner of conflict, you may have developed the expectation that couples should seek peace at any price. So if there's disagreement and conflict, it may seem to you that the world is going to end. Or if you observed your parents being very affectionate, you may have come to expect that in your marriage. If your parents divorced, you may have some negative expectation in the back of your mind that marriages don't really last. If you observed your parents having devotions together, you may have arrived at the belief that this expression of spiritual intimacy is vital for a healthy Christian marriage. You get the idea.

Nancy and John had terrible conflicts about parenting their five-year-old son Joey. Nancy came from a Christian home, but her mother and step-father were extremely harsh in their discipline. Her stepfather would chase the kids around the house when he was angry. If you were caught, you were spanked—sometimes very hard. Worse, almost, was that both parents were perfectionists who screamed or nagged about the slightest mistakes. John came from a family in which the kids could pretty much do whatever they wanted. There were limits, but they were pretty loose. Whenever

Joey acted up, John responded by raising his voice and calling Joey by his first and middle names. Other than that, there were no real consequences. So Joey had learned to all but ignore John's raised voice and only stirred when his middle name was used.

With her background, Nancy expected that someone was about to get spanked when John raised his voice. Her expectation was based in the past but still had real power. She'd even get sick to her stomach from the tension when Joey was about to get in trouble. It was as if her stepfather were chasing her all over again.

At times, she saw John as being abusive even though he wasn't. Her expectations became powerful filters, distorting her perception of what was really going on. Actually, John, like his parents, was quite lenient. Sure, he could lose his temper and yell from time to time, but he was a softy.

As a consequence of their expectations, neither of them provided consistent discipline for Joey, who suffered from their inconsistency. His teacher reported that he was one of the most difficult kids in the school. He didn't understand why she was so insistent that he observe the class rules. What kind of expectations do you think Joey will have when he grows up? In this example, you can see how expectations from our families of origin can have ongoing effects from generation to generation.

If we had the space, we could give thousands more examples. The point is that you each have powerful expectations that come from your families of origin. Understanding this can be an important first step to dealing more effectively with those expectations and to reducing the conflict that arises as a result of them.

Previous Relationships

You have also developed expectations from the other important relationships in your life such as previous dating relationships or marriages. You have expectations about how to kiss, what is romantic, how to communicate about problems, how recreational time should be spent, what church to go to and how often to attend, who should take responsibility for the first move to make up after a fight, and so on.

Suppose, for example, that you got dumped in a previous dating relationship when you began to open up about painful childhood events. Logically, you might have developed the expectation that people can't be trusted to accept the deepest parts of who you are. If so, you'll pull back and withhold this kind of information, and this could reduce the potential intimacy in your present relationship.

Studies show that people who have come to expect that others can't be trusted have more difficulties in relationships. If you look at such a person's past experiences, their reasons for their expectations usually make sense. Yet it can lead to trouble if the mistrust is so intense that you can't allow someone you really love to get close. This would be all the greater reason to learn how to make it safer for verbal intimacy in your relationship.

Many expectations are about such minor things that it's hard to imagine they could become so important—but they can. It all depends on what meanings are attached to the expectations. Paul, for example, told us that his past girlfriend had drilled it into him that she didn't want him opening doors for her. He thought, "OK, no big deal." Now with his wife Janet, he was finding quite the opposite. She liked men to hold doors, and she'd get upset with him if he forgot. He had to work hard to unlearn the expectation he'd finally learned so well.

Door-opening events happen pretty often in life. For Paul and Janet, they triggered conflict because she'd interpret his trouble remembering as a sign that he didn't care about her. This is another example of negative interpretation causing more damage than the actual event. Believing his devotion was being challenged, he'd get angry at her. This just confirmed what she already believed—that he didn't care.

Are you aware of the expectations you have for your partner that are really based in your experiences with others? It's worth thinking about, because your partner isn't the same person as those you've known in the past.

Cultural Influences and Backgrounds

A variety of powerful cultural factors can influence your expectations: books, television, movies, and so forth. What expectations would you have about marriage, for example, based on watching thousands of hours of TV in America? For most of us, this is not a hypothetical question. Shows like "Married with Children," "The Simpsons," "Home Improvement," "Friends," "Cosby," and "Roseanne" all send powerful messages about what is expected or normal. Some of the expectations from television are reasonable; many more are not. What expectations do people learn from daytime soaps and talk shows with topics like "Women who have affairs and the men who love them?"

What about your cultural backgrounds? Did you grow up in the same country and in the same culture, or do you have very different backgrounds? When couples come from different cultures (even different parts of the same country), they have learned different rules, values, and expectations for all kinds of things. These expectations cover areas as wide-ranging as child discipline, sexuality, money management, and roles in marriage. It's very important to understand these differences and how they affect your relationship rather than to assume that you come from the same viewpoint. You may not, and in some ways, that will surprise you.

Core Beliefs: Religious, Spiritual, and Otherwise

In addition to all the general expectations you have for marriage and your relationship, you also have key beliefs about life, God, and how it all fits together. These beliefs make up your core belief system. Everyone has a core belief system. Even if you do not see yourself as being religious or spiritual, you have a core belief system. For many, that belief system is reflected most clearly in spiritual beliefs and religious practices. More specifically, what was the spiritual or religious tradition of your upbringing? How is that similar or different from where you are now? Did you grow up in a Christian home?

What kind? If so, did your home growing up present a more traditional or a more egalitarian view of marriage? Or what if you and your partner are from very different spiritual backgrounds? How will you, or are you, handling that?

Studies have consistently shown that greater differences in religious background translate to greater risk for a marriage. It's not that a marriage is somehow doomed to fail when there are significant differences in this area, but there usually is more to work out and more room for conflict. In contrast, it's probably easier for couples to construct a shared vision for their future when two partners have a clearer, shared core belief system. This makes it easier to see why Paul warned the Corinthians about being bound together with those holding different beliefs. "Do not be yoked together with unbelievers" (II Corinthians 6:14).

These are not issues we address in great detail in this book, but they can be very big issues in marriage. Sometimes, young couples from different spiritual backgrounds marry, believing that the differences will not matter. But people tend to return to their roots when they have children or as they age. What does not seem too important now may become much more important later.

One more point of caution. Don't be misled into thinking that just because you may both have a Christian background that you automatically see all spiritual issues similarly. We know many couples that come from seemingly similar backgrounds but still get into intense conflicts over many areas touching on core beliefs. For example, say you both believe strongly in giving to the Lord's work, but for one of you that means tithing your gross income and for the other it means giving a good deal less (or more). How are you handling that? You can see how the spiritual belief combines with what is already a major conflict area for many couples, leaving room for real fireworks. What about prayer together or how often you attend church together? These issues are associated with very real expectations in marriage—expectations that too many couples do not directly discuss.

Whatever your cultural and religious backgrounds, we strongly recommend that you spend time thinking and talking about the many kinds of expectations you have for your marriage—for the day-to-day things, for the big issues of life, and especially for the practice of your faith.

WHAT TO DO ABOUT EXPECTATIONS

Expectations can lead either to massive disappointment and frustration or to deeper connection. There are four keys to handling expectations well: be aware of what you expect, be reasonable in what you expect, be clear about what you expect, and be willing to listen to the Lord.

Be Aware of What You Expect

Even when you are not fully aware of them, unmet expectations can lead to great disappointment and frustration. And when they continue to be unmet, they can shift from disappointed expectations to angry demands.

Clifford Sager, a pioneer in this field, noticed how people bring a host of expectations to marriage that are never made clear. These expectations are found in the fine print of our unwritten "contracts" for our marriages. The problem is, people don't know what's in their partner's version of the contract when they get married. They don't get to "read the small print." Sager went further to suggest that many of our fine-print expectations are virtually unconscious. We don't mean to say that all expectations are deeply unconscious, but many do become such a part of us that they function automatically. Like the invisible walls mentioned earlier, they are there whether or not you have learned to talk about them and to avoid bumping into them.

One clue that unmet expectations are functioning is the experience of disappointment. Disappointment usually means that an expectation hasn't been met. It's a good habit to stop a minute when you are disappointed, sad, or angry and to ask yourself what you expected. Doing this can help you become more aware of important expectations that otherwise may be unconsciously affecting your relationship.

Jim, for instance, would get very sad when he'd ask his wife to go boating with him and she'd say, "That's OK. Go ahead without me and have a great time." She'd rather stay home and garden. He worked very hard during the week as a repairman, and boating was the greatest relaxation for him. Dawn didn't care for boating but really wanted him to feel OK about having a nice time without her.

His sadness was a clue that some important expectation was at work. In thinking about it, he realized that he expected they'd share this very important interest of his. If she didn't, what did that mean? Although she loved him dearly, the hope that she'd become interested in his hobby stirred sadness about the hidden issue of wanting to feel cared for. Once he was aware of his expectation and the reasons for his sadness, he was able to express what boating with her meant to him. She had no idea. Although she didn't love boating, she was glad to join him more often, once she knew it meant so much to him.

After being aware of an expectation, the next step is to consider whether your expectation is really reasonable.

Be Reasonable in What You Expect

As we noted earlier, many important expectations people have just aren't reasonable or realistic. Some unreasonable expectations are very specific. For example, is it reasonable to expect that your partner will never seriously disagree with you? Of course not. Many newly married couples feel that because they love each other so much they will not experience conflict in their marriage the way their parents did. And many Christians expect that they shouldn't have conflict, simply because they are Christians.

When expectations are unreasonable, studies show that relationships are more likely to be distressed. For example, Barb and Bill have been married for eleven years. He's a plumber and she does bookkeeping for several small businesses. Sex has become a huge issue for them. If he had his way, they'd make love every night of the week and some mornings too. Not only does he have a strong sex drive, he also believes that there is something wrong with a marriage if a couple doesn't make love at least five or more times a week. As Barb seems interested only once or twice a week, Bill believes something is wrong with her, and he tells her so. Bill's expectation is just not reasonable. Unless they can negotiate some way through this problem, it may threaten their future.

Sometimes, couples who progress well with the material we are presenting here develop an unreasonable expectation that they will not have to keep at it, that conflicts will be a thing of the past because they have worked productively on issues for some period of time. We do hope couples who consistently apply our principles will have fewer, and less intense, negative events. But events will always happen, and sometimes we fall back into our old patterns. There's a difference between being perfect and handling issues well.

One of the most destructive and unreasonable expectations you can have is that your partner will meet all your unmet needs and heal all your wounds from life. Talk about hope that will be disappointed! Whereas marriages in which the fullness of the promise is experienced can be healing, a mate cannot satisfy the deepest longings of your soul that only God can touch. The fact is, our partners make lousy substitutes for God. One of the wisest things we can do is recognize this and give up the unreasonable expectation. It puts a lot of pressure on your mate to expect him or her to do things in your life that only God can do. Likewise, you'll not find heaven on earth, no matter how good your marriage. Jesus said we'll have tribulation in this life (John 16:33).

Be Clear About What You Expect

Bill and Natalie, a couple who were beginning to enjoy retirement, were pretty stressed out when they attended one of our workshops.

They decided to follow up on the workshop with a few counseling sessions to fine tune some of the things they had learned. In the course of our work we discovered that they loved to travel together, but many of their excursions ended up in periods of cold silence in the car. One of these periods began when they were traveling on a turnpike together.

An exploration of their expectations revealed that Bill had been a U.S. Army wing commander before he retired. He took his driving seriously and drove with the dedication of a fighter pilot determined to keep the two of them safe on the mission. Natalie hadn't realized that he expected a copilot's dedication from her and that this included having the money ready when they approached the turnpike toll booth. When she failed to "do her part" he would become upset and would silently stew for days. When his expectation was clarified, it changed the whole travel experience for them. Natalie simply hadn't known what Bill expected and was happy to comply by having the money ready and in other ways that were important to him. Natalie couldn't read Bill's mind.

An important expectation such as this one may be perfectly reasonable when understood between two partners, but it's not reasonable if it's never clearly expressed. Your partner can't do anything about something he or she doesn't know about. So, it's crucial to tell your partner about your important expectations. We all tend to assume that our partner's model of the ideal marriage is the same as ours. If so, then why should we have to tell them what we expect? In effect, we are assuming they already know, or should know, what we expect.

How many people make the assumption that their partner should know exactly what is most pleasing or displeasing sexually? We see this over and over again. One or both partners are angry that the other is failing to meet a desire or expectation. But more often than not, they've never expressed that expectation. What this amounts to is expecting your partner to be good at mind reading, which is unrealistic. When this is going on and key expectations are not being "read" by one partner, it's all too easy for hidden issues to be triggered. The one with the unmet expectation can feel that the partner doesn't care because he or she didn't figure out the expectation. We'll deal with the problems this causes sexually in Chapter Thirteen.

Unless you make your expectations clear, you'll have trouble working as a team. You simply can't work from any kind of shared perspective if you don't share your perspective. You need to be aware of your expectations, willing to evaluate them, and willing to share them with your partner. Otherwise, expectations have power to trigger meltdowns over some of the hottest issues and hidden issues in your relationship.

Be Willing to Listen to the Lord

Agreement is essential to walking together in oneness. Being aware, being reasonable, and being clear are central to reaching a deeper agreement. There's one more level here we'd like you to consider. As the creator of life and designer of marriage, God has a critical part to play in how your life unfolds. God has expectations too. Couples who learn about His expectations and take them into account are much more likely to have a lasting marriage. Fortunately, God's expectations are not hidden, nor are they unclear or unreasonable. Consider a little background from history.

Amos the prophet was called by God to preach to the Israelites about their unfaithfulness to Him. God spoke to them through Amos, including this often-quoted line, "Can two walk together, except they be agreed?" (Amos 3:3, KJV).

Matthew Henry (the Bible commentator) stated the simple point of the message this way: "They could not expect any comfortable communion with God unless they first made their peace with him" (Matthew Henry's Commentary, Amos 3:3). Unless we are each willing to listen to the Lord's direction in our lives, we cannot be in agreement with His purposes, and we cannot have the deeper fellowship implied by the metaphor of "walking" with Him.

Although there are many traditions within Christianity about what and how God has revealed Himself, there would be wide agreement that God both designed and has expectations for marriage and relationships in general. Do you take the Lord into account when thinking about what your marriage should be like or in how you should treat your mate? Many passages in scripture teach about marriage and other relationships. We cover many of them in this book. Will you (or do you) consider such teachings and what God is asking of you in your life together?

Additional teachings address many matters related to marriage having to do with love, respect, leadership and submission (mutual or hierarchical or both), roles, sex, parents, and parenting. In choosing not to discuss such matters in more detail we do not mean to suggest they are unimportant. Rather, it is simply not the purpose of this book to clarify our views on all of God's expectations for marriage. First, there are too many complicated passages to consider here that various denominations interpret differently. Second, plenty of other books are available for the serious student of scripture and the history of Christian teaching for us to want to attempt such a discussion. However we do encourage you to discuss your views of such matters—what you believe God has revealed and how that affects the two of you in your marriage. We also encourage you to discuss such matters with your pastor.

We emphasize this point because we believe that blessings in life come from being on the path God wants you to be on. He says two cannot walk together without agreement, and we encourage you to work on this agreement as a couple before the Lord. We believe that the more you spend time as a couple getting to know God and listening to what He desires of you, the more you will experience the richest fruit of the promise in your marriage. You'll be listening to the very designer of your union and the one who can bring fruit from your love.

The exercise we are about to present is as important as any in this book. It will take time and perseverance to do it well. Combining the insights you will gain with the other skills you are learn-

ing can have a major impact on the depth and strength of your relationship, both now and into the future. God bless you as you seek
to further understand one another's expectations and bring them
into line with His expectations.

> May the God of hope fill you with all joy and peace as you
> trust in him, so that you may overflow with hope by the power
> of the Holy Spirit [Romans 15:13].

EXERCISES

The following exercises are designed to help you explore some of
your expectations. Plan to spend time thinking carefully about each
area that is applicable to you. Both of you should write your
thoughts down on a separate pad of paper, then share them. Each
point is meant to stimulate your own thinking. You may also have
expectations in numerous other areas. Please consider every expectation you can think of that seems significant to you, whether or
not it is listed here. Remember, you won't get much out of this exercise unless you are able and willing to put time into it. Many couples, whether already married or planning to be married, have found
this to be extremely beneficial for their relationship.

General Relationship Expectations

In this first section, we ask you to consider all manner of expectations about marriage in general. The goal is to clarify your expectations for how you *want* your marriage to be or how you think it
should be. You are not to evaluate how your marriage is or how you
guess it will be. Write down what you expect, whether or not you
think the expectation is realistic. (The expectation will affect your
relationship whether or not it's realistic, so you need to be aware of
it.) It's essential that you write down what you really think, not
what sounds like the correct or least embarrassing answer.

It can also be valuable to think on what you observed about each of these areas in your family growing up. This is probably where many of your beliefs about what you want or don't want come from. With many areas of expectation, we have provided some references to key passages of scripture that deal with that area. These are provided for further thought, reflection—even struggle—as you work through your expectations in this exercise.

1. Write about what you want (or how you think things should be) regarding each of the areas that seems significant to you:

    A. What do you expect in the area of loyalty? What does "leave and cleave" mean to you? (Genesis 2:18–24; Ruth 1:16,17)

    B. What are your expectations and concerns about the longevity of this relationship? About "till death do us part?" (Mark 10:7–9)

    C. "Marriage should be honored by all, and the marriage bed kept pure" (Hebrews 13:4a). What does this say about God's expectation for marriage? What do you expect about fidelity, including whether your partner should have friends of the opposite sex, and so forth?

    D. What does being loving and caring mean to you? Do you expect you should always have loving feelings? Do you expect this to change over time? (I Corinthians 13)

    E. What about your sexual relationship? Frequency? Practices? Taboos? Who should initiate lovemaking?

    F. What are your expectations about romance in your marriage? What is your particular language of love?

    G. How about having children (or having more children)? Who should discipline the kids? How? What about spanking?

    H. If you married before and have children from that marriage, where do you want them to live? How do you expect that you should share in their discipline?

I. Think about work, careers, and the provision of income. Who should work in the future? Whose career or job is more important? If there are or will be children, should either partner reduce work time out of the home to take care of them? What about work after your nest is empty? Retirement?

J. What are your expectations and concerns about the degree of emotional dependency on the other? Do you want to feel taken care of? In what ways? How much do you expect to rely on each other to get through the tough times? What about depending on family and friends for emotional support? In what areas would you expect to be more emotionally independent?

K. What should be your basic approach to marriage? As a team or as two independent individuals? What about the implications of the roles described in scripture? (Ephesians 5:20–31)

L. How should you work out problems? Do you want to talk these out, and if so, how? What about the expression of strong emotions like anger?

M. Think about power and control. Who do you expect will have more power in what kinds of decisions? For example, who will control the money, or who will discipline the kids? Who should make the final decision when you disagree about a key area? Who seems to have the most power in your relationship now, and how do you feel about that? (Ephesians 5:20–31; Colossians 3:18–21; I Peter 3:1–7)

O. Consider household tasks. Who should do what? How does the current breakdown match up with what you expect?

P. What are your expectations, desires, and concerns about time together? How much time do you want to spend together (versus time alone, with friends, at work, with family, and so forth)?

Q. What do you expect about sharing all of your thoughts and feelings? Are there feelings that shouldn't be shared?

R. How do you envision friendship with your partner? What is a friend? Should your partner always be your best friend?

S. Think about some of the "little things" in life. Where should you squeeze the toothpaste? Should the toilet seat be left up or down? Who sends greeting cards? Think about the little things that have irritated you in the past. What do you want or expect in each area?

T. What should happen when there is a need for forgiveness? How important is forgiveness in your relationship? (I John 4)

U. Now, with your mind primed from all of the work you have done, consider again the hidden issues we described in the last chapter. Do you see any ways now that some of these deeper issues of yours might influence your expectations? What do you expect, want, or fear in each of these areas? Power? Caring? Recognition? Commitment? Integrity? Acceptance?

V. Write about any other expectations that come to mind. Some other areas might include money (saving, spending); free time, recreation, TV; use of alcohol and drugs; your interactions in public; relatives; and so on.

2. Go back to each area just listed and rate each of your expectations for how reasonable you think it really is. Use a scale of 1 to 10 where 10 = completely reasonable ("I really think it is OK to expect this in this relationship.") and 1 = completely unreasonable ("I can honestly say that, although I expect or want this, it just is not a reasonable expectation for me to have in our relationship."). For example, suppose you grew up in a family where problems were not discussed, and you are aware that you honestly expect or prefer to avoid such discussions. You might now rate that expectation as not very reasonable.

3. Place a big check mark by each expectation that you feel you have not clearly discussed with your partner.

4. Share your expectations. After you and your partner have finished the entire written exercise, schedule times together to discuss each of the areas either of you thinks is important. Please don't try to do this all at once. You should plan on a number of discussions, each covering only one or two expectations. Discuss the degree to which you each felt the expectation being discussed has been shared clearly in the past and how it may have affected your relationship. Talk about the degree to which you both feel your expectations are reasonable or unreasonable and discuss what you will agree to do about these. (This might be a great place to use the problem-solving model you learned earlier.)

Religious and Spiritual Beliefs and Expectations

The goal in this section is to help you identify what you believe, where those beliefs came from, and how they affect or will affect your relationship in the future. As we said earlier, these kinds of expectations are very critical because they are associated with your ability to construct a shared vision together. Even when you do not share a similar view on such important matters, it's still much better to be able to handle these differences openly and with respect than to ignore them. In fact, for many couples, talking together about what each believes and why can be a key element of the mutual friendship, even when you don't see eye to eye at this point in life.

The following questions are designed to get you thinking about a broad range of issues related to your beliefs. There may be other important questions that we've left out, so feel free to answer questions we don't ask as well as those we do. We would like you to write down an answer to each question as it applies to you. This will help you think more clearly about the issues and will also help you when it comes time to talk with your partner about them. As you think about and answer each question, it can be especially valuable to note what you were taught as a child versus what you believe or expect now as an adult.

1. What is your faith (core belief system or worldview)? What do you believe in?

2. How did you come to believe in this viewpoint?

3. What is the meaning or purpose of life in your beliefs?

4. What was your religious affiliation growing up? How were the key beliefs practiced in your family of origin? Religious practices? Other?

5. What is the meaning of marriage in your belief system?

6. What vows will you say, or what vows did you say? How do these tie into your belief system?

7. What is your belief about divorce? How does this fit in with your faith or belief system?

8. How do you practice, or expect to practice, your faith in your relationship? This could mean church attendance, prayer, scripture reading or sharing, discussions of spiritual matters as you go through life, and so forth.

9. What is your understanding of sexuality? Are there specific beliefs about sexuality or birth control in your faith?

10. Do you give, or expect to give, financial support to a church or other ministry? How much? How will this be determined? Do you both agree?

11. Do you see potential areas of conflict regarding your beliefs? What are they?

12. What about observance of major religious holidays? What did you do growing up? What do you like to do now?

13. Can you think of any other questions to consider in this area?

After you and your partner have finished the entire exercise, plan to begin spending time together discussing these expectations. You should plan on a number of discussions. Discuss the degree to which you each feel the expectation being discussed has been shared clearly in the past. Use the Speaker-Listener Technique if you would like some additional structure to deal with the more difficult issues.

The key in all these questions is to get you thinking and talking together. This takes real time and effort to do well. But when you do that work, it can go a long way toward helping you develop and express your overall, long-term vision for your unique expression of oneness.

8

Understanding Commitment

So they are no longer two, but one.

Matthew 19:6

Most married couples consider commitment the glue that holds their relationship together. The kind and depth of your commitment has a lot to do with your chances of staying together and being happy. To begin our discussion of commitment, let's look again at Jesus' answer to the Pharisees' trick question about divorce.

> "Haven't you read," he replied, "that at the beginning the Creator 'made them male and female,' and said, 'For this reason a man will leave his father and mother and be united to his wife, and the two will become one flesh'? So they are no longer two, but one. Therefore what God has joined together, let man not separate" [Matthew 19:4–6].

Jesus covers some crucial ground about commitment in His response to their question about whether divorce was OK. The word united He used is the Greek word *kollao*, which means to "join fast together" or "to glue." This gets right to what commitment is all about. It's the glue that sticks two people together. It's hard to fully convey in English just how strong the image of this uniting is in the Hebrew and Greek texts. It's more profound than simply glue. Jesus went on to connect commitment to oneness, driving home the point that marriage means two people in a lifelong relationship of unbroken oneness. That our marital promise and oneness should never be broken is the ideal that springs right from the heart of God.

Although the intention of God's heart is clear, we find that commitment is a complex concept with many facets. Let's look more deeply into what commitment is about on various levels. (We want to emphasize again that this is a book about what it takes to avoid divorce, not a book that focuses on the biblical teaching regarding divorce. We do not attempt to address some of the difficult questions that people sometimes face.)

THE COMPLEXITY OF COMMITMENT

We believe that the research on commitment has revealed some fascinating things—some findings that fall in nicely with what scripture tells us about it. To explore what we have discovered, we'll discuss two couples in some detail. Both marriages reflect commitment, but the type of commitment is very different. Notice what's similar and what's different as you compare commitment in these two marriages.

Bob and Mary Anderson: Feeling Trapped in Their Relationship

Mary and Bob married thirteen years ago. They have a four-year-old son and a seven-year-old daughter. Bob manages the meat department in a large grocery store, and Mary works part-time as a secretary in a medical office. Like most couples, Bob and Mary started out feeling very much in love. But the normal strains of life, especially the stress of a major job change for Bob, have left both feeling distant and weary of trying to make things better.

Mary has considered divorce on more than a few occasions and finds herself thinking about leaving more and more often. Like many men, Bob also feels unhappy with the marriage but hasn't considered divorce as often. He hopes for more but hasn't told Mary this, and he thinks trying to get closer just doesn't work. When he does try to do something positive, he feels Mary shuts him out. He's become anxious about the thought of her leaving. He senses that any energy put into the relationship at this point is wasted effort and is afraid to try anything at all, for fear of rocking the boat. "Maybe things will get better when the kids leave home," he thinks. "I've just got to stick with it and hope for the best."

Mary and Bob both work around others they find attractive. Larry, an attractive, single man at Mary's office, has been sending signals that say he's interested in her. Hungry for connection, she has been seriously contemplating an affair and finds herself thinking about it a lot more often.

Mary is aware of the disappointment her heart has gone through over the years and has come to the conclusion that Bob will never be the kind of lifelong partner she had hoped for. Furthermore, she feels she has put a lot more into the marriage than Bob has, with little in return for her time and effort. She resents it that he's never seemed to appreciate all she's done for him. When he does make some minuscule effort to move toward her, she never trusts it and usually thinks, "Too little too late, buster. You've got to do more than that to get my heart back." Like Bob, she is thinking it's just not worth the effort to try any more.

As Mary thinks about leaving Bob, difficult questions plague her. First, she has strong beliefs that divorce is not God's will. She struggles most over what God would think if she left Bob. She also wonders how a divorce would affect the kids. Would they ever get over it? Would Bob fight for custody? She also asks herself how hard it would be to get a divorce. Would Bob try to stop her? She wonders whether she could support herself and the kids on her income alone, who would get the house, and whether another man would accept the children if she should remarry.

For Mary, thinking about all the costs of divorce led her to conclude that staying is better than leaving, at least for now. Sure she's in pain, but she balances this against the greater pain and stress a divorce could bring. Bob has thought about many of these same questions, but he's not as unhappy as Mary, so he thinks less about all the "what ifs?" He assumes their marriage will continue for the long haul, but it's not an idea that he draws much comfort from. A feeling of despair hangs over each of them.

Deirdre and Eric Templeton: Constraint and Dedication

Deirdre and Eric were married fifteen years ago. They have one girl, age thirteen, and two boys, ages eleven and seven. Although they have had their stressful times too, both Deirdre and Eric have few regrets about having married one another. They met when they worked for a large insurance company—he in sales and she as manager of the claims department. They are also quite involved in their church as a couple and as a family.

Their kids present some real challenges. The younger boy has a serious learning disability and requires a lot of attention and support. Their daughter is beginning to show more signs of rebellion than they ever imagined, and this too causes concern. Despite this, Deirdre and Eric usually feel the other's support in facing the struggles together.

Eric does occasionally become aware of his attraction to women he meets in his work. However, because of his commitment to Deirdre he's decided not to daydream about other possible relationships. He is happy with Deirdre, and he chooses not to dwell on thoughts of being with someone else. Everyone has regrets at times in marriage, but for Deirdre and Eric these times are few. They genuinely respect and like each other, do things for each other, and talk fairly openly about what they want out of life and marriage. Because of their spiritual convictions, each resists thinking about divorce, even during the times they're not getting along well. Each is still willing to help the other reach for what they desire in life. Simply put, they feel like a team.

As you can see, the Andersons and the Templetons have very different marriages. The Andersons are miserable, and the Templetons are pretty much enjoying their life together. But it's not just the level of happiness that separates these two marriages. Both marriages are likely to continue for the time being. But the two relationships reflect two different kinds of commitment. To understand the difference, we need to look at the research.

A MODEL OF COMMITMENT

Michael Johnson, a colleague of ours at Penn State, points to a useful distinction in how we use the word commitment. The sentence "John sure is committed to his career" conveys one meaning. This statement expresses the dedication commitment that John has to his work. The second way we commonly use the word is seen in a statement such as "Mary made a commitment to organize this project, and she can't back out now." In this use, commitment conveys a sense of obligation or what we call constraint. Mary doesn't feel free to quit the project. Based on this distinction, we believe relationships have two kinds of commitment: dedication and constraint.

A commitment characterized by personal dedication refers to the desire of an individual to maintain or improve the quality of the relationship for the joint benefit of the both partners. Personal dedication is reflected by an intrinsic desire (and associated behaviors) not only to continue in the relationship but also to improve it, to sacrifice for it, to invest in it, to link personal goals to it, and to seek the partner's welfare, not simply one's own. Scripture is filled with teaching about this kind of commitment—most often in the framework of teachings about *agape* love. In fact, we Christians often refer to agape love as committed love.

In contrast, a commitment characterized by constraint refers to forces that keep individuals in relationships whether or not they're dedicated. Sometimes, people stay in unhappy marriages simply because of constraint commitment. Here, commitment feels like a negative force, preventing freedom and happiness. For other couples, constraint commitment is perceived positively, adding a sense of stability to their relationship.

Bob and Mary Anderson have a commitment characterized by constraint. Mary, in particular, is feeling a great deal of constraint and little dedication. She feels compelled to remain in an unhappy marriage for a host of reasons—kids, money, family pressure, and so on. Bob also has high constraint commitment and little dedication, although he's less intensely dissatisfied with their day-to-day life.

Unlike Mary and Bob, Deirdre and Eric Templeton have an abiding sense of dedication to one another. But they also have a good deal of constraint commitment. Any thriving marriage will produce a significant level of constraint over time. In fact, happier, more dedicated couples are just as likely to have considerable constraints as less satisfied, less dedicated couples at similar points in life. Happier couples just don't think a lot about the constraints, and when they do, they often draw comfort from them. For happier couples, constraint commitment feels like a positive force, adding a sense of stability to the marriage.

Together, the forces of constraint and dedication produce a deep bond that takes couples through the thick and thin of the relationship. As with the Templetons, there's a comfortable sense of being rooted together in the complexities of living together.

Let's look in more detail at how constraint and dedication are reflected in relationships.

The Commitment of Constraint

Commitment theorists and researchers have identified many factors that characterize commitment in relationships. These dimensions are described in the research literature, especially in the work of Michael Johnson and of Caryl Rusbult at the University of North Carolina, as well as in our own studies at the University of Denver.

As we discuss these factors, consider the kind and level of commitment that you have in your relationship. You'll probably notice that many of the dimensions we'll focus on can also be understood as areas where people have important expectations as to how things should be.

Constraint commitment may arise from either external or internal pressures. They make the ending of a relationship seem more costly—morally, spiritually, economically, socially, personally, or psychologically—than staying in it.

Moral Constraints. Some constraints are directly related to issues of moral importance. The immorality of divorce refers to one's belief's about whether, and under what circumstances, divorce is morally acceptable or morally wrong. People vary in their reasons for believing divorce would be wrong. Research shows that those with stronger, traditional religious beliefs, for instance, are much more likely to believe that divorce is wrong. By contrast, those who have previously divorced are less likely to believe it's wrong than those who have never been divorced.

Although we aren't covering the theology and dynamics of divorce here, it remains utterly clear that God's heart for marriage is that it be a permanent union. However, some passages refer to situations in which divorce is considered permissible (Malachi 2:16; Matthew 5:31,32, 19:3–9; I Corinthians 7). So, those who have a stronger view about divorce being inconsistent with God's desire in most circumstances are more committed in this respect.

Meta-commitment is another type of moral constraint. This term refers to the belief that you should finish what you start. This kind of belief could serve as an element of constraint because it says you must keep on trying. In our definition, meta-commitment means commitment to commitment. We have heard people say that they remain committed partly because they don't want to be quitters. This dimension is less related to religious standards and more related to the individual's personal value system. Bob Anderson, for instance, isn't particularly religious, but he has a strong sense of duty. He simply doesn't want to give up. Unfortunately, he doesn't seem to know what to do more constructively, either.

Concerns for children's or a partner's welfare is another dimension with a moral flavor. Many people stay married simply because they believe it is best for their children. For Mary Anderson, this seems to be one of her greatest concerns. She's especially concerned about custody, living arrangements, and standard of living in thinking about the effects divorce would have on the kids. Likewise, some dissatisfied people stay married because of their compassion for their mate. Clearly, it is best for any marriage when people have compassion for one another. When it comes to constraint, the interesting point is that some people stay primarily for this reason.

All of the types of constraint just mentioned come from a sense of compassion, guilt, or moral duty—often in combination.

Pragmatic Constraints. Other dimensions related to constraint are more pragmatic than moral. These constraints relate to your perception of what would be gained and lost if you ended your relationship.

Irretrievable investments are the source of one kind of pragmatic constraint. The key here is your perception of investments that would be lost if you ended your relationship. These investments might be in the form of physical possessions or less tangible factors.

Some couples decide to stay together because they can't bear to divide up some of their precious possessions. Less tangible investments relate to comfort level with the present predictable patterns. For instance, you may feel that you've invested a lot of energy in getting your partner "broken in" and would not want the hassle of a new partner squeezing the toothpaste in the wrong place. Or, you may derive comfort from knowing that your spouse knows a lot about you from all the years you've been together. The key here is that you have put a lot of time and energy into the relationship, and you may feel this investment would be lost if it all ended. So there's motivation to stay.

The Templetons are dedicated, but they have also invested a lot with one another. This adds to their constraint commitment. Neither would want to lose what's been invested. For them, the investment is simply further evidence of their ongoing dedication.

Social pressure refers to the forces that third parties exert on a couple to maintain their relationship. Social pressure will be greatest when a couple knows many people who want to see their relationship continue. This is an area of great similarity between the Templetons and the Andersons. Both couples have been together a long time and have many friends and family members (especially the kids) who would be shocked if they split up. In both cases, friends and family would ask a lot of questions about the decision to end the marriage.

Couples sense greater social pressure the longer they have been together. Time spent together and changes such as having children raise the stakes. The effects of social pressure may explain why so many couples end up making monsters of each other to their friends and family in the midst of a separation or divorce. Statements about the awfulness of the partner serve to reduce pressure from others to work it out. Some partners really have been terrible to their spouses. But in most cases, these complaints are probably exaggerated for the purpose of reducing social pressure. It's a bad strategy because it not only is judging another morally and publicly (something we are told not to do), it makes it much harder to turn things around if you decide to try to later.

Termination procedures refer to the immediate steps needed to end a relationship. Here, the focus is not on the long-term consequences of leaving as much as the difficulty of the things you'd have to go through to end the relationship. Ending a casual relationship may be no more difficult than not making another date, but ending a marriage requires legal negotiations, changed residences, detailed financial untangling, and custody battles. The greater these hassles, the more likely you are to stay.

Mary Anderson is very focused on the hassle factor. She has considered the legal steps required and the likelihood that Bob would make it difficult to obtain a divorce. The steps would be just as difficult for Deirdre and Eric if they had the desire to divorce. But they don't.

The quality of the alternatives is a very important dimension of constraint commitment. This dimension represents the degree to which you would be unhappy about any or all of the broad range of possible life changes that would occur if your relationship ended:

residence, economic status, friendships, and so on. In fact, one way to think about commitment is that you have chosen one alternative over others. In general, the poorer the other alternatives, the greater the constraint.

You can't really weigh the alternatives in a vacuum. When people think about the alternatives, they're weighed in contrast to the current quality of life. Some key dimensions related to the alternative lifestyle are economic and social. We'll focus on these separately.

Economic dependence is a constraint falling within the general category of alternative quality. Some people stay in relationships because they can't afford, or don't want to afford, living without their partners. Although the current situation may be unpleasant, the alternatives look worse, adding to constraint. For both the Templetons and the Andersons, ending the marriage would lead to a reduced standard of living.

Unavailability of partners refers to the social constraint resulting from the perception that there would be no one else available to replace your present partner. All things being equal, you are more likely to stay in your present relationship when you perceive the alternative as aloneness.

Both the Templetons and the Andersons have a good deal of constraint commitment. For the Templetons, there's a comforting feeling of stability in that; the Andersons feel trapped—a huge difference in the levels of satisfaction. But that's not all. There is also a great difference in the levels of dedicated commitment. Now we'll explore just what that means.

The Commitment of Personal Dedication

As with constraints, we want to help you understand dedication by describing ingredients that are consistent with fully developed dedication in relationships. If you think about agape love as defined by the apostle Paul, you are thinking about the heart of being dedicated to one another as research reflects what dedication is all about.

Love is patient, love is kind. It does not envy, it does not boast, it is not proud. It is not rude, it is not self-seeking, it is not easily angered, it keeps no record of wrongs. Love does not delight in evil but rejoices with the truth. It always protects, always trusts, always hopes, always perseveres. Love never fails [I Corinthians 13:4–8].

Agape love is a powerfully active kind of love. Keep the actions just described in mind as we describe some of the actions of dedication revealed in research.

Desiring the long-term refers to wanting the relationship to continue into the future. It's a core part of dedication. If you feel this way, there's both an expectation and a desire for the relationship to last. Your marital promise is not a burden but a real live hope. As with agape love that "always hopes, always perseveres," and "never fails," there is a clear and positive sense about the future. This kind of dedication says "I'm expecting to be here for you, and I'm looking forward to it." This long-term expectation for the relationship to continue plays a critical role in marriage.

Mary Anderson isn't thrilled by the idea of her marriage continuing. It's likely to continue for now, but she doesn't really want it to. Bob is unhappy too, but he does want the marriage to continue. By contrast, both of the Templetons want their marriage to continue. In fact, like other dedicated couples, they talk a lot about their shared future together, reflecting this aspect of healthy dedication.

The priority of relationship refers to the importance that you give your relationship relative to everything else. When people are more dedicated to their partners, they are more likely to make decisions for the relationship when it comes into competition with other things. By contrast, when dedication is weaker the relationship is more likely to take a back seat to things like work, hobbies, kids, and so forth. To some degree, this can reflect as much a problem with over-involvement elsewhere as with a lack of dedication.

At some point, we all have to accept the reality that how we live reflects what's really most important to us. Unfortunately, the Andersons have allowed their marriage to become a lower priority, and now they're suffering for it. Their marriage isn't so bad as it is neglected. They no longer think it worthwhile to try, so they invest their energies elsewhere. If they are going to make it, they will have to turn this pattern around.

The Templetons have the attitude that each is truly important to the other. There are times when Eric is angry about what he sees as Deirdre's over-involvement in her work, but he doesn't seriously doubt whether he matters to her. Likewise, she sometimes thinks he is too involved in sports with the boys but believes he is dedicated to her and the family all the same.

We-ness refers to the degree to which one views the relationship as a team rather than two separate individuals who each focus mostly on what's best for themselves. This has been called "we-ness" because "we" transcends "I" in your thinking about your relationship. It's crucial to have a sense of an identity together if the relationship is to be satisfying and growing. Without this sense of being a team, conflict is more likely, as problems are seen as "me against you" instead of "us" against the problem.

As Paul says, love is not self-seeking or envious. Agape love in marriage is reflected by this sense of being a team. When you feel like you are a team, you don't feel you have to fight to get your way. It's easier to put your own needs and desires aside as you think about what's good for the team and about what's best for your partner as part of the team.

As we said in the first chapter, we aren't suggesting that you merge your identity with that of your partner. Rather, we are suggesting that it is healthy to have a clear sense of two individuals coming together to form a third element: us. Dedicated couples enjoy this sense of being a team. Instead of selfishly grappling to get their own way, they feel that the team's goals are at least as important as their individual goals. What a difference this makes in how you view your life together.

There's a huge difference in the Templetons' marriage and the Andersons' marriage on this dimension. In the Andersons' marriage, each feels quite alone. There's no abiding sense that they are a team working through the great ups and downs of life. In contrast, the Templetons draw comfort from their history of working together.

Satisfaction with sacrifice is the degree to which people feel a sense of satisfaction in doing things that are largely or solely for their partner's benefit. The point is not to find pleasure in martyrdom but to find joy in an authentic choice to give of yourself for your partner's good. This aspect of dedication reflects the very character of God in giving Himself for us. It is frequently encouraged in scripture.

> Do nothing out of selfish ambition or vain conceit, but in humility consider others better than yourselves. Each of you should look not only to your own interests, but also to the interests of others [Philippians 2:3–4].

> Greater love hath no man than this, that a man lay down his life for his friends [John 15:13].

The research about this is crystal clear. People who are doing the very best in their marriages are those who feel the best about giving to one another. In these marriages people actually derive pleasure from giving to one another. Marriages are generally stronger, of course, when both partners are willing to make sacrifices, as is true with Deirdre and Eric.

In the absence of this attitude of sacrifice, what do you have? You have a relationship in which at least one of you is in it mostly for what you can get, with little focus on what you can give. That's not a recipe for satisfaction. With Bob and Mary, you can see how each has stopped really giving to the other. Bob does not think he'll get anything back if he gives more, and Mary already feels she's given more than her fair share. Neither feels like sacrificing anything at this point. They each feel they are giving up a lot just by staying.

Alternative monitoring refers to a notion discussed by several commitment theorists. In our research, we have specifically focused on how much one keeps an eye out for—monitors—potential, alternative partners. The more one is attracted to or attuned to other potential partners, the less likely they are to be dedicated to the current partner. Do you find yourself seriously or frequently thinking about being with people other than your spouse? We must emphasize "seriously," because almost everyone is attracted to other people from time to time. Dedication is in jeopardy if this attraction to others has become intense, especially if you have a particular person in mind.

One study showed that people who are highly dedicated mentally devalue attractive, potential partners. This research amplifies a point written hundreds of years ago by Malachi, following the verse in which God says He hates divorce. In fact, this statement is repeated twice in Malachi. "So guard yourself in your spirit, and do not break faith with the wife of your youth" (Malachi 2:15).

People who are more dedicated are more likely to think in ways that protect their marriages—to "guard their spirits" with regard to their marital relationship. This is something you have a choice about. You can choose not to dwell on tempting alternatives, and when you are aware of options that are attractive to you, you can choose to look for what is not so good about those options. You can choose to look less and think less about attractive alternatives. This amounts to focusing on why the grass *isn't* greener on the other side of the fence when you are tempted to look.

Over the years Eric has been tempted a time or two to let his mind dwell on women at work. At one point he was finding Nancy to be very attractive. He was very aware of this attraction and considered it a threat to his marriage. As a matter of will, he decided not to think about Nancy and what he liked about her. At times, when aware of her, he'd think about what wasn't so great about her, compared to Deirdre. It's not that Nancy wasn't a great woman. She seemed to be just that. But he couldn't see any percentage in letting himself fantasize about Nancy because of his commitment to Deirdre.

COMMITMENT IN MARRIAGE OVER TIME

Dedication commitment is believed to develop mostly out of the initial attraction and satisfaction in relationships. Think back about your relationship. Because you liked being together, you wanted to be together more and more; you began to develop "want to" commitment. That's a big part of what dedication is about.

As your dedication to one another became more apparent, you may have noticed that you became more relaxed about the relationship. In most relationships, there's an awkward period in which the desire to be together is great but the commitment is unclear. That produces anxiety about whether or not you'll stay together. As your mutual dedication became clearer, the relationship seemed safer to invest in.

Because of your dedication, you made decisions that increased constraint. For example, as dedication grows a couple will decide to go from a dating relationship to an engaged relationship. As dedication grows further, they decide to marry, buy furniture, buy a home, have children, and so on. Each of these steps, taken as a reflection of dedication, adds to the constraint. Essentially, today's dedication becomes tomorrow's constraint. If you have these kinds of constraints, you probably took these steps out of the dedication commitment that was in your relationship at the times you made the decisions.

Research shows that couples at different developmental points show predictable changes in the levels and kinds of constraints in their marriages. In essence, it's normal for levels of constraint to grow in marriage. There's just more that holds you together as you go through life together.

Like the Templetons, couples who are more dedicated tend to be much more satisfied with their marriages. The relationship between satisfaction and dedication is reciprocal. Greater dedication will usually lead to greater satisfaction; dedication grows due to satisfaction in the relationship. When they are truly dedicated, people are more likely to behave in ways that protect their marital promise and please their partner. So, the effect on satisfaction is positive. It's also comforting to see that your mate really cares about you and protects your relationship from all the other options available.

Perfect Love Casts Out Fear

Dedicated commitment reflects the kind of love that takes the fear out of the relationship. Consider this profound point made by the apostle John. "There is no fear in love. But perfect love drives out fear, because fear has to do with punishment. The one who fears is not made perfect in love" (I John 4:18).

If you read the context of this marvelous verse, you'll find that John is talking about the love of God shown to us by Christ's death on the cross. That is perfect love. But we see John laying out a more general principle here as well. Because dedication can be thought of like agape love, you can think about dedication being about the kind of love that leads you to actively give to one another. And when this love is evident in your marriage, it adds to an overall sense of security, that is, the feeling that it is safe to be open and one with your mate. This kind of dedicated love promotes deeper levels of oneness and intimacy.

How Does Dedication Erode?

Studies show that nearly all engaged and newly married couples have high levels of dedication. So what happens that weakens it for so many couples? For one thing, if conflict is not handled well the satisfaction in marriage will go down steadily. And because satisfaction fuels dedication, dedication begins to erode along with satisfaction. When dedication is in jeopardy, giving to one another is eroded further, and satisfaction takes a big dive. It's a spiral that leads downhill. Dedication also erodes as we take our mates for granted and fail to nurture the kinds of loving attitudes and acts that build such a strong bond in the first place.

The secret to satisfying commitment is to maintain dedication at high levels. Although constraint commitment can add a positive, stabilizing dimension to your marriage, it can't give you a great relationship.

Dedication is the side of commitment that is associated with healthy, satisfying, and growing relationships. In fact, dedicated couples not only report more satisfaction with their relationships, they also report less conflict about the problems they have and greater levels of self-disclosure. Are you just existing in your relationship, or are you making it what you hoped it would be? Don't be satisfied with just constraint commitment alone.

In this chapter, we've given a detailed understanding of commitment. Although this material doesn't lend itself to the kinds of specific steps mentioned in other chapters, you can get plenty of ideas about preserving dedication by reflecting on this chapter and the next. Furthermore, we can think of no better way to strengthen your dedication than by working together on the suggestions contained in this book.

Making your marriage a high priority is your choice. You can choose to sacrifice more for your partner. It's your choice to protect your relationship from attractive alternatives. Fundamentally, these are matters of the will. We recognize that in some relationships, increasing your dedication to your partner will not make much appreciable difference. Far more often, however, people respond positively—and in kind—to evidence of their partner's dedication, especially when that person persists in the expression of dedication over time.

In the next chapter we will discuss some important implications of commitment and what you can do to build a stronger marriage. But before we move on, we want you give you the opportunity to assess the level of commitment in your relationship.

EXERCISES

We would like for you to approach this exercise in a couple of ways. First, think about your past experiences with commitment and how these experiences may have set up expectations or caused hidden issues (for example, fears) about commitment that may affect your ability to be vulnerable in your relationship. Referring back to Chapter Six on hidden issues or Chapter Seven on expectations may help.

Second, assess your current commitment by answering the questions that follow. Write your answers to the current commitment questions independently from your partner, using a separate piece of paper. We suggest you keep your answers to yourself. The exercises on assessing constraint and dedication commitment are best done individually, for your own reflection.

Commitment in Other Key Relationships

1. Describe the type of commitment you witnessed in your parents' relationship. How would you describe their dedication? Their constraint?

2. Were you involved in other relationships prior to your marriage? What kind of commitments were present in these relationships, and how has that affected how you feel about commitment today? How about your friendships? Have you had loyal, committed friends throughout your life?

3. Think about any times when you felt abandoned for any reason. How has that experience affected your present relationship? If you have suffered from abandonment, we strongly urge you to draw strength from Him who said "Never will I leave you, never will I forsake you" (Hebrews 13:5b). Meditating on Christ's commitment to you can help you be less insecure about commitment issues in all your relationships.

Constraint Commitment

Answer each item by choosing a number to the left to indicate how true the statement seems to you. Use the scale for your answers:

1 = Strongly disagree, 4 = Neither agree nor disagree, 7 = Strongly agree.

1 2 3 4 5 6 7   The steps I would need to take to end this relationship would require a great deal of time and effort.

1 2 3 4 5 6 7   A marriage is a sacred bond between two people that should not be broken.

1 2 3 4 5 6 7   I would have trouble finding a suitable partner if this relationship ended.

1 2 3 4 5 6 7   My friends or family really want this relationship to work.

1 2 3 4 5 6 7   I would lose valuable possessions if I left my partner.

1 2 3 4 5 6 7   I stay in this relationship partly because I am concerned that my partner would be emotionally devastated if I left.

1 2 3 4 5 6 7   I couldn't make it financially if we broke up or divorced.

1 2 3 4 5 6 7   My lifestyle would be worse in many ways if I left my partner.

1 2 3 4 5 6 7   I feel trapped in this relationship.

1 2 3 4 5 6 7   It is important to finish what you have started, no matter what.

Your answers to these few questions can tell you a lot. We can't give you an average score on these items because we don't use them in research in quite that way. Instead, we want you to use your responses for reflection. Are you aware of the power of your constraints? Which constraints seem to be the greatest?

Most important, do you feel trapped? Just about everyone does from time to time. This is normal. You should be more concerned if you feel trapped a lot of the time. Having a good deal of constraint but not feeling trapped is normal in a healthy marriage. The best marriages have two partners who are each dedicated to one another and who feel comfortable with the stability implied by constraint.

Dedication Commitment

The following items will help you gauge your level of dedication.
Use the same scale you used earlier.

1 2 3 4 5 6 7   My relationship with my partner is more important to
me than almost anything else in my life.

1 2 3 4 5 6 7   I want this relationship to stay strong, no matter what
rough times we may encounter.

1 2 3 4 5 6 7   It makes me feel good to sacrifice for my partner.

1 2 3 4 5 6 7   I like to think of myself and my partner more in terms
of "us" and "we" than "me" and "him-her."

1 2 3 4 5 6 7   I am not seriously attracted to anyone other than my
partner.

1 2 3 4 5 6 7   My relationship with my partner is clearly a part of
my future life plans.

1 2 3 4 5 6 7   When push comes to shove, my relationship with my
partner comes first.

1 2 3 4 5 6 7   I tend to think about how things affect us as a couple
more than how things affect me as an individual.

1 2 3 4 5 6 7   I do not often find myself thinking about what it would
be like to be in a relationship with someone else.

1 2 3 4 5 6 7   I want to grow old with my partner.

We can give you an idea of what your score means on these dedication items. To obtain your score, simply add up the numbers you
selected. In our research, with a sample of people who were mostly
happy and quite dedicated in their relationships (including those
dating for a few months to those married for over thirty years), the
average person scored about 58 on this scale. If you scored at or
above 58, we'd bet you are pretty highly dedicated in your relationship. However, your dedication may be quite low if you scored below
45. However you scored, consider what it may mean for the future of
your relationship. In the next chapter, we will talk more about maintaining and acting on your commitment to one another.

9

The Power of Commitment

Love . . . is not self-seeking . . . love . . . always hopes, always
perseveres.

I Corinthians 13:7

God designed marriage with lifetime commitment in mind.
And, as always, there are great advantages to embracing a biblical
worldview. In this chapter, we'll explore the incredible benefits
of taking a long-term view in marriage. Then we'll discuss self-
centeredness and its destructive effect on relationships. Both of
these have crucial implications for making your marital promise a
lasting promise.

THE IMPORTANCE OF A LONG-TERM VIEW

At the heart of it, when people are committed, they have a long-
term outlook on the relationship. Both dedication and constraint
combine in a healthy chemistry to produce this gratifying sense of
permanence. The long-term, positive view is critical because *no relationship is consistently satisfying*. The marriage experience can be
very ungratifying at times. What gets couples through these times
is the long-term view. There's an expectation that thick-and-thin
times will come and that the relationship will make it through.

The long-term perspective is crucial for a marriage to thrive
over time. It frees you to grow closer because you feel secure enough
to take the risks of disclosing more about yourself. Great security
comes from knowing your mate will be there when it really counts.

Otherwise, it's just not safe. In fact, when it comes to safety, the first part of this book focused on safety in your day-to-day interactions. When we talk about the long-term view, we are really talking about a deeper kind of safety that comes from the assurance that you will always be there for one another, no matter what. It's the same kind of wonderful security we feel with God when we really believe His promise: "Never will I leave you; never will I forsake you" (Hebrews 13:5b).

When the long term is uncertain, partners begin to focus on the immediate payoff. They naturally concentrate on what they are getting in the present, so they keep score on each other's performance as in "What have you done for me lately?" Essentially, the short-term view selfishly says "Give it to me now and give it to me quick."

In contrast, couples with a clear long-term view have a strong expectation of a future rooted in solid commitment, in spite of the imperfection of their marriages. Their belief in their future is reflected in frequent talks about plans they have for life *together*. They have protected their commitment, especially dedication. They do things for one another, show respect, and protect their marriage, giving it priority and protecting it from temptation. Having this sense of a future together is poetically captured in what Ruth said to Naomi: "Where you go I will go, and where you stay I will stay. Your people will be my people and your God my God" (Ruth 1:16).

This statement powerfully expressed Ruth's commitment to her mother-in-law and their future together. In your marriage, this kind of commitment is a *promise* that you both can rest your hearts in. It's a wonderful "want to" kind of commitment.

Marriage and the Stock Market

In the stock market, investors generally do best when they don't react to the day-to-day swings in stock prices. Investors tend to do poorly when they look in the newspaper each day, see if their fund is doing as well as another, and constantly move their investments in and out of the market or from one stock to another. They move their money around so often that long-term growth is compromised. They tend to lose more money than those who just keep on investing, whether the market is up or down.

Think of your marriage as a long-term investment. The ups and downs in the stock market and the value of a good mutual fund are like the ups and downs of satisfaction in marriage. These ups and downs are inevitable and normal. Unending bliss is just not what marriage is like for most people. It's wonderful at times and very hard at times—and sometimes it's wonderfully hard. In good marriages, satisfaction can be down for long periods of time, only to rebound later to mutual joy—just like the stock market. If you get too focused on the down cycles, you can bail out too quickly and lose much of what you've invested. Successful couples just keep on investing, whether the relationship feels great or lousy. That's why it takes commitment—a long-term view.

Are You Hedging Your Bets? People with short-term views scrutinize the costs and benefits of their relationship on a day-to-day basis, just like the investor who checks the paper daily in search of a better deal. These people are likely to "move their investments around" so much (affairs, commitments to priorities other than their spouse, and so forth) that the marriage is weakened. They're hedging their bets. Their energies are so divided that there isn't enough left over for the marriage.

Investment experts also tell us to diversify. And the healthy way to diversify in marriage is to multiply the number of ways you invest *within* the relationship. (It's like having a mutual fund that includes a wide variety of stocks.) In addition to sexual and sensual connection, for instance, you can share spiritually, learn to talk as friends, increase your fun together, learn to work on problems as a team, and so on. In all these ways, you are diversifying your avenues of connection—but diversifying *within* the marriage. At times during your life, some of these avenues may not work as well as others but, having diversified, you still stay connected. Regular, diversified investment is the key to preventing erosion in your commitment.

Investing for the Long Haul. Nothing is gained and much is lost if you wait around for what feels like the right time to act positively. Regular investment in the marriage is critical for those who want to prevent problems in the first place or who want to begin turning things around.

Because investors with short-term views tend to get burned in the stock market, financial experts often advocate a strategy called dollar cost averaging. In this strategy, you choose a good mutual fund and you stick with it. You are advised to invest a set amount in the fund at regular intervals (for example, $50 a month) over the long haul. Unless one is good at timing the market (and even professionals fail at this), this strategy is considered very effective for beating inflation and saving something for the future. Whether the market is up or down, you send in the investment.

We believe marriage works much the same way. It is best if both partners are regularly investing in the marriage whether the market—their satisfaction level—is currently up or down. You make investments when, among other things, you communicate well and validate each other, when you handle conflict well, when you do fun things together, when you put self-interest aside to do something that helps your partner, when you preserve friendship, when you forgive, and when you are able to resolve some problems that have been bothering you. These are the very things we're teaching you in this book.

Sometimes, we take our mates for granted because of the security we feel in their commitment. In the rush of life we fail to put all we should into the marriage because we're confident our mate will be there for us and will, therefore, wait to get our attention. Don't take your mate for granted. Keep investing regularly. Many marriages flounder because of one partner's neglect. If you believe you are the neglected partner, don't remain silent about it. Do not let the neglect of your relationship continue.

Score Keeping

One indicator of low commitment and the short-term view is score keeping, that is, the tendency to monitor what you are getting out of the relationship relative to what you are putting in. People who are experiencing the erosion of dedication tend to be more attuned to the day-to-day, short-term payoffs. They ask, "Am I getting what I deserve for what I'm putting into this?" They're keeping score. When the future is uncertain, the score today is all that matters.

Score keeping be very destructive. One variation of this is to strongly believe that one should get out of a marriage equal to what one has put into it. Although that may sound fair, such a belief is actually predictive of future unhappiness in marriages. Obviously, it is only fair that both partners pull their weight in a marriage. But when you are tuned in to what you're getting, and always expecting to get back something equal to what you're putting in, you'll probably feel you're getting cheated. The problem is that score keeping is fundamentally and hopelessly biased in favor of the one keeping score. You can see everything positive you do for your mate, but there is no way you can see all the positive things your partner does. Hence, even when both of you are pulling equal weight in your own ways, score keeping will foster resentment that can grow to a root of bitterness. You'll begin to think it's unfair even when it's not. Are you keeping score? If so, you may be headed for trouble.

Trust and Commitment

In our workshops we are often asked about the relationship between trust and commitment. The answer also relates to the importance of the long-term view. *Webster's New World Dictionary* defines trust as "the firm belief in the honesty, reliability, etc. of another; faith . . . confident expectation, hope."

Trust means being able to count on your partner to be there for you. The relationship between trust and commitment is best described with another financial metaphor.

Suppose you were looking for a new savings and loan to start a savings account. You notice that one opens up on the corner near your home, and a sign goes up that says "Conditional Bank: We're Here to Serve You (at least until the end of the month)." Are you going to deposit your hard-earned money there? No way! You'll have doubts about the long-term stability of the institution, so you won't trust them to be there for you in the future.

Marriage works the same way. Without the long-term view, who's going to trust enough to invest in a marriage? If you don't see reasons to trust your partner, you're less likely to invest, period. At the same time, if you don't let your partner see your own dedication, how is your partner supposed to trust you and keep on investing?

Trust and commitment depend on one another. You'll commit more when you trust more, and you'll trust more when you see commitment—especially dedication—from your spouse. When you both actively express dedication, you help build mutual trust. If you want your partner to trust you, give some solid evidence about the security of his or her investment. Controlling *your own* expression of dedication is key, but there is another important part to the equation.

Trashing the Long-Term View

Commitment sometimes becomes a weapon in a fight. Although Bob and Mary Anderson are not planning to get a divorce any time soon, the topic sometimes comes up in bad arguments. Consider the following conversation and its effect on trust and commitment.

BOB: Why does this house always look like a pigpen? You are never here to get things done.

MARY: I am out doing so many things because we have kids, and kids need a lot of attention.

BOB: I end up having to clean up all the time, and I am tired of it.

MARY: Oh, and I don't clean up? When you are here, you disappear in your shop. I don't see you doing all that much cleaning up. I do most of it, not you.

BOB: Yeah, yeah, I disappear all the time. You just don't care about this marriage. I don't even know why we stay together.

MARY: Me neither. Maybe you should move out.

BOB: Not a terrible idea. I'll think about it.

By the end of the fight it seems each was trying to convince the other that they were not committed. You can't get much more short-term than to suggest divorce. We call this trashing the long-term view. If you are trying to keep your marriage on track, it's important not to bring up divorce, period. Such statements erode trust and reinforce the perception that it's too risky to invest.

SELFISHNESS

Our culture encourages devotion to self. Notions of sacrifice and teamwork, as well as placing a high priority on your partner and the dedicated relationship, have not enjoyed much positive press lately. In fact, our society seems to glorify self and vilify whatever gets in the way of our self-seeking. As it says in I Corinthians 13, "Love is not self-seeking." Agape love constrains us to live for Christ selflessly.

For the love of Christ constraineth us; because we thus judge, that if one died for all, then were all dead: And that he died for all, that they which live should not henceforth live unto themselves, but unto him which died for them, and rose again [II Corinthians 5:14–15, KJV].

The Lord made it so clear. Living for Him means to love one another and to give ourselves to one another unselfishly (for example, John 15:13–17). This goes to the center of God's heart about relationships. He has designed us to give ourselves to one another in love.

We believe that this kind of selfless dedication is fundamental to healthy relationships and that selfishness is fundamentally destructive. Selfishness may sell in our consumer-oriented culture, but it doesn't bring lifelong, happy marriages. Godly love is the kind of love that leads us to serve another. It works powerfully against the tendency to use our partner for our own good—as if that person were just another product to be consumed (see Galatians 5:13–15). You can either try to get your way all the time, or you can try to outdo one another in love and enjoy the rich blessings of oneness. It's your choice.

Dedication is more about what you can give to one another than what you can get from one another. Part of being team-centered is being sensitive to your partner, trying to hear your partner's perspective, seeking to build up and protect that person in loving ways *because you are a team*. It means making your partner's happiness, rather than your own, a priority. It means doing what you know is good for your relationship, like listening to your partner, even when you don't particularly want to. It means protecting your commitment from alternative attractions. These are the kinds of things that research shows dedicated people do in their marriages. These are the actions of pure love.

To be selfish and self-centered is to be insensitive to your partner, to see things only your way, to seek your own good above all else, and to protect yourself first and foremost. Few people will argue that these things are good, but many Christians live this way and then are disappointed that a great marriage never materializes. One of the best things about the early days of many relationships is the relative lack of self-centeredness. When courting, people think up ways to put their partners first and spend lots of time listening. Sadly, such a focus on the partner's needs often fails to last.

Martin and Jennifer had a serious problem with selfishness. Jennifer described her frustration with Martin to us during a break at a workshop. She said things went pretty well until they had a baby four years into the marriage. While Jennifer was caring for the baby, Martin would disappear into the basement. Jennifer asked him to be more involved, but he didn't seem interested. She had been very clear in her expectation, but he had not responded.

Martin loved spending time on his projects. Jennifer seemed to be doing all right with the baby, so he felt free to disappear. Although we can't know all of his motives, it did seem to us that he was being pretty selfish. He left Jennifer to do most of the child care, so he could do what he wanted to do instead of giving himself to the needs of his wife and daughter.

Such attitudes aren't compatible with dedication. Over time, they can kill a relationship. Whereas dedication reflects "we-ness" and sacrifice, our culture asserts the singular value of individual rights, including the "right" to protect ourselves from all pain and discomfort. You can't have a great marriage when each partner is primarily focused on what feels best for himself or herself. In a culture that justifies self-centeredness, it's hard to ask "What can I do to make things better for you?" It's a lot easier to ask "What can you do to make me happier?" But that's not the question we are to live our lives by.

It's no coincidence that the "me" attitude of the seventies and eighties was coupled with all-time highs in the divorce rate. The kind of lasting and deeply intimate marriages most people seek are built and maintained on dedication to one another expressed in the kinds of constructive action we advocate throughout this book.

Codependency or Commitment?

You may be wondering if we aren't encouraging some kind of codependency here. Rest assured, this is not the case. However, we do disagree with some of the ideas that have come out of the codependency movement. Part of the problem is that the term *codependent* has come to mean just about anything. People have labeled virtually everything bad—and even some things that are good—as codependent.

The original idea of codependency came out of work with alcoholism. Professionals noticed that significant people in the life of the person who was dependent on alcohol would "help" that person in ways that served to keep the alcoholism going. For example, they would "enable" the alcoholic to avoid the consequences of drinking by calling the boss on the day after a binge to say the alcoholic was sick.

Counselors began to recognize a need in some people to feed the alcoholic's dependency. They were dependent on the alcohol too (codependent) out of their own need to be a caretaker and the one in control. The central idea was that people sometimes "help" or do things for others in ways that are destructive to both parties out of their own deeper insecurities and issues of control. Such behavior can look like dedication, but it's not. Although it is usually unconscious, it's actually very selfish, because the codependent person allows bad things to go on in order to get their own needs met. Counselors have been wise to spot this destructive pattern and to label it as unhealthy.

But now, people might be labeled codependent for choosing to give of themselves to others in truly good ways. In some circles, sacrifice is now considered codependent, as is having the attitude of being other-centered or team-centered. Try, however, to have a really great marriage without giving of yourself, at times sacrificially. It just won't happen. Christ laid down His life for us, and we are to lay our lives down for one another. This is not codependency; it is one of the greatest expressions of love.

Sure, you *can* relate in ways that look patient and giving but that actually harm the relationship and yourself. Does it really show dedication to tolerate a spouse's neglectful, demanding, or impolite behavior, for instance? No. This is not dedication. It shows far more dedication to constructively confront the behavior that threatens to destroy you, your partner, or the marriage. We are, in fact, plainly told in scripture to confront a variety of destructive patterns in the lives of others (for example, Matthew 18:15f; I Corinthians 5; Hebrews 3:12,13).

The bottom line is this. Whether it's through unabashed selfishness or the martyr-like selfishness of codependency, many people are too self-centered too much of the time to experience the kind of relationship they deeply desire.

HOW CAN YOU KEEP COMMITMENT ALIVE AND THRIVING?

Instead of asking "What have you done for me lately?" ask yourself, "What am I doing to improve and strengthen my marriage?" You have the most control over your own dedication and behavior, not your partner's. In most relationships, positive behavior is eventually reciprocated, so the best thing you can do to encourage your partner to be more positive is to act more positively yourself. *It's your choice*.

You can decide to make the relationship better by refusing to fall into the score-keeping trap. Show how you value the relationship and want to build it up. Do the things that foster teamwork. Keep at it and don't keep score.

One couple, Elizabeth and Frank, told us how they reinvigorated their marriage at the seven-year point. They'd been so busy building a home and family that each was feeling distant in the relationship. The long-term view was still intact, but they'd lost something they had at first. They decided to talk it out and, in a way, were each relieved to hear the concerns the other was feeling. They risked by sharing and listening to the hurt—an act that is, in itself, evidence of dedication.

ELIZABETH: (*catching Frank after dinner one night, while the kids played outside*) You know, I've been thinking.

FRANK: What about?

ELIZABETH: I think we've been doing pretty well, but I don't think we're putting enough into our relationship.

FRANK: I see that, too. It's like we put so much time into the house, the kids, and work that there's not a lot left for us.

ELIZABETH: Have you been reading my mind? Yeah, that's just what I'm thinking. And it's been painful for me when I have the time to think about it. I never thought it'd happen to us.

FRANK: (*moving closer, looking at Elizabeth*) It's really been worrying you, hasn't it?

ELIZABETH: Yeah. This isn't the way it was supposed to go for us.

FRANK: I know what you mean. I've felt sad about us losing something, but it's hard to put my finger on it. I've just known something's been missing.

ELIZABETH: I'm glad to hear you say that. I was most afraid that you hadn't noticed.

FRANK: (*putting his arms around her*) I have. I'm glad you brought it up to talk about. We have too much going for us to let the distance grow further. Let's sit down and talk about what we can do to about it.

ELIZABETH: I'll get some coffee.

This talk ignited a positive chain reaction in their marriage. Elizabeth and Frank renewed their dedication to one another in several ways. They made time together a greater priority—and followed through. Each began to look for ways to do more special things for the other. They redoubled their efforts to handle conflicts and disagreements with respect. They also confirmed their dedication by talking more openly about plans for the future, developing a greater sense of the long term and being a team again.

This example illustrates that it's possible to recapture the strength of dedication when both partners really want to do it.

However, we need to emphasize that *it's your choice*. You can't make your partner do anything. But, assuming you want to make your marriage work for the long haul, you'll be best off reflecting on how *you* can boost or maintain *your* dedication. As with Elizabeth and Frank, the bottom line was action.

Help! All We Have Is Constraint Commitment

This section is for those of you whose marriage might be in serious trouble. If that's not you, you might skip to the end of this section. Unfortunately, many couples are like Bob and Mary Anderson, whom we focused on in the last chapter. As you recall, all they had was constraint, with little of the sense of the companionship they both wanted. Our primary focus in this book is to prevent marriages from getting to that point. But even if you have come to that place, we don't think you have to stay there. If that's where you are, it's not too late to turn things around, if you both want to do the work.

Because you are reading this book, we assume you want to make your marriage work. So, what can you do if you find yourself in a marriage characterized by constraint without much dedication? How do you redevelop dedication?

First, you need to believe that it's possible, especially with the Lord's help. We cannot predict the future of your relationship, but we find that most couples are able to repair and strengthen the most lifeless, frustrating marriages. Second, you must really be willing to work at it, because it will take *sustained* work before the feelings of dedication return, and you will have to work against your present feelings and some tendencies that now exist in the relationship.

If you want to breathe life into your marriage, follow Christ's comments to the church at Ephesus. He told the Ephesians that all they were doing was wonderful, but they lacked one thing—they had forsaken their first love for Christ (Revelation 2:1–7). Note what He suggested they do about it. "Remember therefore from where you have fallen, and repent and do the deeds you did at first" (Revelation 2:5, NASB).

Note the simplicity here. This is not complex theology or psychology. He says *remember, repent,* and *do the things you did at first.* Although the Lord is talking about our dedication and love for Him, the process applies to restoring one's love in marriage as well. Remember, when we are talking about dedication in commitment research we are talking about what the Bible calls agape love. That's the kind of love Christ is talking about regaining here. So, consider these steps in light of this simple message. These steps will be most powerful if you sit down together and really think them through as a couple.

Remember What You Used to Have Together. Spend some time reminiscing together about the good old days. What were things like when you first met? What attracted you to each other? What did you do on your first date? What kinds of things did you do for fun? Do you still do any of these things? Although it can make you feel sad, most couples find this kind of reminiscing enjoyable and enlightening. It can be fun to remember the good old days. It reminds you that at one time you had some pretty great feelings for one another. Beware of the tendency to rewrite history and see experiences that were truly positive at the time as negative now.

It's nearly impossible to recapture the euphoria many couples felt early on, but you can recapture some of the good feelings that once characterized your relationship. There was a spark there, a delight in getting to know one another. In some ways, this step is an attempt to regain an appetite or desire for the relationship again—to light the candle again.

Repent: Decide to Turn Things Around. You can do this whether or not your partner is willing to, although making a commitment to do it together is far better. This is fundamentally a decision of your will. Repentance means to change your mind and your direction. We believe most people have enough control over their own lives to make a decision and stick with it when they want something badly enough. Repentance brings the Lord into the equation as you ask Him for help in turning things around.

Do the Things You Did at First. The point is simple but the impact can be profound. Early in a relationship couples talk more as friends (see Chapter Eleven), do more fun things together (see Chapter Twelve), are more forgiving (see Chapter Ten), are more likely to look for the good and not the bad in the other (see Chapters One, Two, and Three), and, usually, do a better job of controlling conflict (see Chapters One through Six).

Commit yourself to becoming less self-centered and more other-centered. When you have been selfish, admit it to yourself and the Lord and decide to turn the pattern around. The things that you can do to restore dedication in your marriage are the same things that couples can do to prevent marital distress and divorce in the first place. This book is filled with concrete tips on the "doing" part. What you must supply, with the Lord's help, is the willingness to act.

These things can work because they allow dedication to grow early in the relationship. As we pointed out in the last chapter, commitment theorists believe dedication develops out of satisfaction in a relationship. And dedication leads to constraint. Well, you've developed plenty of constraint. Now you need to come full circle by allowing your level of constraint to motivate you to rediscover satisfaction and dedication. We believe you can do this if you are both committed to the task. As a first step in your efforts, it's critical that you control conflict—that you make it safer to try again. Poorly handled conflict is incredibly damaging to the tender hope you are letting yourself feel and to everything else that's good in your relationship.

———

We hope we've given you a feel for how powerful commitment can be in your relationship. Where you think the relationship is heading (long-term view) and what you are putting into it (dedication) are critical issues. There are many actions you could take based on these ideas, but you're the best judge of what needs to be done. Only you know to what degree a short-term view, score keeping, or selfishness might be placing your marriage at risk.

EXERCISES

First, reflect on the questions that follow and write some of your thoughts on a separate piece of paper. We recommend you think about your answers individually, then meet and talk about your reflections. You'll notice that we ask you to reflect more on your own behavior and perspectives than on your partner's. Where are *you* and what are *you* doing? We're only called to change the part we control (for example, Romans 12:18).

1. Has the dedication between the two of you eroded to a dangerously low level? What do you want to do about it?

2. What is your basic outlook on this relationship? Do you have a long-term view? Why or why not? If you have a long-term view, are you comforted by it, or do you feel trapped?

3. To what degree do you engage in score keeping? Do you see the positive efforts your partner makes for you and the relationship? Are you willing to notice the positive more?

4. Does your basic orientation in your marriage reflect more selfishness or team-centeredness? What kinds of things do you do that express selfishness? What do you do to demonstrate a more selfless desire to meet your partner's needs? How can you enlarge these things?

5. If things are going well, how can you keep it that way? What things might become threats to your dedication if they are not dealt with?

Second, consider some of the following ways to increase dedication in your relationship:

1. Pray about *your* commitment to your relationship. Also, pray that both you and your partner will make the commitment to your relationship a priority.

2. Decide to give of yourself for your partner's good (Philippians 2:3,4). Are there ways you can be more giving to your partner

without expecting anything in return? What positive things did you do for your partner in the past that you might have let slide a bit?

3. Actively look for the good in your relationship. Make a list of these things. Try to notice the good things and keep adding these to the list each day. It can be deadly to catalogue the bad things in a marriage but great to keep a clear eye on the good.

4. Schedule some time to talk about these matters. These talks should be handled carefully. We suggest you use the Speaker-Listener Technique to share some of your more sensitive impressions. Determine to use this as an opportunity to come together rather than an opportunity to get defensive and angry. Dare to openly share your decisions of repentance. Talk openly about what you want and how you are going to get it. If dedication has been severely eroded between the two of you, consider the steps we presented in this chapter for turning things around.

10

Forgiveness and the Restoration of Intimacy

Bear with each other and forgive whatever grievances you may
have against one another. Forgive as the Lord forgave you.
Colossians 3:13

Someone once likened married people to two porcupines
who lived in Alaska. When winter came and the snow began to
fall, they felt cold and began to draw close together. However, when
they drew close to get warm, they began to stick one another with
their quills. When they separated, they became cold once again.
They wanted to stay close, but they didn't want to keep getting
stuck. Marriage is like that. In order to keep warm, we have to en-
dure getting hurt from time to time. Therefore, we have to learn to
forgive one another.

Unless you have been dating only a few weeks, chances are
you've been hurt deeply by your partner. Many things can cause
minor or major hurts: put downs, avoidance, negative interpretations, cruel comments, forgetting something important, making decisions without regard for the needs of the other, affairs, addictions,
impoliteness, and so on.

SINS OF OMISSION AND COMMISSION

You married (or intend to marry) an imperfect person—and so did
your mate! Both of you will commit sins of omission and commis-
sion over the course of your marriage. At these times, it's far wiser
to learn how to move on than it is to expect not to ever get hurt.

The more significant the hurt, the more effort that will be needed to put the event in the past.

Let's look at two different Christian couples in need of making forgiveness happen. Both examples demonstrate the need for forgiveness. But the infractions are very different—one's minor and one's major—and they have very different implications.

Oops, I Forgot!

Mary and Tony met in a church support group and later married. Each had been married once before. Each had primary custody of the children from their first marriages. They found they had much in common. There's been nothing remarkable about their marriage and blended family except that they have done a great job of making it work. They have handled the myriad stresses of bringing two sets of kids together, and they've become a loving family where Christ is honored. They've had their ups and downs, but they have handled their problems with respect and skill.

Tony, who is an engineer with a construction firm, had saved the company from financial disaster by noticing a critical design flaw in the company's plans for a high-rise office building. For this and other reasons, Tony was chosen to be honored as employee of the year at a yearly company luncheon. He was happy for the award and happier still to receive a substantial bonus for his "heads up" work. Tony asked Mary to attend the luncheon, and she said she'd be glad to come. He was proud to be honored and wanted Mary to share this moment with him. Tony told his fellow workers and his boss that Mary would be coming. A place was kept for her at the front table, right beside Tony.

Mary became distracted on the big day and completely forgot about the luncheon. While she was out buying groceries, he was at the party feeling very embarrassed. He was also a little bit worried; it was unlike Mary to forget something so important. Here were his peers, honoring him, and his wife failed to show up—without explanation. So, he fumed and made the best of the embarrassment, telling his colleagues that she must have gotten hung up at the doctor's office with one of the kids.

As soon as Tony walked in the door that evening, Mary remembered what she had forgotten:

MARY: (*distressed*) Oh no! Tony, I just remembered . . .

TONY: (*cutting her off*) Where were you? I have never been so embarrassed. I really wanted you there.

MARY: I know, I know. I'm so sorry. I really wanted to be there with you.

TONY: So where were you? I tried calling.

MARY: I was at the grocery store. I completely spaced out your lunch. . . . I feel terrible.

TONY: So do I. I didn't know what to tell people, so I made something up about you maybe being at the doctor's office with one of the kids.

MARY: Please forgive me, dear.

Should he? Of course. What does it mean for him to forgive in this context? How would you recommend he apply the command of Colossians 3:13? Now consider a very different example—one in which the same questions have much more complicated answers.

The Grass Seemed Greener

John and Megan have been together fourteen years. They met in college where both majored in business. They married shortly after they graduated and then moved to the Midwest. He took a job as a buyer in a retail chain, and she took a job as the business manager of a firm that makes windows and frames for home construction. Everything sailed along just fine until about the eighth year of marriage. At that time, Megan noticed that John was gone more and more. His job demanded a lot, but she wondered whether he really needed to be gone that much. She became suspicious. Without much time for open communication together, it was hard to know what was going on. They also drifted in their relationships with God, their church, and one another.

She began to feel as if she did not know John any more and suspected he was having an affair. She'd make phone calls to the office when he was supposed to be working late. He was rarely there. When she asked him about this, he'd say he must've been down the hall, in the copy room, or talking with a colleague. These excuses didn't wash with Megan. She went to their pastor for help. He suggested she and John come in for some counseling to alleviate her fears, but John would not have anything to do with that. Megan got sick and tired of being suspicious so she took matters into her own hands. One night, she told him she was going to see a friend and left. They had arranged for a baby-sitter to watch the kids so he could go in to work. Borrowing her friend's car, she followed him as he left the neighborhood. She followed him right to an apartment complex, noting the door where he went in. She sat in the car for three hours before she got up the courage to look at the name on the mailbox—Sally something-or-other.

"Not good; this is not good," she said to herself. It felt like gravity was pulling her stomach down through her intestines. Now what? She decided to knock on the door. After fifteen minutes, Sally came to the door, in her bathrobe.

SALLY: (*seeming quite tense*) Can I help you?

MEGAN: (*appearing calm but falling apart on the inside*) Yes. Please tell John I'm out here in the car and I'd like to talk to him.

SALLY: (*gaining composure*) John? Who's John? I'm alone. Perhaps you have the wrong address.

MEGAN: (*with sarcasm*) Perhaps I could take a look.

SALLY: I don't think so. Look, you have the wrong address, whatever your problem is. Good-bye!

MEGAN: (*yelling out as Sally closes the door*) Tell John I'll be at home—if he remembers where that is.

John rolled in an hour later. He denied everything for about three days. Megan was quite sure of herself and wasn't about to back down. She told John to get out. "An affair is bad enough, but if you can't even admit it, there's nothing left for us to talk about."

John fell apart. He began drinking and disappeared for days at a time. Megan felt even more alone and betrayed. Although she still loved John, her rage and resentment grew. She told the pastor, "I thought I could trust him. I can't believe he would leave me for someone else." The pastor listened to her anger and encouraged her to seek the Lord's comfort in the crisis. He had lost count of the number of couples he had counseled when one had been unfaithful. He prayed for them both and for the time they would talk about the affair.

The more John was alone with his thoughts, the more the Lord's grace became real again. His denial finally crumbled, and his sense of shame was so great that he was afraid to deal with Megan head on. He'd just stay away from home; but as he did, he pondered. "She told me to get out, anyway," he told himself. Yet he was really bothered that Megan was being so tough. "Is it really over?" In a way, he found new respect for her. No begging or pleading from Megan, just strength and determination. The Lord used all this to help John with his decision. He liked Sally, but didn't want to spend his life with her. It became clearer to him who he wanted to be with—Megan.

Of course Megan didn't feel tough at all. She was in agony. But she was very clear about what she saw. There was no chance she'd go on with John unless he dealt with God and with her honestly. He'd also have to go to counseling with her. As time went on, her anger turned to ambivalence. She was not sure whether she wanted to stay or leave.

Megan came home one night to find John sitting at the kitchen table with a terrible look of pain and conviction on his face.

JOHN: (*desperately*) Please forgive me, Megan. I don't know . . . I'll get help. I don't know . . . I'm not sure what happened.

MEGAN: (*cool outside, raging inside*) I'm not sure what happened either, but I think you know a lot more than I do.

JOHN: (*looking up from the table*) I guess I do. What do you want to know?

MEGAN: (*icily, controlling her rage*) I'd like to know what's been going on, without all the lies.

JOHN: (*tears welling up*) I've been having an affair. I met Sally at work, we got close, and things sort of spun out of control.

MEGAN: I guess they did. How long?

JOHN: What?

MEGAN: (*voice raised, anger coming out*) How long have you been sleeping with her?

JOHN: Five months—since the New Year's party. Look, I couldn't handle things here at home. There's been so much distance between us.

MEGAN: (*enraged*) So what! What if I couldn't have handled it? I didn't go looking for someone else. I don't want you here right now. Just go. (*turning away, heading into the next room*)

JOHN: If that's what you want, I'll go. I'll call our pastor and talk with him.

MEGAN: (*as she walks away*) Right now, that's just what I want. Please leave me alone. Just let me know where you'll be for the kids' sake.

JOHN: (*despondent*) I'll go to my parents' house. That's where I've been lately.

MEGAN: (*sarcastically*) Oh, thanks for telling me.

JOHN: I'll leave. Please forgive me, Megan. I know I've been unfaithful to you. I've asked God to forgive me, and now I'm asking you to forgive me.

MEGAN: I don't know if I can. (*She goes upstairs, while John slips out the back door.*)

At this point, Megan had some big decisions to make. How could she forgive John? She'd already decided that she might have trouble trusting him again. He realized that he had sinned against God and her. He clearly wanted to come back, but how would she ever know he wouldn't do this again the next time they had trouble together? What do you think? How would you recommend she apply Colossians 3:13?

WHAT IS FORGIVENESS?

Forgiveness is a decision to give up your perceived or actual right to get even with, or hold in debt, someone who has wronged you. Webster's New World Dictionary says it this way: "1. to give up resentment against or the desire to punish . . . 2. to give up all claim to punish . . . 3. to cancel or remit (a debt)." The picture of forgiveness is a canceled debt.

Forgive is a verb. It's active. It's something you must decide to do. When one of you fails to forgive, you can't function as a team because one of you is kept "one down" by being indebted to the other. When you forgive, you are committing to no longer, "hold anything against the other" (Mark 11:25).

In scripture the Greek word for forgiveness is *aphiemi*. Strong's exhaustive concordance defines aphiemi in this way: "to send forth, in various applications (as follow): [to] cry, forgive, forsake, lay aside, leave, let (alone, be, go, have), omit, put (send) away, remit, suffer, yield up."

Forgiveness is a vital ingredient for maintaining oneness in marriage. Wounds will come, but it is through forgiveness that we apply a tourniquet that stops the bleeding. This is vital so that relationship healing can begin. The theme of forgiveness is commanded throughout the scripture (for example, Matthew 6:12, 18:21–35; Colossians 3:13). To refuse to forgive not only reinforces barriers to oneness in marriage, it builds barriers between us and God. Forgiveness honors God. "And when you stand praying, if you hold anything against anyone, forgive him, so that your Father in heaven may forgive your sins" (Mark 11:25).

The act of forgiveness gives it up—sends it away—so your marriage can survive in the present to build for the future. It's a choice. It's a decision. It preserves the promise in your marriage.

This is hard for some of us. We read the scripture, we have the information, but we sometimes don't want to let go. The lack of forgiveness is the ultimate in score keeping, with the message being "You are way behind on my scorecard, and I don't know if you can ever catch up." In that context, resentment builds, conflict increases, and hopelessness grows deep roots. The real message is "Maybe you can't do enough to make this up." People often walk away from debts they see no hope of paying off.

As we have seen, infractions can be small or large, with the accompanying sense of debt being small or large as well. Mary has a much smaller debt to Tony than John has to Megan. Either way, the opposite of forgiveness is expressed in statements such as

"I'm going to make you pay for what you did."

"You are never going to live this down."

"You owe me. I'm going to get even with you."

"I'll hold this against you for the rest of your life."

"I'll get you for this."

These statements may sound harsh, but the feelings can be quite real in marriage. When you fail to forgive, you are acting out these kinds of statements, whether or not you state them openly. As we forgive, we keep our relationship in the present rather than in the past. Through this process of keeping short accounts, debts are forgiven and the evil one is not given a foothold he can use to make matters worse (Ephesians 4:26,27). It is your choice.

Now we'll focus on some of the most important issues people have raised when we talk about forgiveness in our workshops. These issues usually have more to do with what forgiveness isn't than what it is.

What Forgiveness Is Not

Maxine, a fifty-five-year-old woman in her second marriage, had been brought up to believe that to forgive means to forget. She asked us, "It seems so hard to forgive and forget. How can you really do this?"

You'll note that we said nothing about forgetting in our definition of forgiveness. But we've all heard the phrase "forgive and forget" so often that the two terms have become synonymous. But they have little to do with one another. We don't believe that you can forget a significant painful experience you have had, even if you want to and even if you have completely forgiven those responsible. The memory of an offense against you is just not something that will quickly go away. This proves the point. Do you think Christ has forgotten the cross? Of course not. Yet are we forgiven? Yes. Completely. In fact, please take a moment to meditate on (remember) the forgiveness that you have in Christ. By fully appreciating the depth of what Christ has done for you on the cross, we believe you are more powerfully freed to be like Christ in forgiving others, including your mate.

Just because you have forgiven and have given up the desire to harm another in return, doesn't mean you have forgotten the event. Fortunately, when people say "forgive and forget," they usually mean you need to put the infraction in the past. There's value in that, but forgiveness should not be measured by the standard of forgetfulness. If putting it in the past simply means you've given up holding it over your partner's head, that's right on.

The Bible's prescription for handling sin is active. It is never to just forget it as if it will go away (see Matthew 11:25 and 18:15–17; James 5:16). First John 1:7 says we have fellowship with one another when we "walk in the light" about our sin. The blood of Christ keeps on cleansing us as we do this. The implication is that our relationships with God and one another are restored as we admit our sin. When we don't bring offenses out into the open so they can be cleansed, that amounts to keeping them repressed in the darkness. But the forgive-and-forget myth may actually help foster unforgiveness rather than forgiveness.

Another misconception related to the forgetting myth is the belief that if a person still has feelings about what happened, he or she has not really forgiven. We believe you can perfectly forgive the person who hurt you and still feel the pain, anger, and grief that the offense has caused. So forgiveness is something different from feeling the effects of an offense.

Megan may come to a point of completely forgiving John, as forgiveness was just defined. Hopefully, she will work through and eliminate her rage and desire to hurt him back. However, in the best of circumstances, what happened will leave her with wounded trust and a grief that will remain for many years. Tony and Mary's case is far less severe, with fewer lasting consequences. As it turned out, he did forgive her for missing the luncheon. He didn't dwell on it and he didn't need to grieve about it. However, when he is reminded of it, such as at company events, he remembers. He still feels the same twinge of humiliation that he felt on that day. That doesn't mean that he's holding it over Mary or trying to get even. He has forgiven her, and he reminds himself of that fact. He just has a painful emotional memory from an event that happened along the road of their marriage.

Forgiveness and Responsibility

We're often asked something like "But in forgiving, aren't you are saying that the one who did wrong is no longer to be considered responsible for what was done?" This is another big misunderstanding about forgiveness. When you forgive, you are saying nothing about the responsibility of the one who did wrong. The one who did wrong is responsible for the wrong they did, period. Forgiving someone does not absolve them of their responsibility for their actions. It does take the relationship out of the mode of one punishing the other, but it shouldn't diminish the responsibility for the wrong done. In this light, it's important to distinguish between punishment and consequences. You can be forgiven from the standpoint of your partner not seeking to hurt or punish you, but you should still accept and act on the consequences of your behavior.

Let's summarize so far. If you have been wronged by your partner, it's up to you to decide whether or not you will forgive. Your partner can't do this for you. It's your choice. If you've wronged your partner in some way, it's your job to take responsibility for your actions, and if needed, to take steps to see that it doesn't happen again. This assumes the infraction is clear and you are both humble and mature enough to take responsibility. The key is that if you want your relationship to move forward, you need to have a plan for forgiving. Even if you don't want to forgive—perhaps because of your own sense of justice—you may still need to do so for the good of your marriage.

Tony and Mary followed this model in the ideal sense. Mary took complete responsibility for missing the luncheon—apologizing and asking Tony to forgive her. He readily forgave her, having no intention of holding it against her. Their relationship was actually strengthened by the way they handled this event. Tony gained respect for Mary in her total acceptance of responsibility. Mary gained respect for Tony in his loving and clear desire to forgive her and move on.

What do you do if one partner can't or won't take responsibility? How can you move forward then? For one thing, you must be open to examining the possibility that your partner didn't intend to do anything wrong, even though you were hurt by what happened. There can be a sincere difference in the interpretation of what happened and why.

When You Don't See the Matter the Same Way

Thelma and Charles, for example, had such an event. On one occasion, he was cleaning out the garage and threw out all sorts of old boxes. He thought he was doing a great job; the garage hadn't looked this good in years. Thelma was away for a few days at the time, and he'd known she wanted the garage cleaned out. When she returned, she was very pleased, just as Charles thought she'd be. The problem was, he threw out a box containing mementos from her days as a track star in high school. It was an accident. He'd even noticed the box and thought he'd put it aside to protect it. Perhaps his daughter, who was helping him, put it with the other boxes by mistake. Anyway, it was gone—for good.

When Thelma realized the box was gone, she went into orbit. She was enraged. She accused Charles of being stupid, insensitive, controlling, and domineering. What happened was unfortunate. Thelma had every right to be upset. Those things meant a lot to her. But it really was a mistake. Thelma was being unfair in accusing Charles of intentionally hurting her—directly challenging his integrity. This was a very negative interpretation.

When harmed in this way, it's OK to expect an apology, not because your partner intended to hurt you but because their mistake did hurt you. Charles can apologize to Thelma. But she has a long wait ahead if she needs to hear him say "You're right. I threw out your things because I'm a control freak, and I think I can do whatever I want with anything in our house. I'll work on it." He's not likely to say that because it's simply not true.

Whether or not you both agree on the nature of the infraction or mistake, you can still move ahead and forgive. It may be hard, but if you don't, you and the relationship will suffer added damage. In fact, there's good reason to believe that when you hang on to resentment and bitterness, you put yourself at risk for psychological and physical problems such as depression, ulcers, high blood pressure, and rage. That's the kind of anger that our friend Gary Smalley believes is so powerful in destroying relationships over time. It's no way to live. As he says, it kills your relationships and it kills you inside.

Before we move on to specific steps you can take to keep forgiveness going, we want to discuss a crucial distinction—the distinction between forgiveness and restoration in a relationship.

Forgiveness Versus Restoration

Forgiveness and restoration usually go hand in hand in a relationship, as with Tony and Mary. Intimacy and openness in their relationship was quickly restored. Each handled their own responsibility without complication. When this happens, restoration will naturally follow. What we mean by restoration is that the relationship is repaired and ready for renewed intimacy and growth.

Now, for the really difficult case. Suppose it's clear to you that your partner did something wrong and isn't going to take any responsibility, as could have been the case in John and Megan's situation. Virtually no one is going to deny that John's affair was wrong. He must be responsible for his own sin if the marriage is to have any chance of moving forward. Sure, they are both responsible for letting their marriage drift. They had grown distant, and neither is more to blame than the other for that. However, in response to this, it was his decision to have the affair. He's responsible for that action, not her. And it was an unequivocally wrong decision.

When John showed up in the kitchen asking for forgiveness, the worst thing Megan could have done would be to go on as if everything had returned to normal. It had not. You can't sweep things like this under the carpet. Megan could have decided then to forgive him, but that's a separate decision from whether or not she should allow a full restoration of the relationship. Here's what we mean. When John came back to the house that night, Megan didn't know what level of responsibility he was taking for the affair. "What if he blames me for it? What if he thinks it's my fault for not being more exciting and available sexually?" If she thought he felt justified or was not serious about changing, why should she allow restoration of the relationship? It really would be a great risk to take him back. Still, she can forgive.

Here is what actually happened. For a few days, they had some very emotional talks on the phone. With so much tension in the air, it was easy to escalate. But John persistently stated his desire to rebuild the marriage. He wanted to come back.

Megan asked John to come to the house one night for a talk. She arranged for the kids to be with her parents for the evening. She met with him and poured out her anguish, pain, and anger. He listened. She focused on how his behavior had affected her, not on his motives and weaknesses. He took responsibility to the point of making a sincere apology. He didn't blame her for the affair. Now, she thought there was a chance they could get through this. Their talk concluded this way:

JOHN: I've had a lot of time to think. I believe I made a very selfish choice that hurt you deeply. It was wrong of me to have the relationship with Sally.

MEGAN: I appreciate the apology. I needed to hear it. I love you but I can't pick up where we left off. I need to know that you will get to the root of this problem.

JOHN: What do you want me to do?

MEGAN: I don't want to say. I don't know. I've got so many questions that I don't know which way is up. I just know that I needed to hear you say you'd done something very wrong.

JOHN: Megan, I did do something wrong. I know it. It's also very clear to me . . . clearer than it's been in a few years . . . that I want our marriage to work. I want you, not some- one else.

MEGAN: I'd like to make it work, but I'm not sure I can learn to trust you again.

JOHN: I know I hurt you very deeply. I wish I could undo it.

MEGAN: That's what I want. With God's help, I suppose I can forgive you, but I also need some way to believe that it won't happen again.

JOHN: Megan, I'd like to come back home.

MEGAN: That's OK with me, but I need to know we'll go and get help to get through this.

JOHN: Like our pastor or a Christian counselor?

MEGAN: Yes. I'm not sure what to do next, and I don't want to mess this up. If you'll agree to that, I can handle you coming back home.

JOHN: That makes sense.

MEGAN: Don't expect me to go on like nothing's happened. I'm very, very angry with you right now.

JOHN: I know, and I won't pressure you to act like nothing happened.

MEGAN: OK.

As you can see, Megan really opened up and John validated her pain and anger. He didn't get defensive or act like nothing bad had happened. If he had, she was prepared to work on forgiveness but end the marriage. She gained hope from this talk. She knew it would take some time, and she also knew they needed help. The future looked uncertain. There was a lot to work through if they were going to restore their relationship.

John did the best he could under the circumstances. Next day, he called their pastor for an appointment. This showed Megan that he was serious about repairing their marriage; this was evidence of long-unseen dedication.

The relationship could not be restored until they got to work. It took time, but they did the work. Megan remembers—she's not going to be able to forget—but the ache in her heart gets weaker all the time. They were able to move forward through forgiveness and on to restoration of their relationship.

But what if John had been unwilling to take responsibility or to change? Then Megan should work through forgiveness as the Lord has told all of us to do. But it might not be wise to restore the relationship, at least not at this time. When someone takes no responsibility to change gross patterns of sin (and we mean clearly defined, overt patterns of sin), scripture teaches us that withdrawing from such a person is a wise course. However, even in these circumstances, we are to be motivated by love in wanting to see the other moved to repentance (for example, Matthew 18; I Corinthians 5). These matters are complex and require a lot of prayer and godly wisdom. Nevertheless, we think it can be helpful to understand that forgiveness is necessary for restoration but that restoration may not be possible or wise until some other things happen.

What About Regaining Trust?

We're often asked how you regain trust when someone has so damaged it. The question is not so relevant for minor offenses. There is no loss of trust in the Tony and Mary incident. But for Megan and John, there's a great loss of trust. Whatever the incident, suppose forgiveness proceeds smoothly and you both want restoration. How do you regain trust? It's not easy. We make two key points about rebuilding trust.

Trust Builds Slowly over Time. As we said in the last chapter, trust builds as you gain confidence in someone being there for you. Although research shows that people vary in their general trust for others, deep trust comes only from seeing that your partner is there for you over time.

Megan can only regain her trust in John slowly. The best thing that can happen is for a considerable amount of time to go by without a serious breach of trust. That takes commitment and new ways of living together. They can't afford to let the same kind of distance build up again. But if John has another affair, it will probably be next to impossible for Megan to trust him again.

Trust Has the Greatest Chance to Be Rebuilt When Each Partner Takes Appropriate Responsibility. The greatest thing John can do to regain Megan's trust is to take full responsibility for his actions. If she sees John doing all he can do to bring about serious change without her prodding and demanding, her trust will grow. In seeing his effort, she gains confidence that things can get better—not perfect but better. As we said in the last chapter, it's easier to trust when you can clearly see your partner's dedication to you.

Megan can also help rebuild John's trust. For one thing, he'll need to see that she doesn't plan to hold the affair over his head forever. Can she really forgive? If she reminds him about it, especially during arguments, he won't be able to trust that she wants him to draw closer to God and her and move ahead with their marriage.

STEPS YOU CAN TAKE TO MAKE FORGIVENESS AND RESTORATION HAPPEN

So far, we've focused on the meaning of forgiveness and what it takes to make it come about. In keeping with our approach in the rest of this book, we want to give you a more specific and structured approach for making forgiveness happen. In suggesting specific steps, we don't mean to imply that forgiveness is easy. But we do want you to be able to move forward with some specific steps to get you through the toughest times.

The steps outlined next are much like the process we suggested in Chapter Four on problem solving. These steps can work very well to guide you in approaching forgiveness when you have a specific event or recurring issue to deal with.

Each step has some key pointers. We'll use the example of Thelma and Charles to highlight the points and to summarize many of the points made in this chapter, as well as provide a road map for working through forgiveness as a team.

Step One

Schedule a couple meeting for discussing the specific issue related to forgiveness.
Pray in advance for strength and peace and grace to release the issue that has been a barrier between you. If an issue is important enough to focus on in this way, do it right. Set aside the time without distractions. Prepare yourselves to deal openly, honestly, and with

respect. As we said in Chapter Five on ground rules, setting aside specific times for dealing with issues makes it more likely that you'll follow through and do it well. Praying together as you begin (silently, openly—whatever works for the two of you in terms of style) demonstrates your humility in recognizing that the work you are about to do is not easy and will flow best from God's grace and strength.

After the initial rush of anger, Thelma and Charles agreed to work through the box incident. They set aside time on an evening when the kids were at a school function.

Step Two

Set the agenda to work on the issue in question. Identify the problem or harmful event.

You must both agree that you are ready to discuss it in this format at this time. If not, wait for a better time. When Thelma and Charles met, the agenda was pretty clear: how to forgive and move on from what happened with her box of mementos. They agreed this was the focus of their meeting, and they both agreed they were ready to work on it.

Step Three

Fully explore the pain and concerns related to this issue for both of you.

The goal in this step is to have an open, validating talk about what has happened that harmed one or both of you. You shouldn't try this unless you are motivated to hear and show respect for your partner's viewpoint. The foundation for forgiveness is best laid through such a talk or series of talks. Validating discussions go a long way toward dealing with the painful issues in ways that bring you closer together. This would be a great place to use the Speaker-Listener Technique. If there's ever a time to have a safe and clear talk, this is it.

Using the Speaker-Listener Technique, Thelma and Charles talked it out for about thirty minutes. He really listened to her anguish about losing the things that meant a lot to her. She edited out her prior belief that he'd somehow done it on purpose. She had calmed down and could see that blaming him in this way didn't make a lot of sense. She listened to how badly he felt for her—for her loss. She also validated his statements that he had specifically tried not to throw out her things. They felt closer than they had in quite a while.

Step Four

The offender asks for forgiveness.
If you have offended your partner in some way, an outward appeal for forgiveness is not only appropriate but it is healing. An apology would be a powerful addition to a request for forgiveness. A sincere apology validates your partner's pain. To say "I'm sorry. I was wrong. Please forgive me" is one of the most healing things that can happen between two people.

Apologizing and asking for forgiveness is a big part of taking responsibility for how you have hurt your partner. This doesn't mean that you sit around and beat yourself up for what you did. You have to accept God's forgiveness of you too.

But what if you don't think you have done anything wrong? You can still ask that your partner forgive you. Remember, forgiveness is a separate issue from the reasons the infraction or mistake occurred. Even if you don't agree that you did anything wrong, you can choose to ask your partner to forgive you (to release you for it) so your partner can more easily choose to forgive you. It's harder to request forgiveness when you don't believe you are guilty, but it's doable.

Listen carefully to the pain and concern of your partner. Even if you feel you have done no wrong, you may find something in what is said that can lead to a change on your part for the betterment of the relationship.

Step Five

The offended agrees to forgive.

Ideally, the one needing to forgive gives a clear, open acknowledgment of the decision to forgive. This may be unnecessary for minor infractions, but for anything of significance, this step is important. It makes it more real, more memorable, and increases accountability between both of you to find the healing you are seeking.

There are several implications of this step. In forgiving, you are attempting to commit the event to the past. You are agreeing that you will not bring it up in the middle of future arguments or conflicts. You both recognize that this commitment to forgive does not mean that the offended will feel no pain or effects from what happened. But you're moving on. You're working as a team to restore the relationship and repair the damage.

Step Six

If applicable, the offender gives positive commitment to change recurrent patterns or attitudes that give offense.

Again, this step depends on your agreement that there is a specific problem with how one of you behaved. It also assumes that what happened is part of a pattern, not just a one-time event. For smaller offenses (for example, Tony and Mary's and Thelma and Charles's cases), this step is not very relevant. For the larger ones (like John and Megan's), it is critical.

If you have hurt your partner, it also helps to make amends. This is not the same as committing to make important changes. When you make amends, you make a peace offering of a sort—not because you "owe" your partner but because you want to demonstrate your desire to get back on track. It's a gesture of good will. One way to make amends is to do unexpected positive acts. This shows your investment and ongoing desire to keep building your relationship.

In Thelma and Charles's case, he scheduled a dinner for just the two of them at her favorite restaurant. He went out of his way to show her that she was special to him. She'd already forgiven, but this gesture took them farther on the path of healing. Besides, it was fun. Their friendship was strengthened.

Step Seven

Expect healing to take time.

These steps are potent for getting you on track as a couple. They begin a process; they don't sum it up. These steps can move that process along, but you may each be working on your side of the equation for some time to come. Relationships can be healed when painful events come between you. Keep praying, keep moving forward, and keep showing your commitment to healing your marriage. It's your choice.

We hope that you are encouraged by the possibility for forgiveness and reconciliation in your relationship. If you've been together for only a short time, this may seem like more of an academic discussion than a set of ideas that are crucial for your relationship. If you've been together for some time, you understand the need for forgiveness. We hope it happens naturally in your relationship. If so, keep at it. Do the work of prevention. The rewards are great.

If you need to initiate forgiveness, and barriers of resentment have built up, start tearing them down. You can do it. These steps will help you get started. Pray for God's blessing as you seek to prevent or take down the barriers to your marital oneness. Seek forgiveness with humility, for God has forgiven you (Colossians 3:13).

Forgiveness is one of God's richest blessings, both for us as individuals and for our relationships with one another. There may be no richer expression of deep acceptance in marriage than seeing the truth about our sinfulness and still choosing to pursue a closer relationship. That's what forgiveness is all about. God moved toward us with the gift of forgiveness even when we were His enemies (Romans 5:10).

In the next part, we will focus on some of the other blessings of marriage, including friendship, fun, sexuality, and spiritual intimacy. These blessings will be most fully enjoyed when your relationship embraces a lifestyle of forgiveness.

EXERCISES

This assignment has two parts, one to do individually and one to do together.

1. *Individually*. First, reflect on and pray about areas in which you may harbor resentment, bitterness, and unforgiveness in your relationship. Write these things down. How long have you had these feelings? Are there patterns of behavior that continue to offend you? Do you still hold things against your partner? Do you bring up past events in arguments? Are you willing to push yourself to forgive (Colossians 3:13; Luke 6:37; Matthew 6:14; Ephesians 4:32)?

   Second, reflect on and pray about times you may have really hurt your partner. Have you taken responsibility? Have you apologized? Have you taken steps to change any recurrent patterns that may offend? Just as you may be holding on to some grudges, you may be standing in the way of reconciliation on some issues if you've never taken responsibility for your part (James 5:16).

2. *Together*. Like everything else we have presented, practice is important to put positive patterns in place. Therefore, we recommend you plan to sit down at least two times and work through some issues with the model presented in this chapter. To start, pick a less significant event or issue, just to get the feel of things. This helps you build confidence and teamwork. We recommend that you use the Speaker-Listener Technique

in step three when you fully explore the issues. That will help you keep things structured and safe.

If you have identified more significant hurts that have not been fully dealt with, take the time to sit down and tackle these tougher issues. It's risky, but if you do it well the resulting growth in your relationship will be well worth it. It's your choice.

PART THREE

The Great Things

People do not get married to learn how to handle conflict well or to have someone with whom they can iron out different expectations in life. People get married to have a lifelong companion in the union of marriage. While that may mean different things to different couples, this part focuses on those areas that allow couples to fully take hold of the blessings of marriage: friendship, fun, sexuality, and spirituality. These positive themes blend together to allow the full mystery of oneness to be expressed between the two of you. Yet, even though these are some of the more wonderful and sometimes lofty themes of marriage, we try to retain our emphasis on practical, clear strategies you can try in your marriage. May God richly bless you as you walk through life together.

11

Preserving and Protecting Friendship

If one falls down, his friend can help him up.

Ecclesiastes 4:10

What people seem to want most of all in a mate is a best friend for life. But for too many couples, this desire for lifelong intimacy is more a hope than a reality. It's not that it is an unreasonable expectation to have your mate be your best friend. Most couples start out with a good taste of it. It's just that friendships need to be nurtured in ways that many couples fail to realize until their friendship is all but gone. We want to help you preserve and deepen your friendship for many years to come.

WHAT IS A FRIEND?

How would you answer this question? When we've asked people, they've said that a friend is someone who supports you, is there for you to talk with, and who is a companion in life. In short, friends are people we relax with, open up to, and count on. We talk and do fun things with friends. In Ecclesiastes, Solomon describes many characteristics of what we would call a good friend. This is also a great passage about priorities in life—and making your friendship a priority in your marriage is crucial, as we shall discuss later.

There was a man all alone; he had neither son nor brother. There was no end to his toil, yet his eyes were not content with his wealth. "For whom am I toiling," he asked, "and why am I depriving myself of enjoyment?" This too is meaning-less—a miserable business! Two are better than one, because they have a good return for their work: If one falls down, his friend can help him up. But pity the man who falls and has no one to help him up! Also, if two lie down together, they will keep warm. But how can one keep warm alone? Though one may be overpowered, two can defend themselves. A cord of three strands is not quickly broken [Ecclesiastes 4:8–12].

You can see the many benefits of a friend as Solomon describes what is lacking in this man's life and what is desirable for a good life. A friend provides companionship (v. 8), productivity in the tasks of life done together (v. 9), support (v. 10), warmth (v. 11), and protection (v. 12). This is a powerful description of a great marriage. It's no wonder that parts of this passage are often cited in wedding ceremonies. With friendship, the support and care for one another help buffer you both from the trials and tribulations of life. A great deal of research confirms this. People who have more friends (especially at least one really good one) do better in almost every conceivable way in life, especially in terms of physical and mental health. Solomon nailed the benefits of having a friend squarely on the head.

Being supportive and encouraging most of the time does not rule out an occasional loving challenge. Solomon also wrote this proverb. "Wounds from a friend can be trusted, but an enemy multiplies kisses" (Proverbs 27:6).

When you are good friends, the positive connection and trust is so great that you can even receive some heat from your friend about patterns that are not constructive in your life. When you are living out a secure love that casts out fear, you can say or hear some things from one another that may not be pleasant but might need to be said.

One of the aspects of friendship that is most powerful is that of deeper intimacy. Intimacy can take many forms. In part, this means being able to share what's really in your heart and have it richly heard by another. That may mean revealing your hopes, fears, dreams, and burdens. It's also important to learn to hear your partner's heart and to listen in ways that make it possible for him or her to readily share it. Sharing at this level will mean different things to different people. In fact, we're all different, so in this area there can be a unique blending of who you each are in the mystery of oneness. Jesus virtually defines friendship along these lines as He tells His apostles that He considers them His friends, because He has disclosed the deeper things of His life with them (John 15:15). Whether you are quiet-spoken or quite outspoken, a key to great friendship in your marriage will be in learning to share, and to listen carefully for, what's within each other's hearts.

BARRIERS TO FRIENDSHIP

Friendship goes to the heart of most people's deepest desires in marriage. But why aren't more married couples good friends? Let's look at some common barriers.

There's No Time

We all lead busy lives. Between work, the needs of the children, the upkeep of the home, church responsibilities, the PTA, or the town council, who's got time for friendship? Friendship, the very core of your relationship, often takes a back seat to all these competing interests.

For example, Julie and Dan are a dual-career couple who'd been together about five years. They had a two-year-old girl named Linda at the time we met them. Although they were happy with their marriage and life together, both sensed that something was slipping away.

> DAN: We used to sit around for hours just talking about things—you know, like politics or the meaning of life. We also have had some great talks in the past about key passages

in the Bible. But, we just don't seem to have the time for that anymore.

JULIE: You're right. It used to be so much fun just being together, listening to how we each thought about things.

DAN: Those talks really brought us together. Why don't we still have those talks?

JULIE: We don't take that kind of time like we used to. Now, we've got Linda, the house—not to mention we each bring too much work home.

DAN: It seems like we're letting something slip away.

All too often, couples fail to take the time to simply chat as friends. The other needs and cares of life crowd out this time to relax and talk. This is often a matter of priorities. When couples date before marriage, they usually find a lot of time for being together. Life is often less busy then, but it's also a higher priority to find the time to be together. But that's not the only reason friendship weakens over time.

We've Lost That Friendship Feeling

Many people have told us that they *were friends* with their spouses to begin with, but not any more. Now they're *just married*. It's as if once you're married you can't be friends anymore; you can be one or the other but not both. Well, that's a mistaken belief.

The strongest marriages we've seen have maintained a solid friendship over the years. Take Geena and Pierre, who've been happily married for over forty years. At one of our workshops, we asked them, "What's your secret?" Their simple answer was "commitment and friendship." They started out with a great friendship and they never let it go. They've maintained a deep respect for one another as friends, who freely share thoughts and feelings about all sorts of things in an atmosphere of deep acceptance. That's kept their bond strong and alive.

Don't buy into an expectation that says because you're married, or planning to be, you can't stay friends. You can.

We Don't Talk Like Friends Anymore

If you've been married for some time, think for a moment about a friendship you enjoy with someone other than your mate. How often do you have to talk with that person about problems between the two of you? Not often, we'd bet. Friends aren't people with whom we argue a lot. In fact, one of the nicest things about friendships is that you don't usually have to work out a lot of issues. Instead, you're able to focus on mutual interests in a way that's fun for both of you.

Friends talk about sports, spiritual matters, politics, philosophy of life, fun things they've done or will do, dreams about the future, and thoughts about what each is going through at this point in life. In contrast, here's what couples talk about after they've been together for a while: problems with the kids, problems with money and budgets, problems with getting the car fixed, concerns about who's got time to do some project around the house, concerns about in-laws, problems with the neighbor's dog, concerns about each other's health, and so on. The list goes on and on.

If couples aren't careful, most of their talks end up being about problems and concerns, not points of view and points of interest. Problems and concerns are part of married life, and they must be dealt with, but too many couples let these issues crowd out the other, more relaxed talks they once shared and enjoyed. And because problems and concerns can easily become events triggering issues, there's much more potential for conflict in talking with a spouse than a friend. That brings us to the next barrier.

We Have Conflicts That Erode Our Friendship

One of the key reasons couples have trouble staying friends is that friendship gets disrupted when issues arise in the relationship. For example, when you're angry with your partner about something that's happened, you're not going to feel much like being friends right then. Or, even worse, when you do have the time to be friends, conflicts come up that take you right out of that relaxed mode of being together. We believe this is the chief reason that some couples talk less and less like friends over the years—they aren't keeping their issues from damaging their friendship.

One couple, Claudia and Kevin, were having real trouble preserving friendship in their relationship. They'd been married fifteen years, had three kids, and were rarely able to get away just to be together. They bred dogs together but hadn't been away to a dog show since they first had children. On one occasion, they'd gotten away to a show and had left the kids with his parents. This was their first chance to be away alone in years.

They were sitting in the hot tub of the hotel, really enjoying talking together about the show and their dogs when a conflict came up that brought a halt to their enjoyable time together.

> CLAUDIA: (*very relaxed*) This is such a nice setting for the dog show.

> KEVIN: (*equally relaxed, as he held Claudia's hand*) Yeah. This is great. I can't believe the size of that shepherd.

> CLAUDIA: Me either. I don't think I ever saw a German shepherd that big. This reminds me. If we're going to breed Sasha again this year, we'd better fix that pen.

> KEVIN: (*tensing up a bit*) But I told you how big a job that was. We'd have to tear out that fence along the property line, build up the side of the hill, and pour concrete for the perimeter of the fence.

> CLAUDIA: (*sensing his tension, and now her own*) Would we really have to do all that? I know we have to get the pen fixed, but I don't think we'd have to make that big of a deal out of getting it done.

KEVIN: (*growing angry*) There you go, coming up with things for me to do. I hate having all these projects lined up. That's a really big job if we're going to do it right.

CLAUDIA: (*getting ticked off, too*) You always make such a big production out of these things. We don't have to do the job that well to make the pen usable again. We could do it on a Saturday.

KEVIN: (*turning away*) Maybe you could. But I don't want to do it unless we do it right, and we can't afford to fix that fence the right way right now.

CLAUDIA: (*looking right at Kevin, with growing contempt*) Heck, if you watched how you spent money for just a couple of months, we could pay someone else to do the whole thing right, if that's so important to you.

KEVIN: (*angry and getting out of the tub*) You spend just as much as I do on stuff. I'm going up to the room.

Notice what happened here. There they were, relaxed, spending some time together, being friends. But their talk turned into a conflict about issues. As Claudia raised the issue of breeding their dog Sasha, they got into an argument in which at least three issues were triggered: projects around the home, their different styles of getting things done, and money. Some hidden issues were probably triggered as well. What had been a great talk as friends turned into a nasty argument as spouses.

When couples aren't doing a good job of keeping issues from erupting into their more relaxed time together, it becomes hard to keep such positive times going in the relationship. The worst thing that can happen is that the couple avoids taking the time to talk as friends. As we said earlier in the book, when conflict isn't managed well the growing perception becomes that talking leads to fighting, including talking as friends. So the baby gets thrown out with the bath water. This is one of the chief reasons some couples lose touch with friendship over time. But as we'll see, you *can* prevent that from happening.

We Are Victims of Reckless Words

One of the major barriers to friendship in marriage occurs when things shared at tender and intimate moments are used later as weapons in a fight. This can be incredibly destructive to your friendship, because "reckless words pierce like a sword" (Proverbs 12:18).

George and Harriet had been married for three years and just had their first child. She'd been feeling overwhelmed by the demands of her career and their new baby, so she'd begun talking with a counselor at church. After one particularly emotional but productive session, she shared with George that she was feeling vulnerable and not very confident about her parenting ability. Later that week, they got into a fight over who should get up with the baby in the middle of the night. As the fight escalated, Harriet accused George of feigning sleep so she'd have to get up all the time. George got defensive and said something like "Why are you accusing me of not holding up my end? You admitted yourself you aren't handling motherhood very well. Why don't you deal with your own problems before you start blaming me for things?"

This devastated Harriet, and she left the room crying, saying that she'd never tell him anything personal again. Unfortunately, events like this happen all too often in relationships. Through positive, intimate experiences as friends, we learn things that can be used as powerful weapons later when we feel more like enemies. But who's going to keep sharing personal and vulnerable information if it might be used later in a fight? That leads to covering up with our fig leaves of self-defense, not to being naked and unashamed.

PROTECTING FRIENDSHIP IN YOUR MARRIAGE

We've found some wonderful principles that help us protect and enhance friendship. If you have a good friendship going, these principles will help prevent your friendship from weakening over time. If you've lost something in terms of being friends, these ideas will help you regain what you've been missing.

Make the Time

Although it's great to be friends no matter what you're doing, we think you can benefit by setting time apart specifically for talking as friends. For that to happen, you must make the time. Otherwise, all the busy stuff of life will keep you occupied with problems and concerns.

We mentioned how Geena and Pierre had preserved and deepened their friendship over the forty years they'd been married. Their strategy for keeping friendship alive included planning regular times to be alone together. They'd take long walks together and talk as they walked. They'd go out to dinner. They'd take weekend vacations from time to time, without the kids. They invested the time, and it's been paying off in big dividends for over forty years.

If couples are really serious in telling us that friendship is important, they need to schedule time to be together as friends. It just won't happen if we don't. This means putting a priority on this aspect of your intimacy. It's one of the most high-paying investments you can make. The problem we all face is that there is much less *quality time* when there is little *quantity time*. Without time for friendship, we too easily end up like the lonely man Solomon described who was very busy and very wealthy but had no friend. That means you need to put some boundaries around all the other things you do in life, like the amount of time you devote to work, to carve out time for being together. But that's not all you need to do to protect friendship.

Protect Your Friendship from Conflict and Issues

In the first part of this book, we focused on skills and techniques for handling conflicts well, such as use of the Speaker-Listener

Technique, good problem-solving skills, and the six ground rules. In the second part, we added to this theme by presenting the issues-and-events model as well as some ideas about forgiveness. These strategies are powerful tools for dealing with conflict. You didn't get married so you could handle conflict, but you do have to handle it well if you want to protect your friendship and intimacy. That means setting regular time aside to deal with issues as issues, taking Time Out when conflicts are intruding on times you set aside for friendship, and forgiving one another for problems in the past so that the trust that friendship thrives on is nurtured.

Never use things shared in moments of intimacy as weapons in a fight. Nothing adds fuel to the fire like betraying a trust in this way. As we said earlier, this is incredibly destructive and creates huge barriers to future intimacy. If you're getting so mad that you're even tempted to do this, you probably aren't handling issues well enough in your relationship. That means you may need to work harder—together—on all of the skills we emphasized in the first two parts of this book. Acting on the material we shared earlier will make it much more likely that you'll have a great friendship that can grow deeper over time.

You might be surprised how powerful it can be for the two of you to simply agree that some times will be "friend times" and therefore off limits for conflicts and issues. For example, you could decide that whenever you take a walk in your neighborhood, it's automatically friend time. Or, you could go out to dinner and specifically agree that "this is friend time tonight, OK?" That way, you are working together to define the times you are "off duty" in your marriage. All the better, you can decide that unless you have both agreed to deal with an issue at a particular time, all your time will be in the friendship mode. Think about how you can work out this principle in your relationship. The key is to realize together that *you are not at the mercy of your issues*. You can keep issues in their place and thereby give place to the promise of deepening friendship in your marriage.

Begin Again to Talk as Friends

To talk as friends, you have to listen like a friend listens. Good friends listen with little defensiveness. So when you're sharing, you don't worry whether your partner's feelings are getting hurt or whether that person is being offended. That's because a friend cares about what you think and feel, and relationship issues are rarely at stake. A friend of ours, Bill Coffin, once said, "A friend is someone who's glad to see you and doesn't have any immediate plans for your improvement." When you're talking as friends, you are not trying to change one another. You can both relax and just enjoy the conversation. Even when we let our hair down and talk about something really serious, we don't want a friend to tell us what to do; we just want them to listen. It feels good to know someone cares. Friends often provide that kind of support, and you can do this for each other in your relationship.

Friends don't focus on solving problems or on giving unwanted advice. Most of the time, when with a friend, you don't have to solve a problem. You may have a limited amount of time together, but there's no pressure to get something done. As we said in Chapter Four, when you feel pressed to solve a problem, it's easy to cut off discussions that can bring you closer together. That's why it's so important not to talk about relationship issues when you're together as friends. With relationship issues, there's too much temptation to solve something and give advice. When your focus is on conflict, it won't be on one another in a positive way.

Like so many other things you've learned in this book, friendship is a skill. To keep your friendship strong, you may have to work on it a bit. We can't think of anything of greater importance for the long-term blessing of your marriage than to stay friends.

In this chapter we've outlined some of the things that make friendships work—especially in how you communicate. As we move to the next chapter, we change the focus to fun. This is another key area of intimacy and friendship in marriage that's often taken for granted. We'll go into that topic after suggesting some friendship exercises for you.

EXERCISES

Plan some time for these exercises. Have fun, relax, and enjoy your friendship.

1. Plan a quiet, uninterrupted time. Take turns picking topics of interest for each of you. Ban relationship conflict issues and problem solutions. Then consider some of the following topics:

   Some aspect of your family of origin that you've been thinking about.

   Personal goals, dreams, or aspirations.

   A recent book or movie. Pretend you're professional critics, if you like.

   Current events such as sports, politics, and so forth.

2. Take turns pretending to be your favorite TV interviewers and interview your partner about his or her life story. This can be a lot of fun, and it's in the spirit of listening as friends. The best interviewers on TV are good at listening and drawing their guests out of themselves. Try to draw one another out in your sharing together as friends.

3. Talk together about how you can build time for friendship into your weekly routine. If you both believe it should be a priority, how do you want to demonstrate that?

12

Increasing Your Fun Together

. . . God, who richly supplies us all things to enjoy.
I Timothy 6:17b

Where did people ever get the idea that God is some sort of cosmic killjoy? How could the creator of something like sex, for instance, be interested in making our lives boring? It is fully consistent with the character of God and the spirit of scripture to assume that enjoying life is something God delights in, particularly when we give thanks to Him for the good things we do enjoy.

The focus for this chapter is on how to continually re-create, re-fresh, and renew your relationship by preserving and increasing *fun*. Like friendship, fun is one of the most delightful ways couples have of drawing close together. But it often gets neglected over time in marriage.

THE IMPORTANCE OF PRESERVING FUN

Fun plays a vital role in the health of intimate relationships. Just as God rested after His work of creation, He expects that we will rest and refresh ourselves regularly. As wise stewards of our lives, we need to care for our health and the health of our partner and family through the wise use of rest. Doing things that are fun is one powerful way to rest our spirits and bodies and rejuvenate our relationships. Making fun memories together can add "big bucks" to your emotional bank account. Knowing that fun times are coming can refresh your daily routine by giving you something to look forward to. But fun doesn't just happen; it must be purposefully planned and nurtured. Otherwise, the demands of life will squeeze it out.

In a nationwide random phone survey conducted in 1996, Scott Stanley and Howard Markman found that fun was a strikingly important ingredient in happy marriages. The couples surveyed filled out over fifty questions on all aspects of their relationships—questions about satisfaction, commitment, communication, sex, and just about anything else you can think of. What is surprising to some is that the amount of fun partners had together emerged as a key factor related to their overall marital happiness. That's not to say that there weren't other good things going on in these happier relationships. But good relationships stay great when you're preserving both the quantity and the quality of your enjoyable times together. Let's look at some of the barriers to fun in marriage. Then we'll show you how to protect and enhance this refreshing part of your relationship.

BARRIERS TO FUN

Most couples start out having a good deal of fun together. This restful time spent playing together builds a relaxed kind of intimacy that strengthens the bond between two people. You'd think it would be easy for couples to maintain something that's so pleasurable. But for too many, fun fizzles out as time goes on. Here are some of the reasons couples tell us this happens.

We're Too Busy

Couples often stop making time for fun. Early in the relationship, they put a high priority on tossing the Frisbee, window shopping, walking hand in hand, going bowling or to the movies, and so forth. That's the way it was for Robert and Cheryl. Recreation was important to them. They'd spent many Saturdays together in the mountains picnicking, hiking, and just sitting on a mountain top talking about their future together. When they got married, they continued to go to the mountains, but less frequently. A few years later they had their first child and began to spend much less time having fun. Hailey was a delight for them, but it became rare for Robert and Cheryl to go out and have fun the way they used to. Over time, they noticed that life wasn't as enjoyable as it used to be. They were happy together, and their eight-year-old marriage was solid, but something was missing.

It's really pretty simple. Life is more satisfying when you take time for fun. But the rest of life will crowd it out if you don't find the time to do playful things that keep the joy alive.

Karen and Frank are a good example of a couple who have preserved time for fun. They've been married for twenty years, and every Friday night for most of those years they've gone out on a date together. Their date night is just one way they've preserved fun in their relationship. They have refused to let other things come between them and this time together. It's a priority in their marriage. They also vary what they do on these dates: dinner and a movie, swimming together, bridge lessons, walking in the park, watching the sun set, and so on. They've tried many things; they make the time for each other, and their marriage has benefited. Their fun experiences have built a positive storehouse of many pleasant memories that help offset the tougher times.

We're Married Now, So We're Not Supposed to Have Fun

One of the expectations people sometimes hold about marriage is that it's not supposed to be fun. Many of us vowed to love and honor our mate, but where is fun mentioned in the wedding vows? It's as if once you get married, you have to be an adult, and adults don't, or shouldn't, have fun. Work and responsibilities are often emphasized over and above the legitimate need for rest and relaxation. There's nothing wrong, of course, with being a responsible member of society. But you also have to let your hair down and enjoy each other. Look at what Solomon said. "Enjoy life with your wife, whom you love, all the days of this meaningless life that God has given you under the sun—all your meaningless days. For this is your lot in life and in your toilsome labor under the sun" (Ecclesiastes 9:9).

As Solomon pondered the meaning of life, he concluded that it was too full of toilsome labor—and he had it pretty good! In the midst of the responsibilities of life, he concluded, it was important to enjoy life with your mate. How many couples have worked hard their whole lives to build a home, send the kids to college, and have a retirement nest egg, but haven't been able to reap the benefits because of death, illness, or divorce? At the end of life, when people are asked what they wish they'd done differently, hardly anyone says "I wish I'd worked harder, sold another car, completed more projects." People usually wish they had played more with the kids or spent more time with their spouse. Don't wait for retirement to start enjoying life. Make sure that fun and play are essential parts of your relationship *now*.

We Have Conflicts That Ruin Our Fun Times

Mishandled conflict is a real killer of fun time together. As we've emphasized so often, handling problems poorly can just about ruin all the enjoyable aspects of a relationship.

Noreen and David were a middle-aged couple who made time for fun. Making the time wasn't the problem, but all too often they'd be out to have a good time and some event would trigger an issue that would kill the lightness of the moment. One night they'd arranged for a sitter for the kids and went out to take a class in couple's massage. They thought, "This will push us a bit to have some fun in a new way." Great idea! The instructor was making a point to the class about paying attention to their partner's reactions. David whispered to Noreen, "That's a great point." Noreen whispered back, "I've been trying to tell you that for years." David was instantly offended. He felt attacked and showed it by pulling away from Noreen, folding his hands across his chest in disgust.

This event triggered some hot issues for David and Noreen. Noreen had felt for years that David didn't listen well to what she said (a hidden issue of caring). She was hurt that he hadn't cared enough to remember her making the same point the instructor was making. On his part, David had been feeling that Noreen was critical of nearly everything he did and now was attacking him when he was really trying to improve their relationship by taking this workshop with her. He felt rejected and dejected, wondering, "Can't she even lay off when we're out to have fun?" On this evening, they didn't recover well. David suggested that they leave the class early and go home. They did—in silence.

There will be occasions for all couples when conflict erupts during fun times. But when it happens too often, the fun times aren't so much fun anymore. The whole idea is to share a relaxing time together that creates a positive experience that feels enjoyable. Poorly handled conflict will blow this all away. The sense that conflict could erupt at any moment isn't compatible with relaxed playfulness. We set ourselves up to fail at fun when we take unresolved problems and anger into our special times. Remember Ground Rule No. 6: "We will agree to protect these (fun) times from conflict and the need to deal with issues."

Now that we've discussed some barriers that can keep fun from being a regular part of a relationship, we want to present a few ideas for keeping it alive and well.

GUIDELINES FOR KEEPING FUN IN MARRIAGE

You may be thinking that you know how to enjoy yourselves together and don't need strategies and skills for something so simple. But don't be too sure. Great fun takes thought and planning. Here are some pointers that can help you stay on track.

Making the Time

"There is a time for everything, and a season for every activity under heaven . . . a time to weep and a time to laugh, a time to mourn and a time to dance (Ecclesiastes 3:1,4). Is there a time for you and your mate to have fun? In this passage, Solomon tells us that there is a time for everything, including laughing and dancing. It's unlikely you'll have fun together without setting aside the time and money to make it happen. Sure, you can and should have spontaneous moments of playfulness just about anywhere, anytime. Even a quick joke together or seeing something funny on TV can be enjoyable. But to get the full benefit of fun times together, we suggest that you make it a priority so that you can really get into the flow of it. *This means you need to be serious about setting aside time to be less serious.*

To do this, you will probably need to schedule these times together. This may not sound very spontaneous or romantic; fun times seemed so automatic earlier in your relationship. In fact, early on, you probably went out of your way to make time to be together doing enjoyable things. But, sad as this reality is, most couples have so much going on that it takes a deliberate act to create free time. People talk a lot about quality time versus quantity time. *The truth is that many of the best quality times come from having set aside a quantity of time.* If you have children, you may need to arrange for a babysitter, and if you don't have a sitter you trust, this may be the time to find one. Nothing helps you relax more than being out to have fun and knowing that your little ones are with someone you trust.

And when you're out to have fun together, try to eliminate all distractions. For example, if your job requires you to wear a pager or carry a cell phone, do you really have to have it when you've carved out time to play with your spouse? It's not very relaxing to know you could get beeped or called at any moment. Set aside time and shut out all distractions for a while. It's worth it.

Protecting Fun from Conflict

As we said in our discussion of friendship in the last chapter, this book's guidelines for handling conflict (Chapters One through Five) are critical if you're going to protect fun in your relationship. You need to control the times and conditions for dealing with the difficult things in your marriage. Blocking out separate times to handle the tricky issues keeps them from popping up during your fun times.

Many couples see the wisdom of a "date night" or weekends to get away and enjoy each other. However, in our experience, many couples try to do too much with the time they've set aside. They try to have fun together *and* resolve difficult issues "while we have this chance for some time together." Avoid this at all costs. *When you've blocked out time to have fun, don't do conflict.*

Frank and Karen, mentioned earlier in this chapter, learned this the hard way before they got into the groove of doing fun right. Earlier in their marriage they went through a period when they were so busy that they'd try to schedule everything into the few times they had together. They'd get a sitter, go out for fun, and mess up the evening with issues. For example, one night they went out to an ice skating show. When they were seated and waiting for the show to start, Frank said "We haven't had time to talk out that budget problem. Let's see what we can get done right now." Big mistake! Their budget was a serious conflict area between them, and it deserved far more focused time than they were going to have while waiting for an ice show to start. As you can imagine, they didn't get anywhere on the budget in the time they had. Instead, they ended up feeling stressed out with each other when they were out to have fun.

Deal with the important issues in your relationship in your couple meetings set aside for that purpose, not during times set aside for fun. When issues are triggers during these times, table them. Call a Time Out and come back to them *later*. It's not hard to do once you try it a few times. It's a wonderful thing to simply agree to keep conflict out of time set aside for enjoyment. When you feel safe and confident that issues won't come up because they are being dealt with at their own time and place, you'll find it much easier to relax and have fun.

Brainstorming About Fun Activities

OK, you've set aside time for fun, and you've agreed to put conflicts aside to protect that time. Now what? For many couples who have become rusty at coming up with fun things to do together, this is a difficult question. Others, like the couples in the research we described, have plenty of ideas. Of course there are many kinds of activities couples do for fun. What do you do? Have you fallen into the common rut of dinner and a movie? Sit down together and think about the most enjoyable, interesting, and fun things you've ever done, or things you would like to do together. Make a list to which you both contribute, putting down all ideas that come to mind, no matter how foolish or outrageous they may seem. Part of the fun is in brainstorming about fun—throwing out the wackiest ideas you can. Avoid getting into ruts. Stretch yourself with some new things, even though it feels uncomfortable at first.

To help you get started, we'd like to mention a few of the great ideas we've heard from couples in our workshops. Maybe one of them will trigger some new ideas in your own mind. These are activities almost any couple can do if they find them enjoyable.

Couples have suggested doing exercise or massage together. You can bake cookies together and make a big mess. You can climb a mountain or collect sea shells. You can go swimming or play tag. How about renting a classic movie and cuddling on the sofa with a bowl of popcorn? How long has it been since you had a soda with two straws? Have you ever tried preparing a meal together, then feeding it to each other?

Here are a few more: float down a creek on inner tubes together; take a ride on a horse-drawn carriage; go to a restaurant that serves ethnic food you've never eaten before; buy a kite, put it together, and fly it on a breezy spring day; go to a park and play on the playground equipment, then finish the evening off with your favorite sundae; build a snowman together; audit an interesting adult education class; go downtown and spend the evening just watching people; try roller blading at a city park; take dancing lessons; wash the car together; take a ride in a hot air balloon; research an interesting topic at the library and share what you've learned over an old-fashioned ice cream soda; read a short story together on a blanket at your favorite spot; take a walk in the rain under one umbrella;

or check out the neighborhood Christmas lights on a snowy night. You get the idea.

Even things that seem like work can be turned into play. It's all in your attitude. According to one husband, "My wife and I found out that it was really fun to do yard work together. It's great to be together sprucing up our home, and at the end of the day, it's rewarding to see what we accomplished. And in the summertime, seeing the flowers we planted together bloom is something that gives us great pleasure and pride. These things are fun for us because we're doing them together."

Don't get stuck because things you want to do are too expensive or time consuming. Little things, like taking a walk or watching the sunset together may be some of your most enjoyable moments. The most important thing is that you plan to do something fun *together*.

Over the years, we've noticed that when we have couples brainstorm about enjoyable things to do, sex usually isn't mentioned until many other matters have been mentioned. Couples tend to forget that sexual intimacy is one of the most fun things they can do together. God created sex as a fundamental part of your oneness together. How about setting aside an evening without the kids to make love in front of the fireplace?

Getting Going

Make a personal "fun deck" by taking a deck of index cards and writing down on each card one of the ideas from your brainstorming session. This fun deck idea goes back to the book *A Couple's Guide to Communication* (1976, Research Press), which was published over twenty years ago. We suggest listing twenty-five to thirty different ideas to start with. Make sure you have a variety of ideas with different time requirements, expense, and so forth. Once you've made the deck, set aside particular times to choose activities and do them. Don't let anything stop you.

Share the responsibility for making fun happen. Because you're going to have more fun if you're working on it as a team, here's one way to make sure this happens. One of you can pick three cards from the deck, describing things you would enjoy doing in the time set aside. Then, the other person chooses one of the three cards your mate selected and takes the responsibility for making that activity happen (buying the tickets, getting the baby-sitter, and so forth). That way, you're picking something you know your partner will like, but because you get to choose from among the three, you're likely to like it too. Don't worry about which one of their three suggestions your partner might want you to pick. Just choose your preference and make it happen. If you don't get to choose one of your favorite ideas this time, you'll have another chance the next time you go out, because then it will be your turn to choose three card ideas and your partner's turn to make one of the ideas happen.

You can derive a lot of pleasure from rituals in your marriage like dinner out every Thursday, but it's also important to stretch yourselves. A lot of times the most enjoyable things are novel, and the newness of the activity is a big part of the fun. Perhaps one week you can say "You know, for a change, I'd really like to hire a baby-sitter and go out to a dinner theater instead of going to the movies. What do you think?" It might feel risky to try something new, and you don't know what your partner will say. But if you get into the spirit of fun together, your partner may say "Great, when do we go?" Or your partner may have another idea you'll find even more appealing. The key is that you're able to work together to collaborate on choosing some new and interesting activities.

You can also choose at times to intensify the effort. For example, you could try a slightly different approach with your fun deck in which you each pick three cards and then, over the next weekend, do all six of these activities. Try breaking the fun barrier. You may think, "My goodness, I can't possibly do all that." But if you think about it, you could go for a walk and watch the sunset (that's one), then go out to dinner (there's two), go to a movie (there's three), come home and make love (four), have breakfast in bed the next morning (five), and then take a shower together (there's six).

So you can do six activities in the course of one evening and morning. When they are dating, couples commonly do many fun things together in a short period of time. If your priorities are on keeping your relationship vibrant, there's no reason not to keep doing this.

If you follow the key points in this chapter, you'll be qualified for a degree in relationship fun. You can do it. Early in relationships, it comes easily. Even after many years in a marriage, it's not all that hard if you make the time, protect that time, and work as a team to make fun happen.

Sensuality and sexuality can be fun, too. All too often, however, the sensual-sexual area also falls victim to the barriers against fun that we discussed earlier. Many professionals believe that sexual chemistry inevitably decreases over time. Yet many couples are able to sustain and even improve their sex lives. We don't believe that couples fall out of attraction. Instead, the biggest reason attraction dies down is that couples neglect the very things that built and maintained it in the first place: friendship and fun. But before we focus on the sexual side of things, we have some exercises to help you break the fun barrier.

EXERCISES

We'd like you to go through the steps we discussed in this chapter. Here they are again:

1. Brainstorm about a list of fun things. Be creative. Have a good time coming up with ideas.

2. Write these ideas out on index cards to build your own fun deck. It will come in handy when you don't have much time to decide what to do, but you're ready for some fun.

3. Set aside the time.

4. Pick out three things from the deck that you'd enjoy doing and hand them to your partner. Each of you should take turns making one of your partner's three things happen in the times you've set aside.

13

Enhancing and Protecting Your Sex Life

Let the husband render to his wife the affection due her, and likewise also the wife to her husband.

I Corinthians 7:3, NKJV

God, who "richly provides us with everything for our enjoyment" (I Timothy 6:17), delights in our enjoyment of sexual and sensual pleasure. He clearly intended marriage for physical oneness as well as all the other kinds of oneness. As a matter of fact, the foundational picture of oneness in scripture is a picture of two coming together in a "one-flesh" relationship (Genesis 2:24). Scripture clearly honors the importance of sexuality in marriage. But sensuality is also portrayed positively. In this chapter, we'll look at these two wonderful aspects of marital oneness and discuss some of the common pitfalls couples fall into that deprive them of some of the blessings God had in mind at creation.

We realize we are speaking to couples at many different places in life. For some of you, this area of your marriage is going great and you are wanting to keep it that way. For others, some problems have crept in, and you may be interested in renewing your physical union. Still others of you are engaged and are working through this book as a part of your preparation for marriage. For you, the key will be to learn some principles that can keep your marriage on the right path from the start.

SENSUALITY IN MARRIAGE

We live in a culture that glorifies sex outside of marriage. One clearly gets the impression that marital sex, especially in Christian marriages, is boring. These impressions couldn't be further from the truth, according to the Bible as well as recent research. The Bible speaks to incredible degrees of love, sensuality, and physical pleasure in marriage. The clearest description of this is in the Song of Solomon. Although many have viewed Solomon as depicting either God's love for Israel or Christ's love for the church (or both), it is also one of the most magnificent descriptions of love, devotion, and passion ever penned. Consider just a few passages:

> Beloved
> While the king was at his table, my perfume spread its
>   fragrance.
> My lover is to me a sachet of myrrh resting between my
>   breasts.
> My lover is to me a cluster of henna blossoms from the
>   vineyards of En Gedi.
> Lover
> How beautiful you are, my darling! Oh, how beautiful!
>   Your eyes are doves.
> Beloved
> How handsome you are, my lover! Oh, how charming!
> And our bed is verdant.
>
> *Song of Solomon 1:12–16*

> Awake, north wind, and come, south wind! Blow on
>   my garden, that its fragrance may spread abroad. Let
>   my lover come into his garden and taste its choice
>   fruits.
>
> *Song of Solomon 4:16*

> I am my lover's and my lover is mine; he browses
>   among the lilies.
>
> *Song of Solomon 6:3*

Place me like a seal over your heart, like a seal on your
arm; for love is as strong as death, its jealousy
unyielding as the grave. It burns like blazing fire, like a
mighty flame. Many waters cannot quench love;
rivers cannot wash it away. If one were to give all the
wealth of his house for love, it would be utterly
scorned.

Song of Solomon 8:6,7

Many couples struggle a great deal in this area. Some rely on the sexual relationship as the sole path to intimacy and oneness. But as we'll see, sexuality without a broader connection (including sensuality) spells trouble for a marriage. Other couples virtually ignore this kind of intimacy and fall into the trap of a lifeless physical relationship of occasional sex. When a balanced diet of intimacy is not maintained, and sex is misused or over-used, couples can lose interest and connection and become bored. Couples who enjoy the most rewarding physical unions realize that, in a sense, all of marriage is foreplay. The foundations of emotional, intellectual, and spiritual closeness, along with nonsexual sensuality, provide the basis for great experiences of love in sexual union. You can enjoy more of the blessings of physical oneness as God created it when you are doing the things to nurture the other kinds of oneness we've discussed in this book so far. Now let's look at sexuality and sensuality and see how couples can become confused.

Sensuality and Sexuality Are Different

Think about *sexuality* for a moment. What comes to mind? For many, the first thought is of sexual intercourse and all the pleasurable things that may come before and after. Or perhaps you think of the things that are arousing to you or your partner or the feelings you have when you want to make love.

Now think about *sensuality*. What comes to mind? People usually think of some pleasant experience that involves touching, seeing, smelling, or tasting, like walking on the beach or being massaged with sweet-smelling oil. How about the roughness of a beard or silkiness of hair? The smell of your partner after a shower or a bath? Chocolate? You get the idea. These are sensual experiences that are not necessarily connected with sexuality. The Song of Solomon is full of sensuality. It includes physical touch and other sensations, but it is not always associated with making love. We'd include hugging, affectionate cuddling, nonsexual massages—all provide physical pleasure in nonsexual ways. This distinction between sensuality and sexuality is important. Your relationship should be growing in both areas. However, in order for there to be growth there needs to be a willingness to explore, discover, listen, laugh, compromise, change, and practice.

In early stages of relationships, touching, holding hands, hugging, and caressing are natural. Over time, many couples tend to either bypass the sensual and move directly to goal-oriented sexual behavior or to drift apart and lose interest. Less time is spent on the kinds of touching that had been so delightful before. The focus is more on the end product of sex than the process of expressing love. This leads to problems, because nonsexual touching is an important part of your overall physical intimacy.

Kristen and Andrew have been married for eight years. They used to spend a lot of time just cuddling and caressing. As time went by, they got busier with kids, work, and other duties, as most of us do. After a year or two of marriage, they had settled into a pattern of having sex about twice a week. Less and less time was devoted to sensuality. One or the other would initiate sex after they went to bed, and they'd quickly have intercourse, usually finishing in about ten minutes.

Kristen and Andrew had become quite efficient at making love or, more accurately, at having intercourse. They didn't make extra time, so they simply made do. In fact, they were making do rather than making love. Their focus on sexual intercourse without much sensuality led to their dissatisfaction. "What happened to all those times we'd just lie around for hours together," Kristen wondered. "It seems like Kristen used to be a lot more responsive when we made love," Andrew mused. We'll come back to them in a bit.

Keeping the Sensual Alive and Well

There needs to be a place for sensual touching in your relationship, both in and outside of the experience of making love. This is similar to the distinction between problem discussion and problem solution. Just as the pressures of life lead many couples to problem solve prematurely, too many couples short-change the sensual, and prematurely focus on sex. That leads to sex without the overall context of touching—and to problems in physical oneness.

It's important to make sensual experiences a regular part of your relationship, apart from sexuality. Sensual experiences set the stage for better sexual experiences. The whole climate for physical intimacy is better when you have preserved the sensual. It's also important to keep sensuality as a regular part of your lovemaking. When you focus on touching in a variety of ways, it elevates the pleasure of the whole experience. Most couples prefer this broader sensual focus to a narrow focus on sex. It provides a much richer expression of intimacy in your physical relationship.

PROTECTING PHYSICAL INTIMACY FROM ANXIETY

Arousal is the natural process by which we are stimulated to sensual or sexual pleasure. It's a state of pleasurable excitement. Although just about everyone is capable of being aroused, this pleasurable feeling can be short-circuited by anxiety. Numerous studies suggest that anxiety inhibits sexual arousal. We'd like to discuss two key kinds of anxiety: performance anxiety and the tension from conflict in your marriage.

The Barrier of Performance Anxiety

Performance anxiety is about having too much concern about how good a job you are doing when you make love. Frequently asking yourself questions such as "How am I doing?" or "Is my partner enjoying this?" reflects performance anxiety. When you're keeping an eye on your performance, you put distance between you and your partner. *You're focused on how you are doing rather than on being in the experience with your mate.* The focus is no longer on the pleasure you're sharing. Instead, your partner's approval feels at stake. It's as if the event of making love has triggered the deeper issues of acceptance and rejection.

The focus on performance interferes with arousal because you are distracted from your own sensations of pleasure. This distraction leads to many of the most common sexual problems people experience: premature ejaculation, problems keeping erections, and difficulty lubricating or reaching orgasm. You simply can't be anxious and pleasantly aroused at the same time. And you can't be relaxed and enjoy being with your partner if your focus is on avoiding mistakes.

Consider Andrew and Kristen again. Andrew became aware that Kristen was becoming less and less pleased with their lovemaking. Without a focus on sensuality and touching throughout their relationship, Kristen began to feel like Andrew was just using her sexually. This feeling was intensified because he'd have orgasms every time they made love, but her climaxes were less frequent. As dissatisfying as their lovemaking was for both of them, it seemed to Kristen that it was still better for Andrew. So her resentment grew.

Andrew became aware of her resentment and wanted to make things better. But instead of talking it out and working on the problem together, he decided he'd just do a better job of making love to Kristen. This wasn't all bad, as ideas go. However, it caused him to become more and more focused on performing, so his anxiety grew. Thoughts about performance were on his mind constantly during their lovemaking. "How's Kristen doing? Is she getting excited? Does she like this? I wonder if she thinks I'm doing this right? Man, I'd better try more of this for a while, I'm not sure she's ready."

Pretty soon he was pleasing Kristen somewhat more, but he was growing more and more tense about how he was doing. Sure, he was meeting some of her needs, but he wasn't feeling at all connected with her or satisfied in their lovemaking. He was performing. Performance anxiety does not foster a sense of deeper connection and oneness. Kristen knew there was some change in Andrew's attention to her arousal, which did please her to some degree. But she had a growing sense that Andrew was somewhere else when they made love. She was reaching orgasm more often, but she still didn't feel they were close while they made love.

The key for Kristen and Andrew was to rediscover the sensual side of their relationship. They had to begin talking openly about what was going on. Fortunately, they still had a lot of love and respect for each other, so once they started dealing with this part of their relationship, things improved quickly.

In the Christian PREP approach, we emphasize that you can *prevent* problems from developing in the first place if you are willing to do so and if you know what to do. It's the same for physical intimacy. You can do a lot to keep sexual problems from developing. For some of you, the story of Kristen and Andrew is very familiar. For others, your physical relationship hasn't deteriorated, and that's great. For you the goal is to protect what you have and to keep your sexual intimacy growing.

The Barrier of Relationship Conflict and Anxiety

Mishandled conflicts can destroy your physical relationship by adding tension, both in and out of the bedroom. Let's face it, when you've been arguing and you're angry with each other, you don't feel like being sensual or making love. For some, the sexual relationship is temporarily enhanced by conflict followed by making up. But for most, poorly handled conflict adds a layer of tension that affects everything else in the relationship. Tension isn't compatible with enjoyable, intimate lovemaking for most people. In fact, your physical relationship is probably more vulnerable to the effects of conflict and resentment than any other area. If you are experiencing unresolved conflict in other areas of your relationship, it can be difficult to feel safe or excited about making love. It's even worse when conflicts erupt in the context of lovemaking.

Earlier, we described how the Song of Solomon portrays such wonderful images of sensual and loving connection in marriage. In the midst of this Hebrew poetry of love and passion is a verse that people often overlook. A friend of ours, Tim Doyle, recently brought it to our attention in a conversation about oneness in marriage. "Catch for us the foxes, the little foxes that ruin the vineyards, our vineyards that are in bloom" (Song of Solomon 2:15).

To get the full impact of the importance of this verse, you need to realize just how much of the imagery in the Song of Solomon is about a garden and the fruit in it (Song of Solomon 2:1–3; 4:13,14; 4:16–5:1; 6:2,3). For example:

> Beloved
> Awake, north wind, and come, south wind! Blow on
>   my garden, that its fragrance may spread abroad. Let
>   my lover come into his garden and taste its choice
>   fruits.
> Lover
> I have come into my garden, my sister, my bride; I have
>   gathered my myrrh with my spice.
>
> *Song of Solomon 4:16–5:1a*

Because love and passion are depicted here as fruit in a garden, the "little foxes" must be those little things that eat that fruit before you ever have a chance to taste it. What are the little things that nip your physical oneness while it's still in the bud? Surely, one of the most common and powerful destroyers of such connection is mishandled conflict. These little day-to-day destructive conflicts build barriers. Love's enjoyable fruit is tender and easily damaged if not nurtured and protected from conflict.

If you can protect your times for physical intimacy from conflict, you can do a great deal to keep your physical relationship alive and well. To do this, you must work to handle conflict well by using the ground rules and other techniques we've been stressing. *It's critical to keep problems and disagreements off limits when you have the time to be together for touching or making love.* And it's just as important to be managing conflict well the rest of the time too, so you don't erode all the ways in which you can stay friends and lovers over the years to come.

COMMUNICATING DESIRES

It's critical for you to talk openly and specifically about your physical relationship. That goes not only for handling potential conflicts around physical intimacy but also for telling each other what you desire. We're talking about frank communication, not mind reading. Mind reading can cause serious conflicts in many areas of a relationship, including the realms of sensuality and sexuality. The problem is that couples often assume they should know what each other wants.

You Should Know What I Like!

It's a mistake to assume that your partner likes whatever you like or that you can read each other's minds. Would you go out to a restaurant and order the same thing you want for your partner? Of course not. It's also too easy for some people to assume that their partner *won't* like the things they like. Either way, you're mind reading—making assumptions about what is in your partner's mind. And because many couples have trouble talking openly about their physical relationship, it's easy for these assumptions to take control. You don't know what your partner's expectations are until they tell you and vice versa.

Because of your history together, you can often assume correctly, of course. And things can work out fine based on these experience-based assumptions. But it is not enough, because people change. Also, how will you ever discover new things in your sexual experience? So regularly checking in with each other about your desires and expectations is necessary. We can't tell you how many couples we've talked with when one expects the other "to just know" what they like or don't like when making love. It's as if people believe that "it just isn't romantic or exciting if I have to tell you what I want. You *should* know!" This is an unreasonable expectation. If you hold this fantasy, you should challenge it for the health of your relationship.

Couples who have the best sexual relationships have ways of communicating both verbally and nonverbally about what they like. Furthermore, there's usually a genuine, unselfish desire to please one another. There's a strong sense of teamwork involved, even in lovemaking, where each gives and receives pleasure willingly. This giving spirit, combined with the direct communication, leads to great lovemaking.

We recommend that you learn to give your partner clear feedback about what feels pleasurable or unpleasant to you *while you are touching or making love*. We're not, of course, suggesting that you have a Speaker-Listener discussion in the middle of lovemaking. (Though if it really excites you that much, let us know how it goes!)

Finally, determine to discover the best ways to give to your partner in your physical relationship. If you're keeping conflict out of the bedroom, handling conflict well in the rest of your relationship, and taking the time and energy to preserve sensuality, this kind of communication will be much easier to do.

Taking a Risk

Although it feels risky at first, open communication is the key. It also helps to try some new ideas to break out of ruts, like reading a book together about your sexual relationship. That might help you get started in talking about this sensitive topic. Agree to set one night aside to surprise each other with some of the things you learn. Determine to make lovemaking a time for fun and discovery. Try something new, even if only once. A good discussion in which you explore the sensual and sexual sides of your relationship may relieve many of your concerns about performance and lead you to the discovery of a lot more joy in this area.

We're not saying every couple can have a perfect physical relationship. Sometimes, real physical problems need attention, or one of you may have to work though sexual mistreatment from the past. But even in these situations, open and clear communication is critical to making your relationship the best it can be. You both have to want it, protect it, and nurture it. If things are going well in your physical relationship, keep it that way by talking about it. If some problems have developed, the things we are emphasizing here can help you get back on track.

In this chapter we've emphasized several keys for keeping your physical relationship growing and vibrant. Now it's up to you.

We don't intend this chapter to be a substitute for sex therapy if you have a history of significant sexual difficulties. Working with an experienced Christian sex therapist can usually accomplish a great deal when there are significant problems. Our focus here has been more to help couples who have moderate problems to begin to deal with them and to help those who have satisfying physical relationships to keep them that way—and to make them even better.

The following exercises can help you enhance your physical intimacy. They are exercises that have worked successfully for many couples over the years. If you're ready for greater sensual and sexual enhancement, read on.

EXERCISES

1. *Giver-Receiver Exercise.* This is an exercise that has benefited many couples, whether or not they were having trouble in their physical relationship. The purpose is twofold: (1) to keep you "in touch" with sensuality in your physical relationship and (2) to help you learn to communicate more openly and

naturally about what you like and don't like in your physical relationship.

This isn't the time for sexual intercourse. That would defeat the purpose; we want you to focus on sensuality. Don't be goal-oriented, other than the goal of relaxing and doing this exercise in a way that you each enjoy. If you want to make love following the exercise, that's up to you. But if you've been having feelings of pressure in your sexuality, we'd recommend you completely separate out these practice times from having sex.

The general idea is that you each take turns giving and receiving pleasure. The first few times, you are either the *giver* or the *receiver* until you switch roles half-way through the time you have set aside. When in the *receiver* role, your job is to enjoy the touching and give feedback on what feels good and what doesn't. Your partner does not know this unless you tell him or her. You can give either verbal or hand-guided feedback.

Verbal feedback means telling your partner what actions feel good, how hard to rub or what areas you like to have touched. Hand-guided feedback consists of gently moving your partner's hand around the part of the body being massaged to provide feedback about what really feels good.

As the *giver*, your role is to provide pleasure by touching your partner and being responsive to feedback. Ask for feedback as often as necessary. Be aware of changes in how your partner is reacting—what feels good one minute may hurt the next. You are to focus on what your partner is wanting, not on what you think would feel good.

Choose roles and give a massage of hands or feet for about ten to twenty minutes, asking for and giving feedback. We recommend massages of areas like hands, back, legs, feet, and so forth, the first few times to get the hang of the technique. This also helps you relax if there are some issues about sexuality between you. Then switch roles. Repeat as often as you like, but also remember to practice these roles in other aspects of your sensual and sexual relationship.

We recommend that you try the Giver-Receiver exercise over the course of several weeks, several times a week. As you work on the exercise, there are some variations of the technique to work in over time. Assuming all is going well in your exercises, begin to move to other areas for touching. Wherever you want to be touched, including the sexual areas, is great.

Over time, you can drop the rigid emphasis on the *giver* and *receiver* roles and work on both of you giving and receiving at the same time, while still keeping an emphasis on sensuality and communication of desires; or you can vary the degree to which you want to stay in these roles as you wish. If you practice this over time, it will become easier for you to communicate openly about touch. It will also be easier for you to work together as you go to keep physical intimacy vibrant and alive.

2. *Exploring the Sensual.* In addition to the Giver-Receiver exercise, set aside a specific time for sensual activities together. This works for all couples, regardless of whether they are engaging in sexual activity. Be sure you will not be interrupted.

At the start of this exercise, talk about what's sensual for each of you and what you'd like to try doing to keep sensual experiences in your relationship. Here are some ideas:

a. Give a massage to your partner, using the Giver-Receiver technique.

b. Share verbally with your partner what you enjoy both sensually and sexually.

c. Cuddle and hug as you talk to your partner about the positive things you love about him or her.

d. Plan a sensual or sexual activity for your next encounter.

e. Plan a wonderful meal together. Prepare it together and sit close together; share the meal.

    f. Wash your partner's hair.

    g. Spend some time just kissing.

3. Read the Song of Solomon aloud, taking turns reading to each other. This could be done a little at a time, a few verses or a chapter a night, or all at once. Set aside time without interruptions (after the children are down for the night). Enjoy sharing one of the most explicit, beautifully written love stories ever written.

4. Consider reading a Christian book about your sexual relationship. There are many excellent ones in most Christian book stores. Then enjoy experimenting with some new ideas.

14

Spiritual Intimacy and Oneness

Unless the LORD builds the house, its builders labor in vain.
Unless the LORD watches over the city, the watchmen stand
guard in vain.

Psalm 127:1

To this point, we have covered many key areas of marriage.
We've left the most wonderful and mysterious topic for last. Spiritual oneness and intimacy may be the most elusive and fragile kind
of intimacy for most couples. It's most likely to thrive when you are
managing many of the more mundane matters of marriage well. If
you are managing conflicts well, solving problems as a team, maintaining commitment, and keeping your friendship thriving, you're
setting the stage for deeper levels of intimacy, including spiritual
intimacy.

There's a paradox here. You will find all of your marriage going
better if you make the Lord the center of your individual lives. But
we think you'll also find that you have the greatest capacity for spiritual intimacy together if much of the rest of your marriage is going
well. That's because spiritual intimacy goes to the deepest and most
vulnerable parts of your soul. To go there together, you need the
kind of trust, safety, and security that are born of commitment and
respectful handling of issues and problems in your relationship.
That's why we've waited to discuss spiritual intimacy until now.

For those of you who are married and do not share the same
faith as your mate, much of what we have to say in the rest of this
chapter will be harder to work out. We acknowledge that some
kinds of spiritual oneness are going to be far more difficult, if not

impossible, when core spiritual differences are great. However, if that is the case for you, we still believe you can strengthen your marriage by discussing these issues as friends rather than fighting about them. So you might find that the skills we have taught you, especially in the chapters on friendship and expectations, can help you strengthen your connection, even while talking about these differences.

For those of you who do share the same faith and spiritual orientation, there are still fine lines to walk as we enter this topic. For example, we don't want to raise unrealistic expectations that every marriage can easily achieve some kind of "soul mate" status. The potential for blessing is great, but it's not easy to find the deepest connections in most marriages. It takes work, and you won't always be as close as you might like, spiritually or otherwise. The Old and New Testaments provide many examples of great men and women of God. However, from what we are told in scripture, many of them were not exactly easy to relate to as people, and many had significant problems at home (for example, Adam and Eve: Genesis 3; Abraham and Sarah: Genesis 12; Moses and Zipporah: Exodus 24:24–26; David and Michal: II Samuel 6:20–23). *Our point is that each of you can be very spiritual people and still struggle in your marriage.* Nevertheless, if you are growing in the various ways we have been discussing, you're ready for exploring ways you can begin to deepen your spiritual connection.

FAILING TO ENTER THE PROMISE

The Israelites were in captivity for many years in Egypt. When they were finally released, God directed them toward the land of blessing that He had promised. When Moses and his people came up to the edge of the land God had promised, they stopped. God told them to first send some spies into the land to check things out. The spies brought back a description of a land as a place "flowing with milk and honey." It was a land of great promise, but they did not enter into the promise that God had for them because of fear and unbelief.

Listen to the fear as the returning spies gave their report:

"But the people who live there are powerful, and the cities are fortified and very large. We even saw descendants of Anak there. The Amalekites live in the Negev; the Hittites, Jebusites and Amorites live in the hill country; and the Canaanites live near the sea and along the Jordan." Then Caleb silenced the people before Moses and said, "We should go up and take possession of the land, for we can certainly do it." But the men who had gone up with him said, "We can't attack those people; they are stronger than we are." And they spread among the Israelites a bad report about the land they had explored. They said, "The land we explored devours those living in it. All the people we saw there are of great size. We saw the Nephilim there (the descendants of Anak come from the Nephilim). We seemed like grasshoppers in our own eyes, and we looked the same to them" [Numbers 13:28–33].

The last sentence is very telling. They seemed like grasshoppers in their *own* eyes. They didn't see themselves as being able to handle what God had promised. You know the rest of the story. The ten spies who did not want to enter the land talked the people into staying out. So the Israelites wandered in the desert for forty years until that unbelieving generation died off.

Marriage is like this. God has given us a "land" of great spiritual promise in His design for marriage, but few enter in. Whether from unbelief or fear of not being up to the task or from a lack of knowing which way the marital promised land lies, too many couples do not take hold of the rich blessing God intends for their marriages. If you are intimidated by the task, you may not even try. And if your marriage is not safe for intimacy in other ways, you won't feel secure enough to try. Intimacy and deeper connection can be a scary place to go in a marriage. This is a fear you must conquer to be able to fully experience the potential blessings. Much of what we've been trying to teach in this book is about ways to act in love and cast out fear. If you are wanting to go deeper in terms of spiritual intimacy, we have some suggestions for which way to head.

WHAT IS SPIRITUAL INTIMACY?

You might have hoped we'd be giving you the five magical steps to spiritual oneness. We're not going to do that. It's not that we wouldn't like to, but we truly believe in what we said at the outset: oneness is mysterious. And spiritual oneness is probably the most mysterious part of all. We don't want to offer any simple formulas. (These might actually inhibit you from developing your own unique spiritual connection.) But we do want to offer you some ideas. In fact, you can think of what follows as a kind of brainstorming. Our aim is to help you think about this topic and to encourage you to move into this kind of intimacy in your marriage. We don't know exactly what will help you draw closer together spiritually, but we have some ideas of things that have helped other couples.

Sharing Your Walk

Spiritual intimacy speaks to some ability to share in each other's spiritual life. That could mean many things. Many couples who are growing in their spiritual oneness have learned to share together about their personal walks with Christ. This is a kind of "as you go" sharing of thoughts about God, struggles in faith, answered prayer, and so forth. This is sharing spiritually as friends. What moves you at the deepest levels of your soul? When have you felt closest to the Lord? What are you most afraid of in your spiritual life?

Martin and Cynthia have cultivated this kind of connection in their marriage. They married seventeen years ago, and neither were very spiritually involved at the time. However, as they have gone through the trials of life and the joys and pains of parenthood, they have increasingly turned their hearts to God. Now they are actively involved with the Lord and with others in their church. Only in recent years have they have begun to talk more openly about their thoughts and struggles in their faith. For example, Martin has always been more on the skeptical side of life, asking "why" and "why not" kinds of questions. Cynthia doesn't have as many questions, but she does struggle more personally with the Lord at times.

When the child of one of their best friends died from liver disease at the age of three, it created a struggle for both of them. For her, the struggle boiled down to anger at God for allowing her friends' child to die. This was not so much a crisis of faith for her as a very personal issue with God about what had happened. For Martin there was much emotion in this event, but it was also a real crisis of faith. "Why would God allow such a thing? Maybe God isn't who I think He is. Maybe He doesn't even exist." Such deep spiritual struggles are not uncommon for deep-thinking Christians. The rewarding thing in this was that Martin and Cynthia began talking much more openly about these deeper matters that they had kept inside in earlier years. This cultivated a spiritual friendship based in the sense of being one in the Spirit. It was about the only thing they could feel thankful for in the midst of the awful thing that had happened.

Many people don't feel comfortable sharing their deeper experiences with their mate. Perhaps most fear rejection. For others, it's a matter of privacy. We've met many people who hold this view. Still others find it difficult to put into words what their spiritual experience with Christ is like, making it hard to talk about with another. These examples illustrate why it is so important for the two of you to find ways of connecting spiritually that work for both of you. This may mean pushing yourself through the discomfort to share what you can. Or it may mean being content to accept your partner's reluctance in this area and to wait for him or her to open up.

Sharing Scripture

Some couples are drawn together by sharing their thoughts and reactions about passages of scripture. This could mean reading the same passage together and then simply talking about it. It's the sharing of what the Lord is impressing on the heart that brings closeness. For some, this comes easiest if they use a devotional guide. One of the great advantages of using such a tool is that it takes the pressure off either of you to teach the other and allows you both to be taught by the devotional. Many excellent couple devotionals are on the market these days, as well as many devotionals not directed toward couples; all would be fine choices for helping you cultivate this kind of sharing.

For other couples, spiritual intimacy is fostered by listening to Christian radio together, especially to teachers that both of you respect and from whom both of you can learn. This is similar to talking together about a sermon you just heard or something a teacher in your church taught that really hit home for you. The key idea here is sharing what you are hearing in the messages from scripture.

One couple we know, Ginger and Josh, tried many times over the years to study scripture together. Nothing seemed to work. Ginger had been a Christian for years before Josh entered the faith, so he felt threatened by her greater knowledge. Not only did they have the typical problems of making time for this, when they did have the time, study would sometimes lead to conflict. As it turns out, both were very sensitive about hidden issues of control. So, when either would assume a tone or manner more like they were teaching the other, conflict would erupt. "Who made you the spiritual genius? What makes you think you understand that passage correctly?"

Ginger and Josh finally found something that worked well for them: listening to one of the radio teachers they both liked. The program came on daily in the evening after the kids were asleep. Although they couldn't have this time together every day, they found that they could listen together on many evenings. That took the control dynamics out of the situation, and they could focus on the message.

There is a passage in the Old Testament that has most often been interpreted to be simply about learning the Torah (literally, direction from God), but much more is implied.

Love the LORD your God with all your heart and with all your soul and with all your strength. These commandments that I give you today are to be upon your hearts. Impress them on your children. Talk about them when you sit at home and when you walk along the road, when you lie down and when you get up [Deuteronomy 6:5–7].

The heart of this passage is about parenting and raising our children to love the Lord by helping them grow in their understanding of Him and His will. In family life, the picture here is one of frequent talking about scripture in the various contexts of daily life. It's about cultivating a regular conversation about the sayings of God. It is noteworthy that the regular discussion of God's desires (which are most clearly revealed in scripture) is so clearly linked to loving God with our whole heart.

Another implication of this passage is that one's spiritual life is not to be compartmentalized in religious activities. It is to permeate all of life. When your spiritual lives are more openly and regularly shared in this way, you will experience one facet of spiritual intimacy. Still, your style may vary greatly from what other couples do.

Praying Together

We don't know how many Christian couples pray together regularly. We've heard it's pretty rare. Perhaps this is a time we are most authentic; therefore it's most threatening, especially when relationships don't feel completely safe. But we believe that praying together can be an important key to experiencing spiritual intimacy. Some couples may not want to do this with great regularity or fervency because of concerns about the privacy of prayer. For other couples, praying together is a regular, desired practice. There's real power in prayer together, whether it's silent prayer or verbal prayer, long or short. Many passages in scripture speak to the power of prayer, especially prayer for one another. Here are just a few to consider.

Therefore confess your sins to each other and pray for each other so that you may be healed. The prayer of a righteous man is powerful and effective [James 5:16].

Be devoted to one another in brotherly love; give preference to one another in honor; not lagging behind in diligence, fervent in spirit, serving the Lord; rejoicing in hope, persevering in tribulation, devoted to prayer . . . [Romans 12:10–12].

Do not deprive each other except by mutual consent and for a time, so that you may devote yourselves to prayer [I Corinthians 7:5a].

There are many ways to pray together. In that last verse, Paul is suggesting that couples agree to abstain from sex from time to time to intentionally devote themselves to prayer. We haven't heard from too many couples who have tried this. But it's in your Bible, and it's a pretty simple suggestion. Although the passage does not necessarily refer to prayer together, the overriding idea is that you are making a spiritual decision to increase the intensity of your prayer life for a time by mutual agreement. That's a form of being together spiritually.

A different approach to prayer together is in sharing prayer needs with one another. This is a sharing of needs, desires, requests, concerns, and praises. It also promotes a sense of oneness in your walk with Christ.

Worshiping God Together

Much has been made in recent years of the fact that couples and families have fewer meals together than they used to have. This decrease in relaxed time together diminishes opportunities for sharing about our lives. Likewise, many couples do not regularly worship together. Worship, of course, can take a variety of forms: church services, giving thanks (Hebrews 12:28,29), and singing praise songs together (Colossians 3:16). You can probably think of other ways as well.

One couple we know of has a tradition of singing praise hymns together as they travel. This is a great example of sharing in worship and communion with Christ. That may or may not be your cup of tea, but that's our key point: find out what *your* cup of tea is when it comes to spiritual intimacy. God has left you great room for the expression of your creativity in marriage. As we said at the beginning of this chapter, we do not want to tell you what to do in this area as much as stimulate you to consider some ways you might grow together spiritually.

Sharing Ministry Together

Some couples find greater spiritual closeness in serving the Lord together. One couple we know, Bill and Joan, have been married for thirty years. They have tried praying together, scripture reading, and so forth, but none of these more typical ways of spiritual connection have worked smoothly for them. But over the years they have noticed how much guests in their home seem to enjoy their hospitality. Now, they think about creative ways to use their home to reach others, even enjoying preparing for the event together and cleaning up and talking about it afterward. As a result, they have begun carving out more frequent times to use their home for ministry to younger families, neighbors, and work associates. This has created a new joy and a spiritual closeness they had not known before.

Ministry may be one of the most important ways we can express our oneness. As a matter of fact, when Christ was praying for us to become one, He twice emphasized the purpose of our oneness: "so that the world may believe that you have sent me" (John 17:20,21). When you minister together as a couple, you are looking beyond yourselves to the world you are called to reach. Your own relationship struggles can seem less important. In addition, your marriage can take on a larger meaning that gives you a stronger sense of oneness.

Taking Communion Together

Before Jesus was crucified, He instituted the ritual we know as communion as a way to remember Him and what He has done for us on the cross (see Mark 14:22–24; John 13; I Corinthians 11:20–34). The key concept here has to do with the idea of sharing our deepest fellowship with the Lord. Communion is to be one of our most personal, deepest acts of relating to Him. Although this is a very personal experience, we are instructed to do it corporately. In fact, part of the imagery Christ is invoking here is the prefiguration of the marriage supper of the lamb, wherein the body of Christ comes to the Lord together as the bride of Christ in heaven.

That's pretty technical, but here's our point: communion is another deep spiritual experience you can share together. It's not an opportunity for talking so much as an opportunity to be side by side in this powerful remembrance. It is a symbol of your spiritual oneness. Because of the many demands of life, even life at church, we know many couples who are not regularly together for communion. One couple, Janis and Quint, have small children and are very active in children's ministry. Therefore, it's become fairly hard for both to take communion at the same time. Often, one is holding down the class of preschoolers while the other slips into the service. Taking communion together will require them to ask a friend to watch the kids while they slip out together. It might add a special blessing to your marriage to make it a higher priority to share communion together from time to time. It's hard to imagine how that could not be the case.

MAKING AND PROTECTING THE TIME

We think two of the very most important ideas in this book are contained in the sixth Ground Rule—to set aside times for the great things and to learn to protect those times from conflict and issues. As we conclude this discussion on spiritual intimacy, we can't think of an area in which this advice is any more important. You can want to make spiritual time together, you can think it's a great idea, but if you don't plan for it in some way, it will not happen.

Just as important, when you have set aside some time for enhancing spiritual oneness, you must protect this time from conflict and issues. It's not that struggling together can't foster spiritual growth, but if you end up struggling much of the time when you are trying to draw together spiritually, you won't be fostering oneness. Use the other skills and strategies we've been talking about to protect this crucial part of your marital oneness.

There's great spiritual promise in your marriage. But you must take hold of it. It does not just happen, any more than the other things in a great marriage just happen. Seek the Lord in prayer for the unique ways the spiritual fullness of your marriage may be developed.

EXERCISE

Our suggestions at the end of this chapter are quite simple but potentially very powerful. Take some time together to discuss what you have read here. Discuss your desires, your fears, and your concerns about spiritual oneness. It might help to discuss how you were each raised in this regard. What have you observed? Spend some time brainstorming together about what you might try to increase your spiritual intimacy. Pray. May God bless you in this.

A Final Word

Above all else, guard your heart, for it is the wellspring of life.
                                                        Proverbs 4:23

We've covered many concepts in this book, including communication and conflict management, commitment, forgiveness, friendship, fun, sensuality, and the importance of spiritual oneness in your relationship. We're confident that these ideas and strategies can go a long way toward helping you keep your marriage strong.

You could think of this book as providing a recipe for a solid, lasting, satisfying relationship. The ingredients are in place: your present level of love, the skills and insights outlined in our approach, the Lord's enabling grace, and so forth. The key for you now is to blend these ingredients with your commitment in order to bring out the best in your marriage. Based on our experience with thousands of couples, these recommendations can help you keep your relationship strong and vital for years to come. We believe they can play a vital part in preserving *A Lasting Promise* in your marriage.

Bill Coffin, a colleague and U.S. Navy specialist in the prevention of marital and family distress, suggests that couples think about relationship fitness as they might think about physical fitness. Just as physical fitness experts recommend that you work out three or four times a week for twenty to thirty minutes, you should devote at least that much time to your relationship fitness.

BUT MY PARTNER WON'T TRY THESE THINGS

What if your partner isn't motivated to learn some of things we've presented? That can be a frustrating problem if you really like the ideas. You could try several things.

For one thing, it's wisest to begin working on what you can change about how you handle yourself in the relationship, regardless of what your partner is willing to do. It's too easy for all of us to get focused on what our partners can do. Instead, focus your attention on where you have the most control—yourself. As Paul said, "As far as it depends on you, be at peace with all" (Romans 12:18). You can only control your side of the equation, but that's quite a bit. We believe your partner is more likely to change in response to the healthy changes in you than to any direct or manipulative efforts you might make to change him or her.

Even though the things we've suggested work best when you're working together, you can accomplish a lot on your own if you're willing to try and your partner isn't actively working to damage the relationship. Do you have a tendency to make negative interpretations? Do you tend to withdraw from talking about issues or to over-pursue your avoidant partner? Do you bring up gripes when you are out to have a fun evening with your partner? You can make substantial changes in such patterns no matter what your partner is doing. In addition, you can work in many ways on maintaining and demonstrating your dedication without your partner ever reading this book.

You can also practice some of the ground rules without necessarily working on them together. For example, you could be out together and begin to get in some conflict and say "You know, we're out to have fun tonight. Let's deal with this tomorrow when we have more time so we can focus on relaxing together this evening." Most partners would get the idea, even if they've never heard of our ground rules.

You can also suggest your partner try some of the lighter topics we've discussed, such as fun or friendship. That could get some potent and positive changes going, which could open up interest in other aspects of this program. As you may have noticed, many of the key ideas about fun and friendship don't necessarily depend on knowledge of other concepts in this book.

WHAT ABOUT SETBACKS?

You may begin using these ideas for a while, only to fall back into some of your old patterns. That's normal. Most successful couples experience setbacks from time to time. Unfortunately, when you have one you may feel like you've not made any progress at all. But don't trust those feelings. Instead, just get up and get going again. We've found that normal growth involves a series of setbacks followed by recovery and more growth, followed by setbacks, and so on. That's a lot like all of our growth in life, beginning with when we're learning how to walk. It's most important not to quit.

KEEP AT WHAT IS MAKING A DIFFERENCE

To get the most out of what we've presented here, be sure to review the material. We all learn better when we go over key concepts again and again. For review, go back and read the sections you may have highlighted. It would be especially valuable to review the rules for the Speaker-Listener Technique, problem solving, and principles on forgiveness. None of these rules or ideas are all that complicated, but you'll want to master them to get the greatest benefit in your marriage. If we haven't said it enough, practice the specific strategies when you don't need them, so you can put them in practice when it matters most.

We've detailed our approach in this book as well as in other materials described in the appendix. We've provided tools that you can use to build a relationship that brings long-term fulfillment and to protect your relationship from naturally occurring storms. But, like anything else, once you have the tools, it's up to you what you do with them. We wish you God's greatest blessings in developing the lasting promise of your marriage.

> Many waters cannot quench love; rivers
> cannot wash it away.
> SO
> Serve one another in love.
> The entire law is summed up in a single
> command: "Love your neighbor as yourself."
> FOR
> There is no fear in love. But perfect love
> drives out fear.

> *Selected scripture: Song of Songs 8:7;*
> *Galatians 5:13,14; I John 4:18*

More Information on the Christian PREP Approach

We conduct workshops for couples, clergy, lay leaders, and counselors who desire to be more fully exposed to the Christian PREP approach. For information about these workshops, please call 303–759–9931 or write to us at the address to follow. We will be glad to give you information about seminars or products to help you in your own relationship or your ministry to other couples.

We also have a directory of people who have been trained in this approach and who do either workshops or counseling using aspects of this model. To obtain the directory, either write to us and request the referral directory or visit our Website.

Our address is Christian PREP, Inc., P.O. Box 102530, Denver, CO 80250–2530. You can e-mail us (Info@PREPinc.com/) or visit our Website (http://members.aol.com/prepinc).

AUDIO- AND VIDEOTAPES AND STUDY GUIDES

To order "Fighting *for* Your Marriage" audio- or videotapes, please call 303–759–9931 or write to us at the address given earlier. You can also order a secular book covering these concepts that is entitled *Fighting* for *Your Marriage*; the book or tapes can also be ordered from Jossey-Bass Publishers, Inc., by calling 415–433–1740. The "Fighting *for* Your Marriage" audiotapes are a six-hour set covering roughly the same content as this book. The "Fighting *for* Your Marriage" videotape series covers the key communication and conflict management concepts. We plan to add other videos to the series in the future. *These tapes are secular in that the material is not presented in a theological context.* Nevertheless, we believe the concepts presented are entirely consistent with biblical truth about healthy marriages.

We plan to continue to create new ways to help couples learn this material. For example, we are developing small-group study materials that can be used in conjunction with this book. Please call or write to us to ask about availability of this and other materials to help you in your marriage or in your ministry to married couples.

Further Reading and Research References

We provide the following list for those interested in further reading in the fields of study underlying this work. Some of the works, like this book, were written for the typical reader. Some were written for researchers and students interested in deeper study.

Arp, D., & Arp, C. (1996). *The Second Half of Marriage: Facing the Eight Challenges of Every Long-Term Marriage*. Grand Rapids, MI: Zondervan.

Baucom, D., & Epstein, N. (1990). *Cognitive-behavioral marital therapy*. New York: Guilford.

Center for Marriage and Family. (1995). *Marriage preparation in the Catholic Church: Getting it right*. Omaha, NE: Creighton University.

Chesterton, G. K. (1956). *Saint Thomas Aquinas: "The Dumb Ox."* New York: Image.

Clements, M., Stanley, S. M., & Markman, H. J. (1997). *Prediction of marital distress and divorce: A discriminant analysis*. Manuscript submitted for publication.

Cowan, C. P., & Cowan, P. A. (1992). *When partners become parents: The big life change for couples*. New York: HarperCollins.

Eidelson, R. J., & Epstein, N. (1981). Unrealistic beliefs of clinical couples: Their relationship to expectations, goals and satisfaction. *American Journal of Family Therapy, 9*(4), 13–22.

Fowers, B. J., Montel, K. H., & Olson, D. H. (1996). Predicting marital success for premarital couple types based on PREPARE. *Journal of Marital and Family Therapy, 22*, 103–119.

Giblin, P., Sprenkle, D. H., & Sheehan, R. (1985). Enrichment outcome research: A meta-analysis of premarital, marital, and family interventions. *Journal of Marital and Family Therapy, 11*(3), 257–271.

Glenn, N. D., & Kramer, K. B. (1987). The marriages and divorces of the children of divorce. *Journal of Marriage and the Family, 49,* 811–825.

Gottman, J. M. (1993). A theory of marital dissolution and stability. *Journal of Family Psychology, 7,* 57–75.

Gottman, J. M. (1994). *Why marriages succeed or fail.* New York: Simon & Schuster.

Gottman, J. M., Notarius, C., Gonso J., & Markman, H. (1976). *A couple's guide to communication.* Champaign, IL: Research Press.

Grych, J., & Fincham, F. (1990). Marital conflict and children's adjustment. *Psychological Bulletin, 108,* 267–290.

Guerney, B. G., Jr. (1977). *Relationship enhancement.* San Francisco: Jossey-Bass.

Hahlweg, K., Markman, H. J., Thurmaier, F., Engl, J., & Eckert, V. (1996). *Prevention of marital distress: Results of a German prospective-longitudinal study.* Manuscript submitted for publication.

Johnson, D. J., & Rusbult, C. E. (1989). Resisting temptation: Devaluation of alternative partners as a means of maintaining commitment in close relationships. *Journal of Personality and Social Psychology, 57,* 967–980.

Johnson, M. P. (1982). The social and cognitive features of the dissolution of commitment to relationships. In S. Duck (Ed.), *Personal relationships: Dissolving personal relationships.* New York: Academic Press.

Karney, B. R., & Bradbury, T. N. (1995). The longitudinal course of marital quality and stability: A review of theory, method, and research. *Psychological Bulletin, 118,* 3–34.

Karney, B. R., & Bradbury, T. N. (1997). Neuroticism, marital interaction, and the trajectory of marital satisfaction. *Journal of Personality and Social Psychology, 72,* 1075–1092.

Knox, D. (1971). *Marriage happiness.* Champaign, IL: Research Press.

Kurdek, L. A. (1993). Predicting marital dissolution: A 5-year prospective longitudinal study of newlywed couples. *Journal of Personality and Social Psychology, 64,* 221–242.

Markman, H. J. (1981). Prediction of marital distress: A 5-year follow-up. *Journal of Consulting & Clinical Psychology, 49*(5), 760–762.

Markman, H. J., Floyd, F. J., Stanley, S. M., & Storaasli, R. D. (1988). Prevention of marital distress: A longitudinal investigation. *Journal of Consulting and Clinical Psychology, 56,* 210–217.

Markman, H. J., & Hahlweg, K. (1993). The prediction and prevention of marital distress: An international perspective. *Clinical Psychology Review, 13,* 29–43.

Markman, H. J., Renick, M. J., Floyd, F., Stanley, S., & Clements, M. (1993). Preventing marital distress through communication and conflict management training: A four and five year follow-up. *Journal of Consulting and Clinical Psychology, 62,* 1–8.

Markman, H., Stanley, S., & Blumberg, S. L. (1994). *Fighting for your marriage: Positive steps for a loving and lasting relationship.* San Francisco: Jossey Bass.

Matthews, L. S., Wickrama, K. A. S., & Conger, R. D. (1996). Predicting marital instability from spouse and observer reports of marital interaction. *Journal of Marriage and the Family, 58,* 641–655.

McCain, S. C. (1991). *Impact of intervention, marital, and individual distress on couples.* Unpublished doctoral dissertation, University of Denver.

McManus, M. (1993). *Marriage savers.* Grand Rapids, MI: Zondervan.

Miller, S., Miller, P., Nunnally, E. W., & Wackman, D. (1991). *Talking and listening together.* Littleton, CO: Interpersonal Communication Programs.

Notarius, C., & Markman, H. J. (1993). *We can work it out: Making sense of marital conflict.* New York: Putnam.

Parrott, L., & Parrott, L. (1995). *Saving your marriage before it starts: Seven questions to ask before (and after) you marry.* Grand Rapids, MI: Zondervan.

Pasch, L. A., & Bradbury, T. N. (in press). Social support, conflict, and the development of marital dysfunction. *Journal of Consulting and Clinical Psychology.*

Renick, M. J., Blumberg, S., & Markman, H. J. (1992). The Prevention and Relationship Enhancement Program (PREP): An empirically based preventive intervention program for couples. *Family Relations, 41*(2), 141–147.

Rogge, R. D., & Bradbury, T. N. (in press). Recent advances in the prediction of marital outcomes. In R. Berger & M. T. Hannah (Eds.),

Handbook of preventive approaches in couples therapy. New York: Brunner/Mazel.

Rusbult, C. E., Buunk, B. P., & Bram, P. (1993). Commitment processes in close relationships: An interdependence analysis. *Journal of Social and Personal Relationships, 10,* 175–204.

Sager, C. J. (1976). *Marriage contracts and couple therapy: Hidden forces in intimate relationships.* New York: Brunner/Mazel.

Silliman, B., Stanley, S. M., Coffin, W., Markman, H. J., & Jordan, P. L. (in press). Preventive interventions for couples. In H. Liddle, D. Santisteban, R. Levant, & J. Bray (Eds.), *Family Psychology Intervention Science.* Washington, DC: APA Publications.

Smalley, G. (1996). *Making love last forever.* Dallas: Word Publishing.

Stanley, S. M. (1997). What's important in premarital counseling? *Marriage and Family: A Christian Journal, 1,* 51–60.

Stanley, S. M., Blumberg, S. L., & Markman, H. J. (in press). Helping couples fight *for* their marriages: The PREP approach. In R. Berger & M. Hannah, (Eds.), *Handbook of preventive approaches in couple therapy.* New York: Brunner/Mazel.

Stanley, S. M., Lobitz, W. C., & Dickson, F. (in press). Using what we know: Commitment and cognitions in marital therapy. In W. Jones & J. Adams (Eds.), *Handbook of interpersonal commitment and relationship stability.*

Stanley, S. M., & Markman, H. J. (1992). Assessing commitment in personal relationships. *Journal of Marriage and the Family, 54,* 595–608.

Stanley, S. M., & Markman, H. J. (1997). *Marriage in the 90s: A nationwide random phone survey.* Denver: PREP, Inc.

Stanley, S. M., Markman, H. J., St. Peters, M., & Leber, D. (1995). Strengthening marriages and preventing divorce: New directions in prevention research. *Family Relations, 44,* 392–401.

Stanley, S. M., & Trathen, D. (1994). Christian PREP: An empirically based model for marital and premarital intervention. *The Journal of Psychology and Christianity, 13,* 158–165.

Stanley, S. M., Trathen, D. W., & McCain, S. C. (1996). Christian PREP: An empirically based model for marital and premarital intervention. In E. Worthington (Ed.), *Christian marital counseling: Eight approaches.* Grand Rapids, MI: Baker Books.

Stanton, G. T. (1997). *Why marriage matters: Reasons to believe in marriage in a postmodern society.* Colorado Springs, CO: Pinon Press.

Sullivan, K. T., & Bradbury, T. N. (1997). Are premarital prevention programs reaching couples at risk for marital dysfunction? *Journal of Consulting and Clinical Psychology, 65*(1), 24–30.

Thurmaier, F. R., Engl, J., Eckert, V., & Hahlweg, K. (1993). *Ehevorbereitung-ein partnerschaftliches lernprogramm EPL.* Munich, Germany: Ehrenwirth.

Trathen, D. W. (1995). A comparison of the effectiveness of two Christian premarital counseling programs (skills and information-based) utilized by evangelical Protestant churches (Doctoral dissertation, University of Denver, 1995). *Dissertation Abstracts International, 56/06–A,* 2277.

Wright, N., & Oliver, G. J. (1992). *When anger hits home: Taking care of your anger without taking it out on your family.* Chicago: Moody Press.

Some Thoughts on Domestic Violence

Because Christian PREP (and therefore this book) deals with communication and conflict between partners, questions about domestic violence arise at times. Domestic violence is a complex topic and not the subject of this book. Nevertheless, we would like to stress a few key points.

o Neither Christian PREP nor this book is a treatment program for domestic violence.

o Some couples can reduce their chances of becoming physically aggressive by learning techniques such as those taught here. This is most likely to be the case for couples who are at risk of crossing the line primarily as a result of difficulty managing conflict well. It is not applicable to couples in which a controlling male uses physical aggression to dominate or subjugate his partner.

o Domestic violence of any sort is unacceptable and wrong and dangerous.

o An alarming amount of domestic violence (at all levels) is taking place in families in our society.

o No matter what the nature of the violence, when males strike females, females are in greater danger and will likely suffer more long-lasting and negative aftereffects. Many females strike males, too; that is just as unacceptable.

o *When there is any kind of domestic violence, the preeminent concern should be safety.* Seek whatever services are necessary to ensure that neither partner is in danger, including counseling from a Christian therapist or a pastor *who has experience in this area* or help from a community shelter for battered women when a woman is in significant fear and danger.

o Those who work with couples should be aware of the complex issues around domestic violence and of local resources for help in dealing with it (for example, law enforcement access, shelters).

To read more about the controversies surrounding domestic violence, we recommend *Current Controversies on Family Violence*, published by Sage (1993) and edited by Richard Gelles and Donileen Loseke.

The Authors

Scott Stanley, Ph.D., is codirector of the Center for Marital and Family Studies at the University of Denver and president of Christian PREP Inc. He has worked with Howard Markman on the research and development of PREP (Prevention and Relationship Enhancement Program) for over twenty years. Christian PREP and this book are based, in part, on that work. Stanley coauthored the book, *Fighting for Your Marriage*, and coproduced the videotape and audiotape series by the same title. He has regularly appeared in print and broadcast media as an authority on marriage and is an expert in research on marital commitment and the prevention of divorce.

Daniel Trathen, D.Min., Ph.D., is a psychologist and the program and development director of Southwest Counseling Associates in Littleton, Colorado. He is a visiting associate professor of marriage and family counseling and codirector of the D.Min. in Marriage and Family Counseling at Denver Seminary. Trathen has conducted outcome research on Christian PREP and brings his longstanding experience in developing premarital programs in church settings to Christian PREP and this book.

Savanna McCain, Ph.D., is a psychologist with Kaiser Permanente in Denver. She has conducted outcome research on the effectiveness of PREP and has worked with the team at the University of

Denver on PREP for over eight years. She has conducted PREP workshops at Kaiser Permanente for many years. In addition to her contributions to Christian PREP, McCain has been working on the implementation of the program in local church settings, especially with a focus on mentor couple models.

Milt Bryan, M.A., has been leading PREP and Christian PREP workshops for a number of years. He is also a therapist in private practice, host of the "Morning Talk" radio show in Denver, and director of The Center for Couple Training in Lakewood, Colorado. He has ministered to couples for over twenty years and has been a counselor to couples since 1987. Milt also coauthored "A Christian's Companion Guide to 'Fighting *for* Your Marriage'" with Stanley, Trathen, and McCain.